How to Prepare a Marketing Plan

To my wife Eileen, love her
and
To our first grandchild
Taylor Barry, born 24 April 1987

JOHN STAPLETON

How to Prepare a Marketing Plan

Fourth edition

Gower

© John Stapleton 1974, 1982, 1989

First edition published by Gower Press Limited 1971
Second edition 1974
Third edition 1982

Fourth edition published 1989 by
Gower Publishing Company Limited,
Gower House, Croft Road, Aldershot Hants GU11 3HR, England

British Library Cataloguing in Publication Data

Stapleton, John
    How to prepare a marketing plan. — 4th ed.
    1. Marketing — Management
    I. Title
    658.8' 02   HF5415.13

ISBN 0-566-02723-2

Printed and bound in Great Britain at
The Camelot Press Ltd, Southampton

Contents

List of Illustrations

Preface

In 1971 the first edition of this book was described by a distinguished reviewer as *the definitive work.* It then contained ten chapters. This fourth edition has 23 chapters.

This expansion reflects the increasing sophistication of techniques, the widespread acceptance of basic concepts, and the unprecedented growth of marketing as both a practice and a profession. Yet the practice of marketing is still highly fragmented. For though almost all companies *talk marketing,* too few *think marketing.* Often a selection of techniques is grafted on to a company which then practises this cosmetic form of marketing. While this procedure may help it to survive it does not ensure growth and prosperity – and even that survival is now threatened. Companies worldwide are seeking greater efficiency, not only by reducing expenditure but also by achieving a better return on each pound, dollar, mark, or yen invested. Marketing is an important item in the budgets of many firms, particularly those which pioneered its development. To increase their productivity in marketing they need to capture the markets of the less progressive companies.

This trend has been apparent for some years and it is growing. Consumption and production are both at record levels – but the goods involved are being produced by fewer and fewer people, and unemployment is one of the unfortunate consequences. Production is achieved by machines while consumption is cornered by marketing. The demand exists and continues to grow and can be tapped only by marketing or by innovation followed by marketing.

Until recently there was a gap between marketing as practised in the USA and in Europe. That gap has narrowed, thanks to the activities of multi-nationals and of international advertising agents. The latest American techniques are now applied almost concurrently in the USA and Europe – but not yet by most indigenous companies. For they have not recognized the degree of modern sophistication. Few companies will survive into the 21st century without formal marketing planning. It is a step to productivity, for while the result of a marketing plan may be a highly creative and artistic promotion, the contents of the plan are essentially scientific in terms of organization and development. They are the raw material of company prosperity and require as much information and attention as the most complex assembled product available today. Marketing is a logistics exercise. In this edition I have included more explanation of current concepts than in earlier editions, primarily for those readers who may not be fully aware of the momentum of change and who would otherwise find some material beyond their immediate experience.

John Stapleton

Part One
Laying the Foundations

Introduction to Part One

The core of all marketing decisions is information. Research-based planning has replaced earlier attempts at intuition or simple guesswork. By using information it is possible to integrate functional business roles and to co-ordinate the many activities necessary to initiate, develop, and sustain a market connection.

In any scientific study the researcher marshals all of the available facts, assembles them into a logical order, and then assesses the probabilities for each possible outcome. In business, companies are able to vary the degrees of order and so may influence the outcome. The probabilities can then be made favourable rather than being left to their natural conclusion. And in business there is no final conclusion – in principle it is infinite.

Part One of this book is about marshalling the facts; strictly speaking it is about gathering facts and provisional judgements, whether inductive or deductive.

On completion of Part One those in business will have a comprehensive grasp of both their own business and of the environment in which it operates. Judicious completion of the questions, both with fact-finding and objective reasoning, will enable Part Two to be undertaken – the planning process – with full awareness of where the business should be heading, how it is to reach its objectives, and what likelihood there is that each potential obstacle can be overcome.

It is tempting to say that those in business will not need all the information suggested, but while there is some truth in this it is likely to mislead. Certainly, the very small firm may find it unnecessary, even prohibitively expensive, but it has to be aware that its larger competitors may have, and be using, the information. Only the executives of small firms can decide at what point the knowledge required becomes essential, and the smallest firm has to be aware of the significance of each piece of research. Moreover, the executives will need to know how little control they have over their company and its marketing effectiveness in the absence of full information. However, for very small firms their market conditions may be so favourable that they can prosper without formal planning so long as those conditions remain unchanged.

To be fully effective a marketing plan has to be operational – it has to be a documentary expression of what particular executives mean to do. It is a co-ordination of individual prospectuses and each executive is held responsible for his or her commitment.

Information is gathered and analysed, decisions are made, and appropriate action is planned (see Figure A). The marketing plan is operational when the actions planned are implemented and monitored. Figure A shows the progressive steps and corresponds to the sequence of chapters in this book, but ignores the loops that arise in structured decision-making.

Information gathering can be tedious, time-consuming, and expensive, but with a little careful thought it does not have to be. Suitably briefed, a local librarian attached to a reference section can be recruited as a researcher.

For more widespread research and for the creation of ideas an approach to a nearby college management studies department and the offer of a prize for a specified piece of research work tied to a class assignment will produce at least one or two accurate and constructive reports. Offering to assess and grade all assignments will bring its own reward.

Carrying out data analysis, including quantitative evaluation, can equally be achieved by recruiting two or three full-time students during their three-to-four weeks work experience time. Briefing for either assignment can often be undertaken in consultation with a course tutor, securing, in addition, an element of consultancy.

Such procedure is normal in many countries of the industrialized world. To ensure the reliability of data contributed in this way, it is prudent to ask the researchers to quote sources; it is surprising how much students are able to obtain from behind closed doors. It is equally surprising how often they provide fresh ideas for product planning, promotions, and market development.

In the UK there is a wealth of data and data sources, often obtainable at little cost. Gathering, marshalling, and assessing the facts is the first step towards organizing the marketing plan.

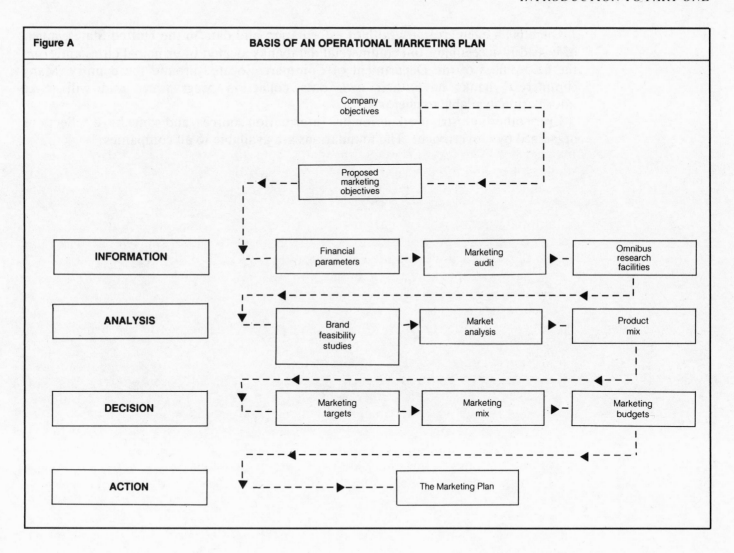

Figure A

BASIS OF AN OPERATIONAL MARKETING PLAN

Company
objectives

Proposed
marketing
objectives

INFORMATION

| Financial parameters | Marketing audit | Omnibus research facilities |

ANALYSIS

| Brand feasibility studies | Market analysis | Product mix |

DECISION

| Marketing targets | Marketing mix | Marketing budgets |

ACTION

The Marketing Plan

There is an even greater wealth of information and data in the United States, much of it readily accessible from commercial databanks located in principal cities and from the field offices of the Department of Commerce located around the country. Many commercial banks have their own data collection programmes and will make information available to clients.

Every other industrialized nation has information sources, and some have collections organized by Government. The foundations are available to all companies.

Auditing Competitiveness 1

Manufacturers make a product: customers buy a brand. Endowing a product with customer recognition, an assurance of value, a clear function, and a unique image makes it a brand. Such is true of consumer goods, industrial equipment, and all services. The success of any brand is determined by the practice of marketing. Marketing provides the bridge between an opportunity and a purchase. Marketing planning is the construction of that bridge.

Every established company has achieved some success in marketing even though the marketing skills may not be apparent. Because techniques in marketing may now be sophisticated it does not mean that those used earlier did not work just as well and so provide a foundation from which many companies still prosper. These companies retain a market connection. Orders come from that connection because of a past innovation, a reliable reputation, a mutual interest, or an established buying channel. The orders are obtained because of marketing practice in the past, even if that practice was not then called marketing. These formalities may continue unchanged until a company within the industry concerned, or entering the industry, introduces modern marketing methods when the picture soon changes. Demand may be stimulated but within that demand shares of the market will change dramatically. Survival requires the introduction of positive marketing action.

This begins with evaluating the market connection in its various forms and using that as a springboard for growth and development. It is not enough to apply marketing cosmetics to the existing product line; this is haphazard and to rely on chance or good fortune is not effective management. The market connection is measured as an element of competitiveness as shown in this chapter.

In the marketing audit it is usual to find a company consists of a complex bundle of issues and consequent subsidiary factors. The audit is undertaken systematically seeking answers to the central issues, separating the significant from the trivial, and facts from opinions. Clearly, one has to be objective and look at the conflicts, the evidence, and the conclusions logically.

In no audit will all of the facts be available. Some may be obtainable, but at a cost in terms of both time and money. So in each situation there will be some aspects on which there is no firm information, and assumptions will have to be made. Quantitative data is often more easily obtained, but it has to be adequate for the purpose for too much reliance on generalizations will tend to support preconceived ideas rather than the revelations required. In addition, data has to be balanced, and consistent, so that conclusions are objective. Qualitative data has to be seen in perspective, and shown in relation to alternatives, particularly where conclusions are drawn in the absence of facts.

Figure 1.1 Company audit

Answering the questions requires considerable thought. Each answer has to be considered in the light of the market connection. This requires an understanding of consumers, customers or clients. They do not buy a lawnmower, they buy a neat garden. They do not want a new lathe, they want greater productivity. They dislike obtaining a loan but they do want its spending power. The brand they choose is the one that gives them what they want. They may even be uncertain as to what they want until such time as they have it clarified.

The main difficulty is separating what a company believes it has to offer and what people in the market perceive as the offer. Every company has an image which may vary within different segments of the market. Successful companies decide on the image they want within the market they choose to serve. This audit should begin the necessary process.

Figure 1.2 Inventory of company resources

As the true company value is its market connection, the emphasis in this audit is on valuing the company's historical marketing. It is the existing state of past investments. While valuation may be difficult, it has to be seen as if a takeover bid is in the offing and how the company would then be valued.

Product evaluation requires classification for each product and a sales analysis of past invoices so that profiles and trends can be formulated. In many companies, products may not be classified by the headings suggested until after the analysis has

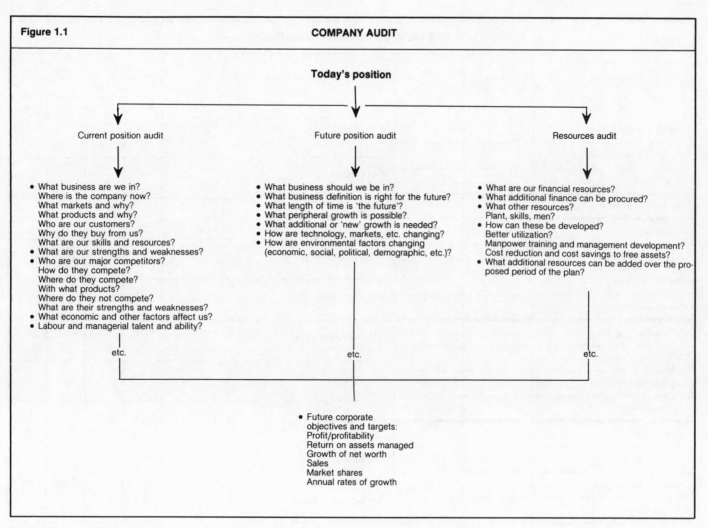

Figure 1.1   COMPANY AUDIT

Today's position

Current position audit   Future position audit   Resources audit

- What business are we in?
  Where is the company now?
  What markets and why?
  What products and why?
  Who are our customers?
  Why do they buy from us?
  What are our skills and resources?
- What are our strengths and weaknesses?
- Who are our major competitors?
  How do they compete?
  Where do they compete?
  With what products?
  Where do they not compete?
  What are their strengths and weaknesses?
- What economic and other factors affect us?
- Labour and managerial talent and ability?

- What business should we be in?
- What business definition is right for the future?
- What length of time is 'the future'?
- What peripheral growth is possible?
- What additional or 'new' growth is needed?
- How are technology, markets, etc. changing?
- How are environmental factors changing (economic, social, political, demographic, etc.)?

- What are our financial resources?
- What additional finance can be procured?
- What other resources?
  Plant, skills, men?
- How can these be developed?
  Better utilization?
  Manpower training and management development?
  Cost reduction and cost savings to free assets?
- What additional resources can be added over the proposed period of the plan?

etc.   etc.   etc.

- Future corporate
  objectives and targets:
  Profit/profitability
  Return on assets managed
  Growth of net worth
  Sales
  Market shares
  Annual rates of growth

Source: D.W. Foster, *Planning for Products and Markets*, Longman, 1972.

| Figure 1.2 | | | INVENTORY OF COMPANY RESOURCES | | | | |

ASSET	Profile (%) Current year	£/$ Valuation Current year times 8	PRODUCT EVALUATION	Profile (%) Current year		Profile (%) +5 years	
				Sales	GM	Sales	GM
Manufacturing capability			Current density sales				
Physical plant and equipment							
Location value			Future density sales				
Raw material reserves							
Financial strength			House accounts specials				
Patents protection			New product development				
Products portfolio							
Distribution network			Sleeper products				
Sales volume			Historical density sales				
Unique market connection							
Significant market share			Filler products				
Innovative history							
Cyclical stability			Inherited problems				
Management calibre			Prestige (EGO) products				
Specialized experience							
Personnel skills			Dormant–High potential				

been completed. The first four headings are the company's future; the others may be deleted now or in the near future. The exception will be *dormant–high potential.* Any in this category have to be assessed for marketability.

Figure 1.3 SWOT Analysis

The key issues in the SWOT (Strengths, Weaknesses, Opportunities, Threats) analysis appear in the marketing plan under each operational activity. The plan is a formalized attempt to exploit strengths, overcome weaknesses, seize opportunities, and counter threats.

The SWOT analysis should indicate possibilities for differentiating company products; the analysis in the chart will show the facts and it is up to the company to seek answers as to why the results are as revealed. Progressing to Chapter 3 it will then be possible to segment and differentiate. And then to Chapter 5 for establishing necessary objectives.

If it is not possible to complete this chart for competing brands it will be necessary to gather relevant information shown in Chapters 2, 4 and 5.

Figure 1.4 Product-line profitability report

It may be necessary for some companies to undertake this report, and the detailed analysis involved, before completing the charts shown in Figures 1.1, 1.2, and 1.3. In firms where a number of product lines are promoted by a single sales team and one advertising budget, it will be necessary to allocate contribution costs to each product line. While it may be quicker to allocate costs pro rata to sales it will be more revealing to do so on 'time absorption' suitably priced. In many companies the products bringing the least in sales and profit require the most time and attention. Pareto's Law may apply in these situations, 20 per cent of products requiring 80 per cent of time, cost and problems.

Figure 1.5 Consumption audit

Although the questions are qualitative it is advisable to develop answers quantitatively. Percentages, by index or profile, ratios and whole numbers, where possible, add substance to conclusions.

This audit is about market movements and how markets are moved and by what, and is therefore fundamental to planning and to marketing activity.

Figure 1.6 Establishing a competitive advantage

Although all products and services are offered to satisfy a need, buyers choose the one that they believe will satisfy them best.

Therefore, every product or service has to have some additional benefit beyond its basic function in order to stand out from others and be chosen. This is differential marketing; it requires a study of markets and the products required, and the recognition of a benefit. This is then incorporated into the product or service, sufficient to give the company a competitive advantage.

Figure 1.7 Auditing the marketing philosophy

In recent years companies have embraced marketing, often as a panacea to solve all business problems, and have poured vast resources into its adoption. Unfortunately too many have seen it as only an effective communications facility. They have spent money on cosmetic marketing with scant regard for its philosophy. Through the checklists shown in this chart it is possible for the company to assess its own true marketing orientation.

Although it is easy to treat the questions on a yes/no basis, it will be more revealing and accurate if every 'yes' is qualified by a reasoned explanation. Try writing a speech incorporating the answers and be prepared for searching questions from the audience.

If 'no' appears more often than considered acceptable then attempt to provide remedial action. What can be done to change the situation?

If, as is most likely, a number of answers suggest partial 'yes' and partial 'no', then regard the answer as 'no' and provide remedial action using the partial 'yes' as the early foundations.

Figure 1.3		SWOT ANALYSIS		
Strength	Opportunity	Measure	Weakness	Threat
		Market share		
		Price index		
		Growth rate		
		Volume sales index		
		Value sales index		
		Profit margin index		
		Rate of stock turn		
		Stock levels		
		Price elasticity		
		Promotional expenditure		
		Return on investment (ROI)		
		Advertising/Sales ratio		
		Advertising unit cost		
		Price relationship		
		Market recognition		
		Segmentation		
		Differentiation		
		Brand loyalty		
		Unique selling proposition		
		Innovative rate		
		Economic		
		Political		
		Fiscal		
		Legal		
		Social		
		Technological		
		Detail OWN BRAND and three MAJOR COMPETITORS		

Source: RMS Wilson, 'The Role of the Accountant in Marketing', *Marketing Forum*, 1971.

Figure 1.4 **PRODUCT-LINE PROFITABILITY REPORT**

Period ending:	Total product line	Brand A	Brand B	Brand C	Brand D
1 Sales volume					
2 Market potential					
3 Sales % potential					
4 Total marketing costs					
5 Total call costs					
6 Total service costs					
7 Total delivery costs					
8 Total advertising and promotion costs					
9 Total marketing research costs					
10 Total marketing admin costs					
11 Marketing costs % sales					
12 Gross margin					
13 Profit contribution					
14 Profit contribution rate					
15 Product net profit					
16 Volume % of total					
17 Gross margin % of total					
18 Profit contribution % of total					
19 Profit % of total					
20 Number of customers					
21 Volume/customers					
22 Call, delivery and service					
23 New profit/customer					
24 Inventory					
25 Cost of goods sold					
26 Total investment					
27 Net profit/sales					
28 Sales/investment					
29 Return on investment					
30 Break-even point					
31 Safety factors					
32 $\dfrac{\text{(Volume} - \text{BE)}}{\text{BE}}$					

Figure 1.5	CONSUMPTION AUDIT
1	Is the total market in decline?
2	Is the brand share in decline?
3	What position does the brand rank?
4	Will brand share increase if promoted?
5	Can retail selling price bear an increase?
6	Can production economies be achieved?
7	Can range be reduced?
8	What other markets are possible?
9	What is the profit contribution?
10	What is the break-even point?
11	Can the brand be revitalized?
12	Can the brand be sold off?
A	Who are the potential buyers?
B	What is the size and scope of the potential market?
C	What is the distribution of the potential market?
D	What are the needs, habits, and buying motives of the potential market?
E	What related products will/do people buy?
F	What is the expected buying frequency?
G	What is the likely buying quantity?
H	Who is the purchasing agent in the target audience family?
I	Who influences brand choice decisions?
J	What price differentials are possible among market segments?
K	Is the buying derived from some other purchase?
L	Is the buying on impulse or predetermined?
M	Is the demand likely to be elastic?
N	Is the brand likely to be price sensitive?
O	Is the demand going to be dependent on merchandising?
P	What factors are likely to limit demand?
Q	What is the effect of fashion/technological changes?
R	What seasonal factors are apparent?
S	What is likely to be the average rate of consumption?
T	What factors are likely to affect the consumption rate?
U	What emotive/psychological factors need to be taken into account?
V	What current legislation exists: safety, packaging, labelling, weights?
W	How are problems related to pre-sales and after-sales?
X	What additional credit/financing is likely to be required?
Y	What guarantees/warranties are appropriate?
Z	What are marked preferences for choice of outlet?

Figure 1.6	ESTABLISHING A COMPETITIVE ADVANTAGE
1	What physical characteristics may be unique?
2	What performance characteristics may be unique?
3	What marketing characteristics may be unique?
4	What uniqueness may be introduced without sacrificing present value?
5	What are present users' attitudes, beliefs or perceptions of the product's competitiveness?
6	What market gaps exist that a slight product modification will fill?
7	What is our present state of market knowledge and can it be extended?
8	How much would buyers be prepared to pay for additional features?
9	Would minor modifications release existing pressure on prices?
10	What existing features could be removed without market dissatisfaction?
11	What other geographical markets exist where current products would provide a major innovation?
12	What other commercial values may be provided to improve the value of the purchase?
13	What commercial values may be placed on these other benefits by each market segment?
14	What opportunities exist for providing turnkey contracts?
15	What variations of the basic product may be introduced so as to provide unlimited specials?
16	What additional scope exists for guarantees, warranties, or penalty clauses?
17	What scope exists for promoting liberal approach to past claims?
18	What additional guarantees would buyers welcome?
19	What existing guarantee restrictions cause the most irritation?
20	What other distribution channels exist?
21	What additional customer/client personnel training facilities would be welcome?
22	What is the normal journey cycle of salesmen?
23	How can we appeal direct to customer management or operational executives?
24	Are there any secondary or alternative uses for our product?
25	What media influence our markets?
26	What company/product image could assist in winning a reputation monopoly?

Figure 1.7   **AUDITING THE MARKETING PHILOSOPHY**

YOUR MARKETING MANAGEMENT
Are you marketing orientated?

Unless your company has some unique quality, whether of substance or image, then you are leaving your future prospects to luck. Although an invaluable asset, luck is not an acceptable marketing policy. Relying on service or quality arguments is irrelevant, for today every competitor uses such clichés, and every customer has a legitimate right to such consideration. Your product is the most important single representative of your company, so it should be given a unique competitive advantage.

1 Do you have an established and formal marketing philosophy; where all decisions are made with prior understanding of the needs of your customers?
2 Have you considered the essential role of the behavioural sciences in your marketing practices?
3 Can you define your market segments and provide a detailed customer profile?
4 Do you have a detailed operational marketing plan?
5 Is there a marketing research programme that aids your commercial decisions?
6 Has your new product development provided a contribution to profits this year?
7 Do you have clearly defined objectives for marketing, selling, advertising, promotions, and media functions?
8 Does your marketing organization provide the essential communications service with your markets?
9 Have your careful deliberations considered every element in the expanded marketing mix; by marketing audit?
10 Do you win orders or do you make customers?

YOUR SELLING PRACTICE
Do your salesmen operate marketing principles?

1 Are you confident you have the most appropriate selling organization?
2 Are you sure you know the essential elements of successful selling?
3 Do you have the full benefits of field sales management?
4 Do your salesmen practise planned selling?
5 Do you have formal sales management planning?
6 Do your salesmen operate with the benefit of a sales manual?
7 Have your sales territories been divided according to measurable market potential?
8 Have you sales literature that sells to the right sort of customers?
9 Is your sales office selling your company image?
10 Do you have sales force documentation that helps management decisions?

YOUR PRODUCT STRATEGY
Do you have increasing demand?

1 Have you yet established a sound reputation monopoly?
2 Do you have a significant competitive advantage?
3 What value leadership do you exercise?
4 To what extent do you have effective product acceptance?
5 Are you ready to innovate your present brand range?
6 Do you provide sufficient supporting services to ensure value for money to your customers?
7 Has your product range been adequately rationalized?
8 What stage in the product life-cycle does each of your brands occupy?
9 Are you able to monitor each brand's performance against competition?
10 Do you have strong product management?

YOUR DISTRIBUTION SERVICES

1 Can you evaluate the effectiveness of your distribution channels?
2 Do you have effective distribution; do your products have prominent positions?
3 Are you practising inventory control?
4 Have you a full understanding of incentive marketing?
5 Do you acknowledge the logistics of distribution?
6 Have you a policy for materials handling?
7 Are you able to evaluate different physical distribution methods?
8 Have you fully considered direct marketing?
9 Do you understand the role of the many different retail/distributor trades?
10 Are you aware of the various techniques in retail merchandising, making full use of the silent salesmen?

YOUR PRICING POLICY
Are you providing real value?

1 Do you have formal pricing objectives?
2 What strategic pricing policies do you have, are you tapping the right market segment?
3 Have you established an appropriate pricing procedure?
4 Does your organization practice value pricing?
5 Can you identify the major pricing determinants?
6 To what extent does price elasticity apply to your main brands?
7 Do you have a comprehensive product line pricing policy?
8 Can you implement flexible pricing techniques?
9 Do you have an acceptable means of increasing prices?
10 Are you able to mount stimulating pricing promotions?

Figure 1.7	AUDITING THE MARKETING PHILOSOPHY *(cont.)*	
YOUR ADVERTISING COMMUNICATIONS **Are your communications cost-effective?** 1 Do you undertake detailed advertising planning; and secure identifiable profits as a result? 2 Are you sure you secure the best from your advertising agency? 3 Do you have appropriate advertising objectives? 4 Are you confident that your communications are highly creative? 5 Do you understand the basic principles of writing copy? 6 Do you know how to brief specialists on layout and design? 7 Can you undertake cost-effective media evaluation, selection, and planning? 8 Have you a full awareness of the methods of advertising research? 9 Do you know the self-regulating advertising controls? 10 Are you able to evaluate a direct mail marketing campaign?	**YOUR PACKAGING SYSTEM** **Does your package or packaging reflect your product?** 1 Do you have specific packaging objectives? 2 Have you formulated clear packaging strategy; is your package part of the product? 3 Do you know how to provide a comprehensive packaging brief? 4 Have you considered proposals from industrial design firms? 5 Have you made full use of the potential from packaging communications? 6 Can you identify the significant packaging parameters? 7 Have you mounted positive packaging promotions, as part of advertising? 8 Do you have a packaging information system? 9 Do you make full use of packaging tactics, promoting other products or services? 10 Have you full information on the requirements for export packaging?	**YOUR PUBLIC RELATIONS ACTIVITY** **Do you have a cultivated company image?** 1 Do you know the scope for top management involvement? 2 To what extent do you use public relations to disseminate real information? 3 Could you write a publishable press release? 4 Are you able to prepare a worthwhile feature article? 5 Are you aware of the guidelines for having photographs published? 6 Do you make your exhibition activities a logistics exercise? 7 Are you able to prepare and distribute a house journal? 8 Have you the means of making a speech? 9 Are you prepared for television or radio interviews? 10 Do you know the public relations codes of conduct?

Collecting Marketing Information 2

Information is the raw material of successful business management. In small firms, owners are in touch with their employees and customers, and with limited information flow are able to carry details in their head and may make intuitive decisions sufficient for the scale of the business. But at each platform of growth the gap between sources of information and decision-makers frequently widens and the amount of information increases.

For larger organizations there are usually intermediaries between management and consumers. In the absence of direct contact and with time lags between consumer purchasing and retail stock replacement management requires instant information and from independent sources. As marketing is discovering, creating, arousing, and satisfying customer needs profitably, it is essential that information be obtained at each stage. How effective the company is depends therefore on how much, how relevant, and how good its information is, and how well it interprets and acts on that information.

Information is essential to each and every chapter in this book. Information and data are the essence of marketing planning and from which successful marketing practice results. Preparing the format for the marketing plan is dependent on the amount and value of available information. The essential criterion for information, however, is management's decision-making needs. If particular information or data is required, it will be obtained, the only proviso being that the cost of securing it is less than the expected return.

Marketing management's decision-making role is related to the careful selection of information, its collection, processing, analysis, interpretation, and communication. Too much information is as frustrating to management as too little. The first action of the marketing executive must be to decide just what is required to make profitable decisions. This book provides the foundations and the formal structure for such a course of action, and this chapter highlights one area of marketing activity; but throughout the book there is the emphasis on the formation of a total marketing information system. Such a system must do more than just monitor orders received and sales recorded; it must help marketing executives to make better decisions on pricing, advertising, promotions, product policy, design, and sales force activity. It needs a set of procedures for the systematic collection, analysis, and presentation of data, and the diagnosis and prognosis of information for making marketing decisions.

There are two types of marketing information: the operational and the investigative. Operational data and information is needed for the planning and controlling of marketing practice, while the investigative is concerned with primary and secondary research in order to generate supporting data. Information is therefore provided for research, planning and control.

The research section relates to market and marketing research, and is concerned with each element in the company marketing mix.

Inherent in a marketing information system is the co-ordination between marketing executives and the production and accounting departments. Such co-ordination in many organizations is undertaken by brand managers.

One of the more important characteristics of a system is the exception-reporting method. All revenues and expenditures are budgeted and variations from such budgets are identified. If the variations appear favourable, they may suggest opportunities for further exploitation. Should they be unfavourable, remedial action may be necessary and a contingency plan implemented. Suitably established, the system provides for a fully-automated monitoring procedure.

Introduction of an information system follows a detailed marketing audit, where a complete study of the company organization is undertaken and a report provided on its information needs. The report will cover each marketing subset, but establishes an integrated reporting system. Such a system will provide for common denominators, so that both regression analysis and correlation potential may be fully utilized, and different types of data will be compatible for comparison and evaluation purposes.

Fully computerizing the system and installing a visual display and retrieval procedure may provide instant response to questions while reducing the amount and complexity of paperwork and its storage. For many companies building a marketing information system based on visual display, and providing microfilm records, enables effective management action.

Figure 2.1(a) and *(b)*   *Sources of information*
These two charts indicate the wealth of information available, which can be obtained by contacting the Market & Statistics Library of the UK, or a field office of the Department of Commerce in the USA. In most cases the required information may be obtained from a local chamber of commerce or reference library.

Figure 2.2   Prestel videotex
Prestel is a registered trademark and part of the British Telecom service. It provides for the distribution of data and information throughout the UK – sales, orders, quotations, schedules, reservations, servicing, pricing, stock holding, and other pertinent marketing information is being relayed by companies large and small.

   Similarly, financial institutions are providing customers with equipment to obtain 24-hour checks and to issue instructions on financial dealings.

Figure 2.3   Retail audits
This company operates a single continuous retail audit panel, producing regular information on market trends. Research can be provided for individual needs – distribution, retail and trade opinion.

Figure 2.4   Tracking advertising and brand strength (TABS)
TABS is a continuous, weekly syndicated monitor tracking brand health and advertising effectiveness across the media. It measures what influence advertising and other marketing activities are really having on the target audience. The information it gains is used to assess the creative execution of client advertising and the planning or buying of media. This brand research covers usage, awareness, goodwill, image, price image, and advertising awareness.

Figure 2.5   The television consumer audit
In the UK, Audits of Great Britain plc (AGB) provides continuing research data appropriate for decision-making on television advertising. This illustration gives a detailed breakdown of available information from AGB. The audit is based on sampling techniques and enables management to secure prompt data on its brand's performance in the market-place, a comparative consumption barometer.

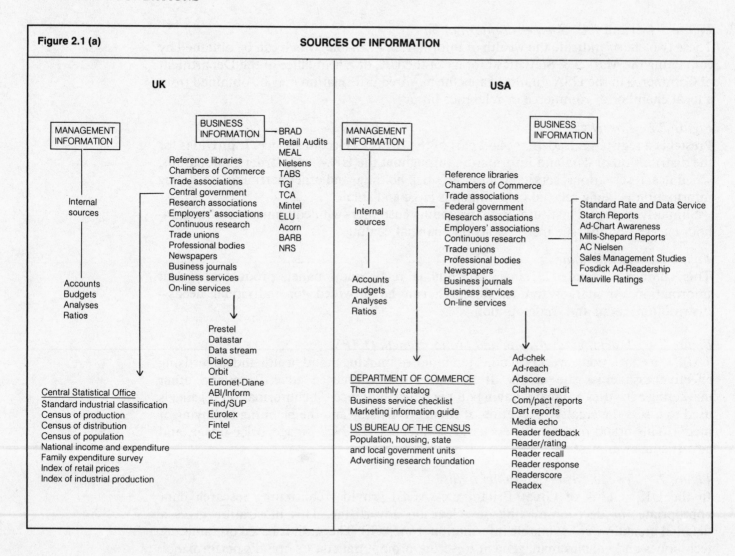

Figure 2.1 (a)   **SOURCES OF INFORMATION**

UK

MANAGEMENT INFORMATION

BUSINESS INFORMATION → BRAD, Retail Audits, MEAL, Nielsens, TABS, TGI, TCA, Mintel, ELU, Acorn, BARB, NRS

Reference libraries
Chambers of Commerce
Trade associations
Central government
Research associations
Employers' associations
Continuous research
Trade unions
Professional bodies
Newspapers
Business journals
Business services
On-line services

Internal sources

Accounts
Budgets
Analyses
Ratios

Prestel
Datastar
Data stream
Dialog
Orbit
Euronet-Diane
ABI/Inform
Find/SUP
Eurolex
Fintel
ICE

Central Statistical Office
Standard industrial classification
Census of production
Census of distribution
Census of population
National income and expenditure
Family expenditure survey
Index of retail prices
Index of industrial production

USA

MANAGEMENT INFORMATION

BUSINESS INFORMATION

Reference libraries
Chambers of Commerce
Trade associations
Federal government
Research associations
Employers' associations
Continuous research
Trade unions
Professional bodies
Newspapers
Business journals
Business services
On-line services

Internal sources

Accounts
Budgets
Analyses
Ratios

Standard Rate and Data Service
Starch Reports
Ad-Chart Awareness
Mills-Shepard Reports
AC Nielsen
Sales Management Studies
Fosdick Ad-Readership
Mauville Ratings

DEPARTMENT OF COMMERCE
The monthly catalog
Business service checklist
Marketing information guide

US BUREAU OF THE CENSUS
Population, housing, state
and local government units
Advertising research foundation

Ad-chek
Ad-reach
Adscore
Clahners audit
Com/pact reports
Dart reports
Media echo
Reader feedback
Reader/rating
Reader recall
Reader response
Readerscore
Readex

Figure 2.1 (b)	**SOURCES OF INFORMATION**
Science Reference Library Official Publications Library London Chamber of Commerce and Industry City Business Library Statistics and Market Intelligence Library Companies Registration Office On-line Information Centre City University London Business School	Stock Exchange Yearbook Jane's Major Companies of Europe Kompass Series Guide to Key British Enterprises Kelly's Manufacturers and Merchants Fortune Top 1000 USA Companies The Times 1000 Who Owns Whom Directory of Directors Gower Handbooks
Anglo-American Trade Directory Extel British Companies Service Extel Handbook of Market Leaders Europa Yearbook Moodies Industries and Commodities Service UK Trade Names Comparative Performance of British Industries (Wood) Dun & Bradstreet Standard & Poor Predicasts	Encyclopedia of Management (Heyel) Handbook of Management (Kempner) How to Find Out — Management and Productivity (Bakewell) Business Information Sources (Campbell) Sources of Business Information (Coman) Business Reference Sources (Daniells) Commercial Information (Davinson) Economics and Commerce — The Sources of Information (Maltby) Guide to Reference Material (Walford) European Companies (C & D research) World Bibliography of Bibliographies (Besterman)

Figure 2.2   **PRESTEL VIDEOTEX (UK)**

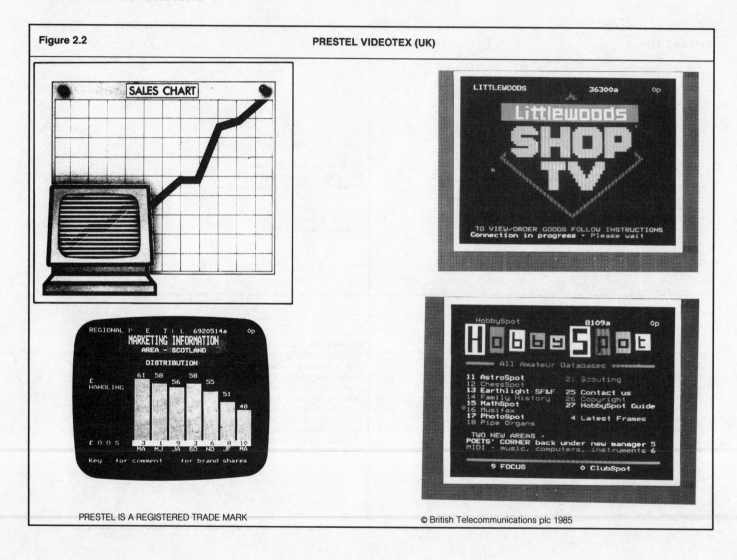

PRESTEL IS A REGISTERED TRADE MARK

Figure 2.3   **RETAIL AUDITS**

- Consumer sales and share
- Retailer purchases and share
- Stock levels and share
- Stock cover
- Prices
- Distribution quantity
- Distribution quality

- Changes in relative market size by shop type/area
- Brand share movements
- Changes in consumer buying patterns
- Impact of new product introductions
- Distribution 'pipe-line lags'
- Seasonal and promotional changes in stock levels
- Effectiveness of advertising campaigns and promotions

RETAIL OMNIBUS
- What sort of company image do you really have?
- Is it what you want – or thought it was?
- How do you rate compared to your competitors?
- How good is your delivery service?
- What does the retailer think of your sales force, trade terms, and advertising?
- Why does the retailer stock some products but not others?
- What would the reaction be to possible new products?
- What are the major current/future trends?

RETAIL LINE
- Which products are stocked
- Their selling price
- How much space they are given
- What point-of-sale material is on display
- The extent to which your product range is stocked

- Percentage distribution of brands or product types by outlet types
- Data from named multiples, a vital sector of the retail trade
- A regional analysis of data by television areas

Figure 2.4	TRACKING ADVERTISING AND BRAND STRENGTH

Brand strength

- Early warning of developing image problems
- Area information — strengths and weaknesses
- How do price changes affect price image/brand goodwill?

Advertising: creative performance

- Is your campaign more intrusive/better branded than competitors?
- Does your campaign build brand awareness?
- Is your campaign benefiting your competitors (and vice versa) — if so to what extent?
- Does improved advertising awareness convert into brand goodwill/usership?
- Is your advertising building the desired image for the brand?

Advertising: media performance

- Which media work best?
- Which media perform for your brand, i.e. deliver awareness/goodwill?
- Area media experiments

Figure 2.5   **THE TELEVISION CONSUMER AUDIT**

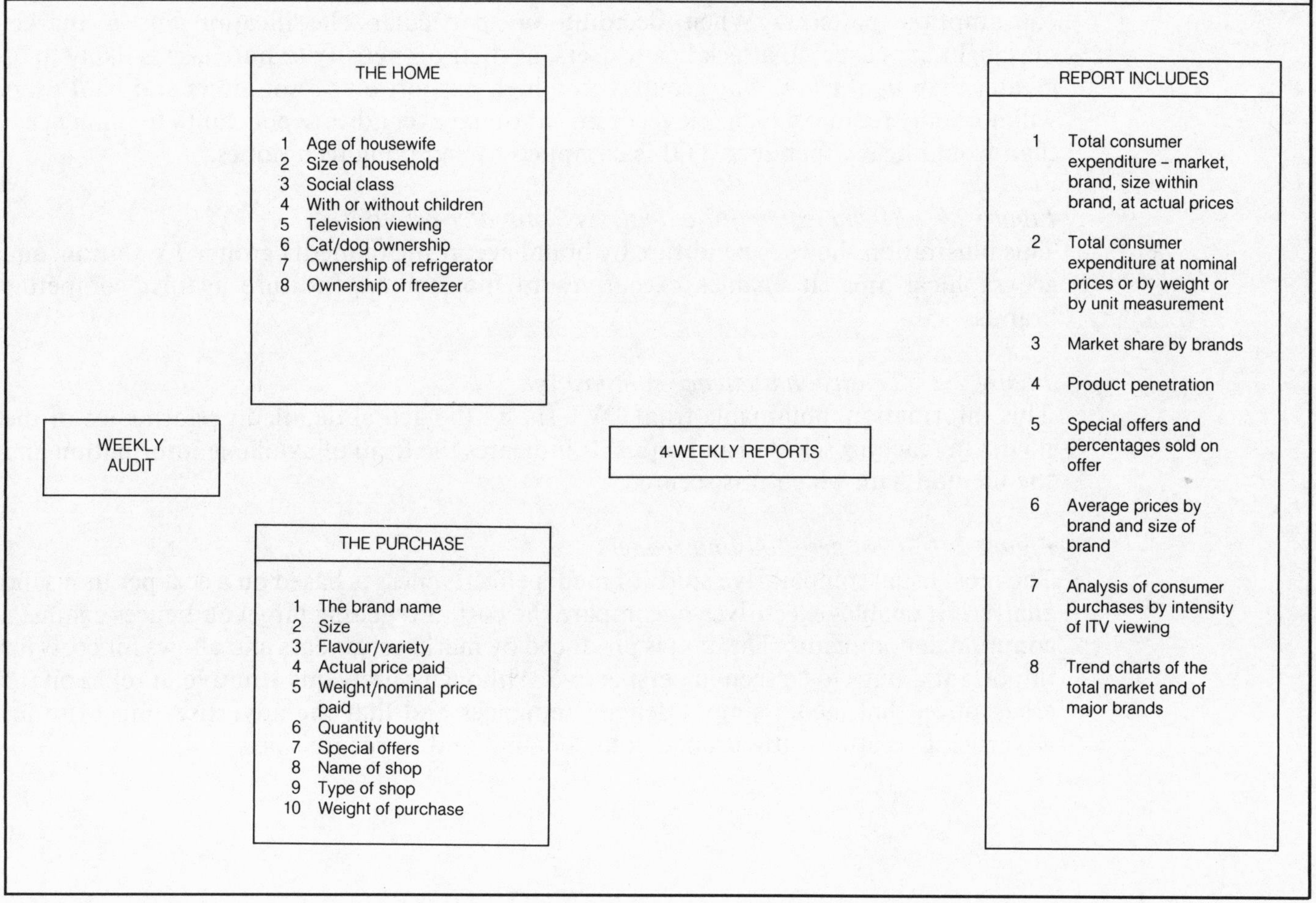

THE HOME

1 Age of housewife
2 Size of household
3 Social class
4 With or without children
5 Television viewing
6 Cat/dog ownership
7 Ownership of refrigerator
8 Ownership of freezer

REPORT INCLUDES

1 Total consumer expenditure – market, brand, size within brand, at actual prices

2 Total consumer expenditure at nominal prices or by weight or by unit measurement

3 Market share by brands

4 Product penetration

5 Special offers and percentages sold on offer

6 Average prices by brand and size of brand

7 Analysis of consumer purchases by intensity of ITV viewing

8 Trend charts of the total market and of major brands

WEEKLY AUDIT

4-WEEKLY REPORTS

THE PURCHASE

1 The brand name
2 Size
3 Flavour/variety
4 Actual price paid
5 Weight/nominal price paid
6 Quantity bought
7 Special offers
8 Name of shop
9 Type of shop
10 Weight of purchase

Figure 2.6   TGI product tables
Target Group Index combines media behaviour of market groups with their consumption patterns. When deciding on particular classification for a market onslaught, it is usual to attack heavy users, as their propensity to purchase is likely to be greater than light users. Any group with a high proportion of non-users and light users will normally require a higher level of promotional expenditure per capita to influence it than would heavy spenders. TGI is compiled by sampling techniques.

Figure 2.7   Media expenditure analysis (computer printout)
This illustration shows expenditure by brand according to media group, TV station, and geographical area. It enables executives to monitor expenditure against competing brands.

Figure 2.8   Television audience composition
This information, obtainable from JWT shows the actual detailed performance of the media in reaching selected audiences. It indicates the form of available information and the method with which it is secured.

Figure 2.9   Cost per thousand readers
The most usual comparative study of media effectiveness is based on a cost per thousand analysis. It enables executives to compare the cost of reaching target audiences against a common denominator. The data is produced by market segments and allows for costs for important groups to be seen in perspective. Although purely quantitative, it relies on the assumption that media simply deliver audiences and that the advertiser must use his advertising to attract attention, create demand, and so secure sales.

Figure 2.6

TGI PRODUCT TABLES

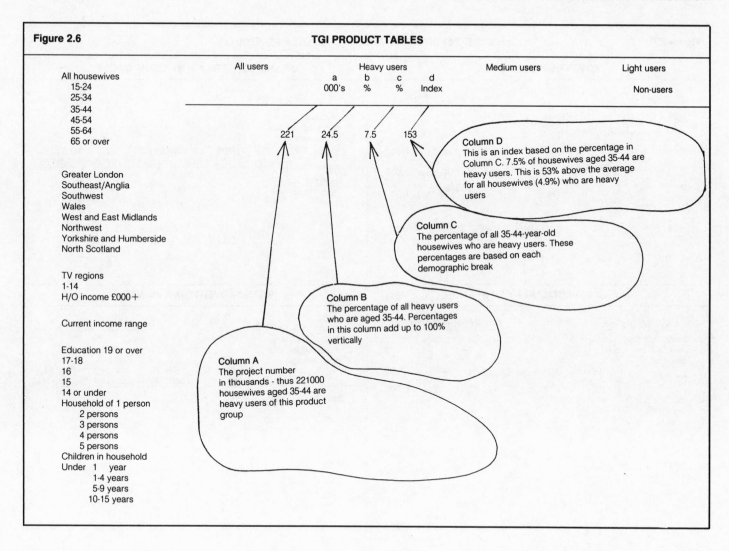

All users

Heavy users

a   b   c   d

000's   %   %   Index

Medium users

Light users

Non-users

All housewives
15-24
25-34
35-44
45-54
55-64
65 or over

Greater London
Southeast/Anglia
Southwest
Wales
West and East Midlands
Northwest
Yorkshire and Humberside
North Scotland

TV regions
1-14
H/O income £000+

Current income range

Education 19 or over
17-18
16
15
14 or under
Household of 1 person
    2 persons
    3 persons
    4 persons
    5 persons
Children in household
Under 1   year
    1-4 years
    5-9 years
    10-15 years

221   24.5   7.5   153

Column D
This is an index based on the percentage in Column C. 7.5% of housewives aged 35-44 are heavy users. This is 53% above the average for all housewives (4.9%) who are heavy users

Column C
The percentage of all 35-44-year-old housewives who are heavy users. These percentages are based on each demographic break

Column B
The percentage of all heavy users who are aged 35-44. Percentages in this column add up to 100% vertically

Column A
The project number in thousands - thus 221000 housewives aged 35-44 are heavy users of this product group

Figure 2.7 **MEDIA EXPENDITURE ANALYSIS (COMPUTER PRINTOUT)**

ADVERTISING ANALYSIS

CATEGORY C DRINK   Product Group 35 SHERRY

BRAND	DAY	SIZE/DURN	DES/TIME	MEDIA	COST £
330C Harvey's Bristol Cream					
	25	30 sec	1946	Trident	1000
	27 1P		4 CLISS	D. Express	20000
	2 1P	4B FH		D. Tel Mag	4000

Total Press £ 000   TV £ 000   Total £ 000

BRAND ADVERTISING BY MEDIA GROUP

CATEGORY C DRINK   Product Group 35 SHERRY

Products spending
over £300 this mth
or on average

	GRAND TOTAL	TV TOTAL	PRESS TOTAL	POPULAR DAILIES	POPULAR SUNDAYS	QUALITY DAILIES	QUALITY SUNDAYS
EMVA £00 mth							
JWT % PR							
HARVEYS £00 mth							
CD % PR							

BRAND ADVERTISING BY TV STATION

CATEGORY C DRINK   Product Group 35 SHERRY

Brand spending
over £300 this mth
or average

	GRAND TOTAL	THAMS	LWT	STH	ANG	WEST
Dry Sack	0015 sec					
	0030 sec					
	£00 mth					
	% PR					
Emva						
JWT						

BRAND ADVERTISING BY AREA

CATEGORY C DRINK   Product Group 35 SHERRY

Brands spending
over £300 this mth
or on average

		LONDON MTH MAT	SOUTH MTH MAT	E.ANG MTH MAT	WALES/W. MTH MAT
Emva	TV £00				
	% PR				
	PRESS £00				
	% PR				
	TOTAL £00				
	% PR				

Figure 2.8

TELEVISION AUDIENCE COMPOSITION

TELEVISION — ITV1

AREA	TOTAL ITV HOMES/ HOUSEWIVES '000s	%	PROFILE NET OF OVERLAP %	30 SEC AVERAGE RATE (MAR '86) JWT Est. £	AVERAGE HOUSEWIFE RATINGS (MAR '86)
London	4,278	20.82	19.73	4,710	14.8
Midland	3,373	16.41	15.26	2,340	15.7
North West	2,510	12.21	11.95	1,890	17.9
Yorkshire	2,222	10.81	10.29	1,510	15.2
Central Scotland	1,264	6.15	6.13	1,000	18.0
Wales & West	1,734	8.44	7.71	1,170	15.7
South & S. East	1,988	9.67	8.97	1,620	13.3
North East	1,143	5.56	5.19	690	18.0
E. England	1,51†	7.35	6.41	990	15.3
South West	605	2.94	2.86	450	15.7
Ulster	464	2.26	2.26	300	19.6
Border	248	1.21	1.18	140	20.6
North Scotland	436	2.12	2.06	250	17.7
Network	20,550*	105.95	100.00	17,060	16.6

* Total excluding duplication of homes in areas capable of receiving more than one station

JULY 1985 — JUNE 1986 AVERAGE MONTHLY RATINGS/INDEX OF INDUSTRY CPT
(Network/All Time)

	J	A	S	O	N	D	J	F	M	A	M	J
Housewives												
TVRs ITV	13.4	14.3	15.3	16.3	17.0	16.6	18.5	17.8	16.6	15.6	13.8	12.7
TVRs Ch4	2.8	3.1	2.5	3.0	3.4	3.5	3.8	4.8	3.9	3.7	3.7	2.8
Combined CPT Index§	92	74	111	119	118	96	79	85	92	97	109	129
Adults												
TVRs ITV	11.1	12.0	12.7	13.6	14.2	14.4	15.7	15.0	14.3	13.1	11.6	10.8
TVRs Ch4	2.5	2.7	2.2	2.6	3.0	3.1	3.4	4.2	3.4	3.1	3.1	2.4
Combined CPT Index§	94	74	112	120	119	94	78	85	90	97	110	128

§ Jul '85 — Jun '86 Ave = 100
Source: BARB/AGB Special Analysis/JWT Estimates

TOP 10 ITV1 PROGRAMMES JULY 1985 — JUNE 1986*

			Audience Millions
1.	Coronation Street	Wed 18/Thur 19 Jun	22.75
2.	The Prince & Princess of Wales	Sun 20 Oct	18.60
3.	Wish You Were Here	Mon 17/Wed 19 Feb	18.35
4.	People Do The Funniest things	Sat 11 Jan	17.85
5.	Blind Date	Sat 11 Jan	17.65
6.	Fresh Fields	Wed 8 Oct	17.50
7.	Duty Free	Wed 8 Jan	17.35
8.	You Only Live Twice	Tue 7 Jan	17.30
9.	From Russia With Love	Sun 8 Dec	17.25
10.	An Officer And A Gentleman	Mon 31 Mar	16.35

* Only the highest rating edition of each programme has been included

TELEVISION — CH4

AREA	PENETRATION OF HOME ITV HOUSEHOLDS '000s	%*	(% FROM HOME STATION)	AVERAGE ADULT RATING (March '86) ALL	ABC1	16—24
London	4,207	98	93	3.0	1.8	1.8
Midland	3,329	99	92	3.2	1.8	1.2
North West	2,474	99	96	3.9	2.6	2.3
Yorkshire	2,192	99	94	3.7	2.7	1.7
Central Scotland	1,224	97	97	4.1	2.9	1.7
Wales & West	1,686	97	89	2.8	2.3	1.5
South & S. East	1,919	97	90	2.6	2.2	1.3
North East	1,133	99	93	4.2	2.9	2.2
E. England	1,479	98	85	2.8	2.3	1.4
South West	594	98	96	3.0	2.5	1.8
Ulster	432	93	93	3.7	3.5	1.5
Border	239	96	93	4.5	3.2	2.3
North Scotland	419	96	94	2.9	2.3	2.0
Network	20,151	98	98	3.4	2.3	1.8

* Receiving CH4 from ANY transmitter

TOP 10 PROGRAMMES JULY 1985 — JUNE 1986*

			Audience Millions
1.	Brookside	Mon 24/Sat 29 Mar	8.00
2.	A Woman of Substance	Thu 15 May	7.55
3.	Athletics	Fri 9 Aug	7.05
4.	It'll Be Alright Late At Night	Thu 11 Jul	6.65
5. =	Man About The House	Mon 14 Oct	6.35
5. =	Treasure Hunt	Thu 27 Feb	6.35
7.	Georgy Girl	Sun 16 Feb	6.25
8	Lord Of The Rings	Sun 5 Jan	6.20
9.	Written On The Wind	Thu 27 May	5.95
10.	Excalibur	Thu 4 Mar	5.80

* Only the highest rating edition of each programme has been included

TV-AM — 30-second Broad Rate — National £4,800
% Total Homes Receiving TV 97%, of which ITV 100%, Colour 88%, Multi Set 43%, VCR 36%

AVERAGE TVR — NETWORK — MARCH 1986	ITV	Ch4	TV-am
Housewives	16.6	3.9	4.3
Adults	14.3	3.4	3.1
Men	12.7	3.1	2.2
Housewives with Children	15.4	3.4	6.9
ABC1 Adults	8.5	2.3	2.0
ABC1 Men	7.5	2.2	1.5
ABC1 Housewives	9.8	2.6	2.6
16—24 Adults	6.0	1.8	1.5
16—44 Men	8.6	2.3	2.3

Sources: BARB/AGB Establishment Survey March '86/ITCA/AGB Special Analyses

J. Walter Thompson, London

Figure 2.9	**COST PER THOUSAND READERS**

SUNDAY NEWSPAPERS

NRS SURVEY			COST PER THOUSAND READERS PER PAGE		IN POUNDS AND PENCE	
ALL ADULTS	OBSERVER		SUNDAY TELEGRAPH	SUNDAY POST	SUNDAY MAIL	
RATE/PAGE	000's	£0000/ PAGE COST				
CIRCULATION	RDRS	PEN				

		London		Profile	National	Publication
ALL		Midlands		15-24	18	26
15–24		North West		25-34	17	20
25–34		Yorkshire		35-44	16	17
35–44		North East		45-54	16	17
45–54		Central Scotland		55-64	16	11
55–64		North Scotland		65 and over	18	9
65 and over		Wales and West				
		South and South East				
Under 35		East of England				
35 and over		South West				
Under 45		Ulster				
45 and over		Border				

				Profile	National	Publication
A				A	3	8
B				B	11	27
C_1				C_1	23	36
C_2				C_2	33	20
D				D	22	8
E				E	9	2
AB						
ABC_1						
C_1C_2						
DE						

Segmenting the Market

Unless a company is able to persuade its potential market that its product or service has some special benefit not offered by competitors, the only way in which it can win and sustain a share of that market is by price-cutting. Many companies do just that, but clearly if all suppliers to one market reduced prices there would be no subsequent advantages. Therefore other benefits are provided.

In any market it is possible to identify suppliers that concentrate on superior quality, or a functional advantage, or additional service elements such as credit, or guarantees, or including product properties such as incentives – gifts, coupons, trading stamps. Each of these companies concentrates on one part of the total market. They each service a core, usually competing against other companies aiming at the same core. Sales growth is confined to expanding that core or widening the core into its fringes.

This process is segmentation – the division of markets into recognizable parts, with each company differentiating its product, making it distinctive, according to the recognizable needs of the segment concerned. The commonest form of segmentation is demographically by age group, geographical area, or socio-economic classification. There is however a limit to this form of segmentation, and a limit to the number of product differentiations that can be made. And because people do not now buy purely on utility but for subconscious desires, contemporary marketing provides subjective values and couples them with economic values for a product. So many products today are pre-sold.

A subjective value is added to a product through abstract association of ideas aimed at a substantial segment of the market, classified by a psychographic peculiarity. The two main techniques are: transference – the coupling of a subconscious emotional desire with its satisfaction from a specific brand purchase; and positioning – taking and owning a position in the consumer's mind by a brand associated with infantile 'imprinting'.

The advantages of segmentation, in whatever form, are important. A company can aim its promotion specifically at a profitable segment of the market. It can develop its product strategy specifically for the chosen segment, and it can monitor that segment closely and adjust its approach according to recognizable trends. Moreover it can develop the most persuasive appeals for the people profile in the chosen market, and select the most cost-effective media reaching the people concerned. It can also time its publicity for maximum response and minimum resistance.

Once a market has been *segmented*, a product *differentiated* and promotion dedicated to the market *segment* and a unique brand *quality*, the company is offering a *unique selling proposition*. From this proposition it is able to develop a *reputation monopoly*, giving it a price haven and protection from competition. The uniqueness may be purely abstract, but if the market perceives it to be unique then it is monopolistic.

Significant brand leaders do not always differentiate their brands. They already have a universal appeal, usually have penetrated more deeply into some segments than others, but recognize that any differentiation could create as much loss as it would gain. Each of their segments has its own perception of the brand's qualities and continue to buy accordingly. Promotions for these companies are geared to *reminder* themes, often based on entertainments.

Segmentation and differentiation are pertinent to the following company audit questions in Figure 1.1: 'What business are we in?' and 'What business should we be in?' These together, are the two most important strategic ploys in contemporary marketing. The future will see the introduction of further psychogenic classifications and the accompanying research data necessary to reach them.

Figure 3.2   Class distinctions

Although surface distinctions are fading between classes, behavioural characteristics persist. These are recognizable as between up-market groups and down-market groups. Although not totally consistent, a form of 'migration' is not an uncommon feature.

Figure 3.3   Demographic classifications

The target group classifications are well established and data is readily available, as is data on product use. *Strategic segments* are core categories for main suppliers, with their own demographic distinctions, while *buyer behaviour* lists the identifiable behaviour characteristics of the market segments at conscious levels of decision-making.

Figure 3.1   **Social classes**

These are recognized groupings in both the USA and the UK.

United States

United Kingdom

Social class system

Incorporated Practitioners in Advertising (IPA).

Social class	Membership	Social grade	Occupation
Upper–upper	Aristocracy	A Upper middle	Higher managerial, administrative or professional.
Lower–upper	New rich	B Middle class	Intermediate managerial, administrative or professional.
Upper–middle	Professionals and managers	C_1 Lower middle	Supervisory or clerical, and junior managerial, administrative or professional.
Lower–middle	White collar workers	C_2 Skilled working class	Skilled manual workers
Upper–lower	Blue collar workers	D Working class	Semi- and unskilled manual workers
Lower–lower	Unskilled labourers	E Those of lowest level of subsistence	State pensioners or widows (no other earner) casual or low grade worker.

The social grade of a housewife is based on the occupation of the primary earner – the head of the household.

Figure 3.4 Acorn consumer targeting

Sets of areas with similar demographic and social characteristics have common lifestyle features and therefore present similar potential for the sale of any product. The purpose of Acorn is to define these different types of areas and to show where they can be found.

Figure 3.5 Psychographic segments – self images

An illustration of penetration by brands according to market segments; two household brands reflecting contrasting images although virtually identical in composition and usage. Brand A is seen as a 'convenience' product, while brand B is seen as a 'gourmet' brand. Either brand can be sold at a premium price because it is perceived to have an advantage over all others – the result of sound planning and promotion.

Figure 3.2	CLASS DISTINCTIONS	
Up-market traits		**Down-market traits**
• Thinks in future terms		• Thinks in present or past
• Respects the long term		• Lives and responds short term
• Indulges in reasoning/logic		• Acts impulsively and compulsively
• Identifies with Suburbia/rural		• Identifies with urban/city centre
• Seeks achievement		• Seeks security
• Investment savings		• Non-investment savings
• Experience-related spending		• Artefact-centred spending
• Abstract thinking		• Functional thinking
• Unlimited horizons		• Narrow horizons
• Politics, economics, dynasty		• Family, self, home

Figure 3.3	DEMOGRAPHIC CLASSIFICATIONS		
TARGET GROUP	**PRODUCT USE**	**STRATEGIC SEGMENTS**	**BUYER BEHAVIOUR**
Sex	All users	Own labels	Brand loyalty
Age group	Heavy users	Genetics	Outlet loyalty
Standard region	Medium users	Franchising	Price sensitivity
TV region	Light users	Licensing	Value sensitivity
Terminal Education	Non-users	Reciprocal	Habitual
Education		Credit cards	Rational
Occupation		Joint venture	Convenience
Nationality		Co-operative	Labour-saving
Marital status		Imitation	Time-saving
Years married		Buy out	Trouble-free
Number of children		Non-differential	Economy
Readership habits		Horizontal	Status conscious
TV viewing	Brand use	Vertical	Responsive
Cinema attendance	All users	Functional	Fashion
Radio listening	Solus users	Quality	Peer group
Annual travel	Major users	Transference	Social Awareness
Income range	Minor users	Positioning	Impulsive
Home owner	Non-users	Modular	Reckless

Figure 3.4				ACORN CONSUMER TARGETING

GROUP		NEIGHBOURHOOD TYPES	1978 HHS	%
A	1	LA and new town housing, high wage areas	286457	1.5
A	2	Mixed housing, young families	292303	1.5
A	3	Recent council housing	861319	4.4
A	4	Modern low cost private housing	417019	2.1
B	5	Modern private housing, medium status	1163365	6.0
B	6	Modern private housing, young families	196817	1.0
B	7	Military bases	75999	0.4
C	8	Mixed housing, older areas	352712	1.8
C	9	Older terraces with low unemployment	921729	4.7
C	10	Mixed development, often in country towns	740500	3.8
D	11	Inner areas, low-quality terraced housing	645105	3.3
D	12	Low quality housing, declining areas	1134135	5.8
E	13	Villages with some non-farm employment	487171	2.5
E	14	Rural areas with large farms	341917	1.8
E	15	Rural areas with own account farmers	298149	1.5
F	16	Peripheral low income LA estates	1106853	5.7
F	17	Small LA family houses (Scotland and NE)	643066	1.5
F	18	Urban LA estates, low unemployment	284508	3.3
F	19	Terraced/LA houses (often mining areas)	401429	2.1
F	20	LA estates with older couples	871062	4.5
F	21	Low income LA estates (often high-rise)	395583	2.0
F	22	LA estates with aged (often high-rise)	309841	1.6
G	23	LA estates with most stress (Glasgow)	354661	1.8
G	24	Tenements and non-permanent dwellings	216304	1.1
H	25	Victorian low status (Inner London)	255278	1.3
H	26	Multi-let housing with immigrants	296200	1.5
H	27	Terraced housing with immigrants	265021	1.4
I	28	Student areas/affluent Inner London	385840	2.0
I	29	High-income areas with few children	450146	2.3
J	30	Modern private housing, high income	927575	4.8
J	31	Medium status, inter-war private housing	991981	5.1
J	32	Established suburbs of high status	726860	3.7
J	33	Established rural commuter villages	302046	1.6
J	34	Very high status areas	765833	3.9
K	35	Areas of elderly people, private housing	902241	4.6
K	36	Areas of elderly people, flats and homes	342969	1.8
		*UNCLASSIFIED	31179	0.2

Acorn census enumeration districts

(a) Modern family housing for manual worker

(b) Modern family housing for higher income groups

(c) Older housing of intermediate status

(d) Very poor quality older terraced housing

(e) Rural areas

(f) Urban local authority housing

(g) Housing with most overcrowding

(h) Low income areas with immigrants

(i) Student and high status non-family areas

(j) Traditional high status Suburbia

Acorn key variables

(a) Level of unemployment

(b) Proportion of students

(c) Number of two-car households

(d) Proportion working in particular sectors

(e) Social class

(f) Age

(g) Five-year migrancy

(h) Tenure type

(i) Proportion of immigrants from Commonwealth

(j) Level of overcrowding

(k) Level of basic housing amenities

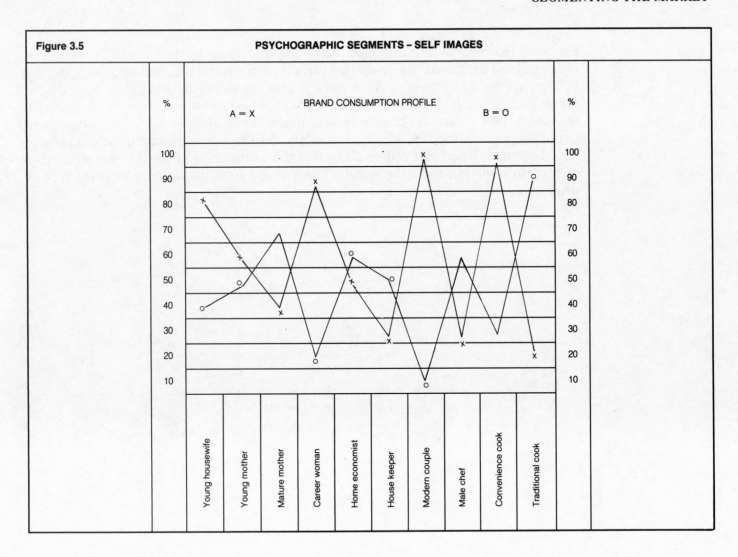

Figure 3.5 **PSYCHOGRAPHIC SEGMENTS – SELF IMAGES**

BRAND CONSUMPTION PROFILE

A = X   B = O

Figure 3.6   Psychological segmentation
Everyone has basic desires although their composition may differ markedly. People in industrialized nations have secondary desires that require satisfaction once basic desires have been catered for adequately. It is clear that secondary desires are extensions and refinements of basic desires; for example, once a basic desire such as thirst has been satisfied by water, taste takes over and the desire for alcohol, coffee, or tea assumes an important role. In modern society, secondary desires have replaced basic desires and have become selected substitutes. Therefore the satisfaction of thirst is not so much a priority in itself, but more the social status one achieves by association of the type of drink selected.

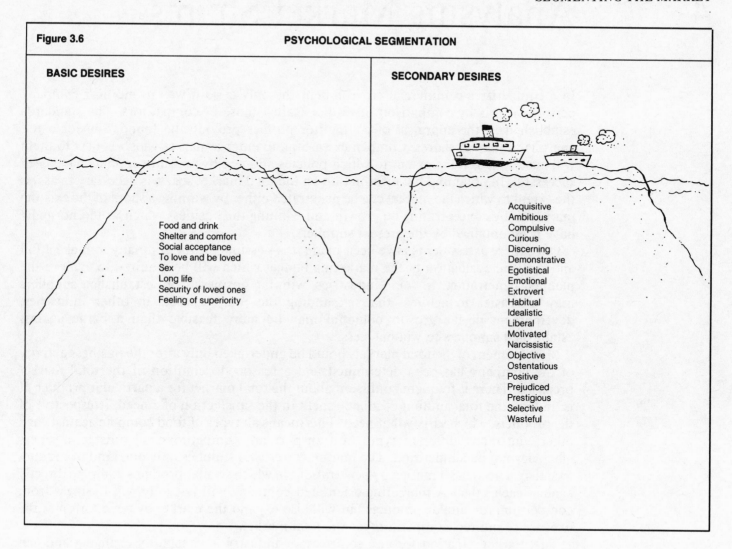

Figure 3.6

PSYCHOLOGICAL SEGMENTATION

BASIC DESIRES

Food and drink
Shelter and comfort
Social acceptance
To love and be loved
Sex
Long life
Security of loved ones
Feeling of superiority

SECONDARY DESIRES

Acquisitive
Ambitious
Compulsive
Curious
Discerning
Demonstrative
Egotistical
Emotional
Extrovert
Habitual
Idealistic
Liberal
Motivated
Narcissistic
Objective
Ostentatious
Positive
Prejudiced
Prestigious
Selective
Wasteful

4   Analysing Market Shares

In a competitive commercial environment the only certain way to monitor company performance is by comparison of results against those of competitors. The standards established in the appraisal of competitor profiles provide the foundation for a full analysis of market shares. Companies wishing to enter a market which is new to them will need to assess the extent to which policies adopted by present suppliers have been successful. In obtaining full information on the total market size it is necessary to assess the extent to which the market can be penetrated either by winning a share of the existing market or by concentrating on growth and winning the business which would normally have been obtained by the present suppliers.

Once these assessments have been made it is possible for the company to make a full and realistic evaluation of the marketing budget which will be required to achieve the planned penetration. In some industries, winning business from established suppliers may be easier to achieve than expanding the total market. In other industries, development of the growth potential may be more feasible than a battle against established suppliers to win business.

Measurement of the total market should be undertaken only after the business activity of the company has been determined and a reasoned definition of the total market prepared. There is frequent confusion about the total market for a particular product. It is, in fact, the total amount of money spent in the satisfaction of a need, irrespective of the products, which satisfy that need. This means all types of food compete against each other; the many different types of transport are competitors; all aids to business efficiency are in competition. The manufacturer who supplies only one kind of product to satisfy a need has a market by penetration, in which similar products compete directly against each other. A marketing-orientated company will not only win business from competitors for similar products but will also expand the market by penetration at the expense of indirect competitors for the total market.

The market situation for any company or industry is constantly changing and can experience violent fluctuations in market shares from day to day. Over a period of time there will be shifts in the pattern of demand and a company must keep constant track of such trends. A steadily rising sales turnover will not, by itself, indicate whether a firm is making best use of its potential. A company may have a reasonable increase in sales each year and yet still have a rapidly diminishing market share. Unless sales volume is rising at a rate not less than that of the industry as a whole, it will be losing sales opportunities.

In a rapidly expanding economy a depression will leave such companies in a very weak position against stronger competitors which have maintained surveillance on market trends. It is also essential for a company to keep track of the market shares for each of its major competitors and to be able to explain any apparent change. If a competitor is expanding its market share at a greater rate than might be expected, there must be an explanation. The cause must be established quickly before the investigating company's own performance is affected by the expanding competitor. If, however, a major competitor which is known to be strong in its marketing activities begins to show a deterioration in market share, it is possible that the company had decided to diversify out of that market, either because it has forecast a decreasing rate of growth or because it has anticipated an increase in supply over demand, and the consequent marketing expense will not bring in the required profit performance. For these reasons it is vital for companies to carry out market share analysis on a continuous basis. It is usually better to carry out inexpensive elementary research at regular periods than to carry out extensive research projects infrequently.

Marketing research is frequently confused with market research. Marketing research is an activity which examines all the elements in marketing practice, including markets, products, distribution channels, pricing behaviour and opinions. Market research is just one element of marketing research, although easily the most widely known and practised. Today the average size of firms is increasing and business decisions are becoming even more critical. Not only are the financial consequences of each business decision becoming greater but the time span between decisions and the consequences is widening. Research into the distributive system will not necessarily determine the future but it can be used to illuminate the scene, eliminate the unlikely and spotlight the probable. It is an aid to reducing business risk.

Although the market research industry is growing rapidly, there are still relatively few firms which spend money in an effort to discover what is happening in the market-place.

Research by manufacturers selling to the general public is more usual than it is with companies selling to industrial markets.

Some manufacturers of fast-moving consumer lines subscribe to continuous research carried out by retail audit investigators. By carrying out regular stock checks among a representative sample of retailers and calculating the quantity of goods sold by brand, the research company is able to appraise the market shares of leading companies and make this information available to its subscribers. In the industrial field, multi-client projects are gaining in popularity and have proved invaluable to the sponsors. A service provided for both consumer and industrial companies is the collection and analysis of detailed financial information which enables a company to compare total performance against the industrial average. Although competitors are not identified by name, it is possible to relate the information supplied to other published information and to make direct comparisons. This work is undertaken by Inter-Firm Comparisons.

The Companies Act 1967 made it possible for an investigator to obtain substantial financial information on competitors. The formerly exempt private company no longer exists, such companies are now compelled by law to file an annual return, including a profit and loss account and a balance sheet. Such information about companies is readily available from Companies' House, London.

Figure 4.1   Market shares analyses – by value, volume and product group

Figure 4.2   Buying behaviour and quantification
Both parts of the chart are essential to customer-orientated companies. Distinguishing by demographic group the psychological reasons for making purchasing decisions provides the bases for brand development, advertising copy, and the critical brand image for specific groups. Breaking down the profiles of buyers and describing their characteristics in detail provides a positive means for formulating marketing strategy. Knowing one's customers and their demand structure ensures appropriate marketing orientation.

Figure 4.1

MARKET SHARES ANALYSIS – BY VALUE AND PRODUCT GROUP

Prior year 1		Prior year 2		Company	Budget year		Plan year 1		Plan year 2		Plan year 3		Plan year 4		Plan year 5	
				Product group	Value	Growth										

MARKET SHARES ANALYSIS – BY VOLUME AND PRODUCT GROUP

Prior year 2		Prior year 1		Company	Budget year		Plan year 1		Plan year 2		Plan year 3		Plan year 4		Plan year 5	
				Product group	Value	Growth										

Figure 4.2			BUYING BEHAVIOUR AND QUANTIFICATION			
Habitual	Rational	Impulsive	Emotional	Experimental	Conceptual	Price conscious
Social class						
Age group						
Distribution State						

Number of actual and potential buyers	Available spending power of all buyers	Influence of price in the market-place	Influence of pricing of substitutes	Distribution of spending power	Expectation of prosperity among consumers	Established reputation of suppliers	Structure of the industry

Figure 4.3   Sales growth/sales strength ratios
Using this chart it is possible to compare sales strength with sales growth and any consistency between the two.

Figure 4.4   Market shares analyses – by value, volume and SIC

Figure 4.5   The purchasing maze
The buying process may be unique to each individual, but each person necessarily moves through a chain of thoughts even if each link does not involve a fully conscious decision. Identifying the pressures on people when making a decision enables the company to overcome obstacles which are likely to arise by building into its sales literature or its promotions the necessary reassurances. Making it easy for customers to buy is a natural marketing philosophy.

Figure 4.6   Market shares analysis – by value and size of outlet
Over the past few years there has been a steady increase in the average size of firm from the very small retail outlet through all industries up to the larger industrial empires. At the same time there has been steady merging among non-competing companies, giving rise to the term 'conglomerate company'. This expression describes a large group of companies with diverse products and markets. It is reasonable to assume that this tendency is occurring more rapidly in some industries than in others. In industries where it is particularly marked, suppliers may be facing an increased marketing problem. With a reduction in the total potential outlets and with the buying strength of those remaining becoming more pronounced, suppliers are faced with increasing competition from suppliers, thus experiencing a serious deterioration in profitability. By carefully assessing and watching closely the tendency towards such rationalization among customers, the companies are able to prepare for the consequences of such events. They may find it prudent to find outlets by acquiring competitors or by diversifying into other markets. In this illustration markets have been segmented carefully so that a trend can be isolated and, where significant, more detailed investigation carried out into the actual industry concerned and also, where possible, into the geographical area which has already been significantly affected.

There are several different methods by which the size of the firm can be determined. It may be by sales turnover, or by capital employed, or by number of employees. The most reliable guide to size is probably that of number of employees and the categories provided are the groupings which can be extracted from the census of production.

Figure 4.7   Market shares analysis – by volume and size of outlet
Where rationalization has already begun it should be possible to establish to what extent it has affected prices by comparing volume in physical units against sales value and producing an average selling price per unit sold. It will also indicate whether rationalization within industrial groupings is causing an increase in growth rate compared with other industrial segments.

These charts will also show the growth rate by size of outlet and indicate profitability by outlet size. The information produced should enable the company to embark upon a policy of selective selling. A decline in the number and the value of a particular size of outlet, if investigated and proved to be consistent with national performance, will provide guidance to the sales manager in directing the efforts and calling pattern of sales personnel.

Figure 4.3   **SALES GROWTH/SALES STRENGTH RATIOS**

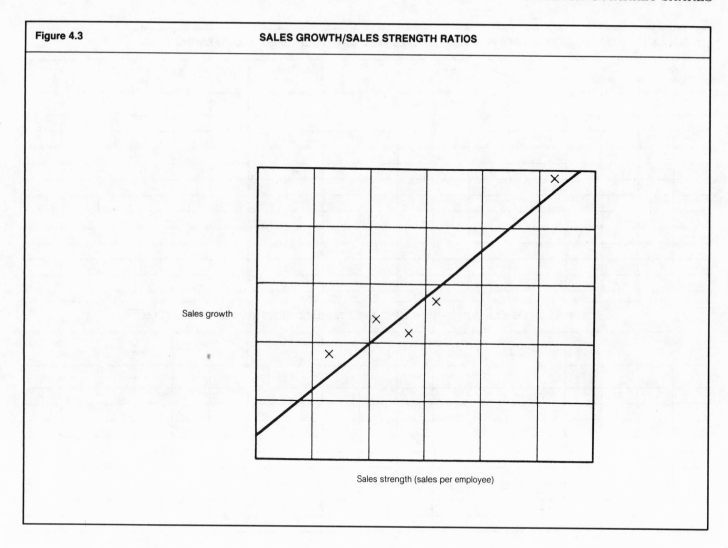

Sales growth

Sales strength (sales per employee)

Figure 4.4   MARKET SHARES ANALYSIS – BY VALUE AND STANDARD INDUSTRIAL CLASSIFICATION

Prior year 2		Prior year 1		SIC	Budget year		Plan year 1		Plan year 2		Plan year 3		Plan year 4		Plan year 5	
					Value	Growth										

MARKET SHARES ANALYSIS – BY VOLUME AND STANDARD INDUSTRIAL CLASSIFICATION

Prior year 2		Prior year 1		SIC	Budget year		Plan year 1		Plan year 2		Plan year 3		Plan year 4		Plan year 5	
					Value	Growth										

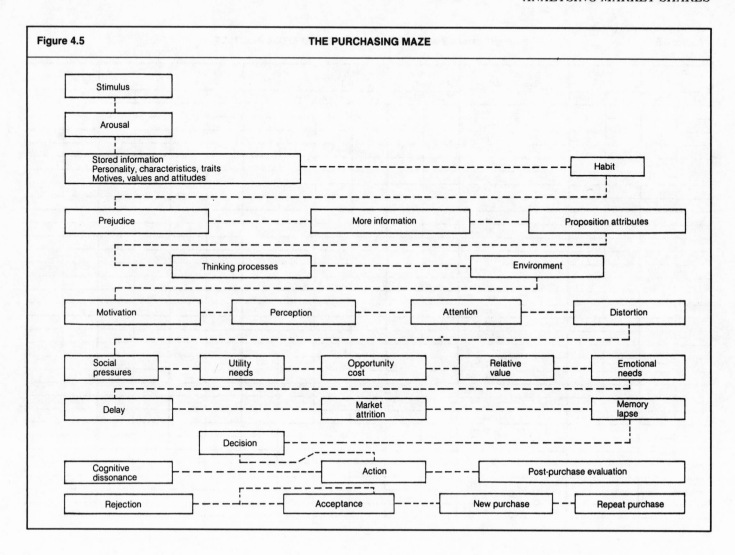

Figure 4.5   **THE PURCHASING MAZE**

Figure 4.6 Date				MARKET SHARES ANALYSIS – BY VALUE AND SIZE OF OUTLET Prepared by														
Prior year 1		Prior year 2		Size of outlet		Budget year		Plan year 1		Plan year 2		Plan year 3		Plan year 4		Plan year 5	
Value	Growth	Value	Growth			Value	Growth	Value	Growth	Value	Growth	Value	Growth	Value	Growth	Value	Growth
				Manufacturing	0–25												
					26–50												
					51–100												
					101–250												
					251–500												
					501–1000												
					over 1000												
					Total												
				Service	0–25												
					26–50												
					51–100												
					101–250												
					251–500												
					501–1000												
					over 1000												
					Total												
				Distributive	0–25												
					26–50												
					51–100												
					101–250												
					251–500												
					501–1000												
					over 1000												
					Total												
				Finance–credit	0–25												
					26–50												
					51–100												
					101–250												
					251–500												
					501–1000												
					over 1000												
					Total												

Figure 4.7
Date

MARKET SHARES ANALYSIS – BY VOLUME AND SIZE OF OUTLET

Prepared by

Prior year 1		Prior year 2		Size of outlet		Budget year		Plan year 1		Plan year 2		Plan year 3		Plan year 4		Plan year 5	
Volume	Growth	Volume	Growth			Volume	Growth	Volume	Growth	Volume	Growth	Volume	Growth	Volume	Growth	Volume	Growth
				Manufacturing	0–25												
					26–50												
					51–100												
					101–250												
					251–500												
					501–1000												
					over 1000												
					Total												
				Service	0–25												
					26–50												
					51–100												
					101–250												
					251–500												
					501–1000												
					over 1000												
					Total												
				Distributive	0–25												
					26–50												
					51–100												
					101–250												
					251–500												
					501–1000												
					over 1000												
					Total												
				Finance–credit	0–25												
					26–50												
					51–100												
					101–250												
					251–500												
					501–1000												
					over 1000												
					Total												

5 Appraising the Competition

There is only one element in the modern business environment which has any marked degree of certainty and that is change. It may be change in the size of a market or its structure, or among the firms operating within the market, or the markets with which it is concerned.

No company or organization in a free society operates in complete isolation, for even monopolies struggle against competition for available purchasing power. Opposition may come from a substitute product or companies providing products or services which indirectly affect performance. Establishing the cause and effect of the forces of competition becomes more and more critical as the degree of complexity of influential factors increases. In order to make an assessment of these factors it is necessary to isolate those which are likely to be most significant in their impact upon the market-place.

Price cutting is the most frequently encountered of all tactical devices in the struggle against competition. This is a negative approach unless the company has made the price cut from a position of strength and anticipates growth in the total market because of increased consumption as a direct result of the price promotion, which will increase its profit.

Product innovation which brings a product closer to the needs of the market will, until it is copied by others, often cause a shift in purchasing habits towards the innovating company. Sometimes consumers will begin to use a substitute because the other product is in short supply or because the substitute has become available at a price which compares favourably against that of the original.

The Government, by producing new legislation, will frequently create a new market or cause a substantial growth or decline in established markets in its attempt to improve the social and economic life of the nation. Sudden changes in taste or fashion usually cause shifts in demand from one source of supply to another. Variations in the climate or fluctuations in the temperature can seriously affect the sales of products which rely upon extremes of temperature for sales volume. Trade recessions, strikes or industrial disputes often bring in their wake changes in purchasing habits.

Fortunately, many of these influences are predictable. Certainly there will be a vast amount of published comment indicating likely possibilities. Occasionally, trade associations and professional institutions sponsor investigations into likely future events, and numerous authoritative writers produce feature articles, news columns, and special reports which can be of value to the company looking into the future. While it is not always possible to forecast accurately the likely consequences of any of these events, it is still possible to prepare remedial measures in advance, at different levels of effectiveness. If the consequences of such events are quantified in monetary terms, companies will be able to equate consequences with sales volume and hence profitability. At this point the contingency plan may be brought into operation.

In investigating and charting the information on competitors, as illustrated in this chapter, a company is forced to assess its competition and its activities in purely financial terms, enabling comparisons to be made and a standard to be developed against which its own performance can be measured. In addition, the detailed investigation necessary to complete the forms creates a self-educating process and will enable managers to plan their future operations based upon the collective experience of the main suppliers and their market or markets. It will also enable the planner to quantify the interactive forces of competition.

Figure 5.1   Financial performance
This simple chart is intended to highlight the profitability and growth of significant suppliers and to compare their performance against each other. Organizations exist which provide considerable detail of the financial performance of companies operating within a given industry but information is made available to subscribers anonymously. Nevertheless this material is invaluable for comparative studies and for planning purposes.

Before analysing the published information on competitors it is advisable for the investigator to prepare definitions for each of the headings in this chart. Sales can mean different things to different companies. Net income for any company at any one time can be influenced by such things as stock evaluation, and total assets are often subject to considerable degrees of variation of interpretation among accountants. Accountants also disagree about the true meaning of profit and for any one company profit performance may vary substantially according to the accounting procedure preferred.

Share prices are usually dependent upon the value of distributed dividends and they will not always be a direct reflection of a company's profitability. They can fluctuate widely in any given period and it may be misleading to adopt a share valuation at any one time. It may be more realistic to take a mean average over a full year, but allow more weighting for the most recent period of trading.

Figure 5.2   Standard comparison

This document is equivalent to a direct comparison of the detailed profit and loss account of each main competitor. Certain items listed will be impossible to extract from published information and, unless the information is obtainable from a reliable unofficial source, an attempt must be made to make an evaluation based upon judgement. If this technique is used the assessment must be qualified and justified in logical terms, otherwise it is best to ignore the items altogether until such time as the information becomes available.

By providing an index, in which the previous year is equal to 100, it is possible to compare successive years against each other and also the relative growth of each asset or investment.

Figure 5.3   Weighted services and performance

In making a comparison between competitive firms it is logical to assume that whatever the extent of market penetration achieved by those firms the success or otherwise of their achievements is attributable to some activity on their part. One company may have a strong sales force, another may spend considerable sums on advertising. Whatever the cause, it should be isolated. In drawing up a 'league table' of competitors, a means of weighting these activities should be formulated. The factors which are typical of competing companies are shown in this illustration.

In order to develop a realistic appraisal so that one activity can be compared against a dissimilar activity, weighting techniques are used. Although each of the factors is totally interdependent and the mix unique to each company, it is subject to constant variation. Each factor will need to be studied and the significance of each activity decided so that the relevance of, for example, price can be compared to sales ability or sales strength.

In the context of this chart the price referred to is a strategic one. The technical specification is the inherent characteristic of the product, which if properly exploited can be the foundation for the establishment of a unique selling proposition.

Delivery services may be the means that are adopted, such as road, rail, sea or air, and may also include the speed of delivery and frequency. The emphasis on packaging is not only restricted to the strength or durability of the container but also its aesthetic design. Supporting services will include such facilities as credit agreements, leasing facilities, consultancy or installation. Often, when faced with a purchasing decision, buyers may choose a particular proposition simply because it has originated from a well-established company which is known to them and in which they have confidence. Similarly, products that have become well entrenched and accepted in the market-place may often be chosen in preference to products that may be superior but are not so well known.

The practice of reciprocal trade agreements has not been well publicized but is established although hidden by pretence of some other arrangement. Some companies have engaged in vertical integration by taking over customers, so ensuring a certain outlet for their products. Because it is captive, sales opportunities will not be left open to competitors. Many businesses have prospered in the past because of personal relationships between prominent members of the firm. This advantage frequently disappears with the departure of one of the individuals involved. Some companies make a positive effort to cultivate other organization which could have a non-competing but nevertheless a vested interest in identical markets. These concerns are frequently able to exercise considerable influence over buying decisions.

Many manufacturers tend to take their products for granted and rarely investigate the use to which they are being put by customers and how relevant the products are to customers' applications. Often, research establishes that features introduced in good faith by a manufacturer are not used by the customer although they have paid for them in the selling price. They may not have recognized their significance nor relevance to them at the time of purchase.

In assessing the product's performance, the application must be related to product characteristics. Many companies have developed their own market share as a direct result of superior finish or design for their product. Buyers can be impressed by stories of long life for certain items, particularly in the mechanical field, and will often make a purchasing decision because the cost of the equipment can be spread over many years of operation.

In some industries, advertising is the most significant factor in influencing sales performance, particularly where expenditure is supported by creative expertise and by shrewd media selection. Merchandising is a comparatively new term, although many of the techniques have been practised since the earliest days of trading. Their prominence has been achieved largely as a result of greater use of advertising, particularly by television where emphasis at the point-of-sale has become a necessity. The adoption of the 'silent salesman' continues to grow. Sales strength relates clearly to the numbers employed, while the section on sales ability relates directly to the knowledge and the skill in its use by sales personnel.

Companies distribute their products through different channels. Some use distributors or stockists, others may deliver direct to the retailer or even the ultimate consumer. Different channels have varying degrees of competence in selling their suppliers' products and their effectiveness can be critical to the sales volume achieved by any one company.

Figure 5.4   Price/market share differential
In arriving at a final assessment, based upon established standards relating each factor to every other factor, it is possible to compare the total significance of these in terms of market share, and the performance of individual companies can be related to the factor or factors upon which they concentrate.

Figure 5.5   Geographical sales distribution
Many sales regions used by companies have grown from historical foundations. In fact they should be closely related to a significant activity, such as the regions used by the Registrar-General in the UK or the US Bureau of Census in the USA, enabling measurement against figures they provide, or they could use the regions adopted so that regional campaigns carry maximum cost-effectiveness.

Figure 5.1 Date	FINANCIAL PERFORMANCE					Prepared by		
Company	Prior year actual £000's (£/$)				Net profit % return on			
Company and competitors	Sales	Net income	Total assets	Ordinary shares	Sales	Total assets	Ordinary shares	
Company performance								

Figure 5.2
Date

STANDARD COMPARISON

Prepared by

Competitor	Prior year = 100	Capital	Reserves	Long-term loans	Funds employed	Stock in hand	Work in progress	Debtors	Cash in hand	Current assets	Creditors	Bank overdraft	Current taxation	Preference dividends	Ordinary share dividends	Current liabilities	Net current assets	Investment associates	Investments subsidiaries	Other investments	Current investments	Depreciation	Goodwill	Total fixed assets	Management and supervision	Office and administration	Manufacturing labour	Salesmen	Total manpower	Agents and distributors	Manufacturing plant (sq. ft.)	Advertising appropriation	Sales office	Warehouses	Distribution vehicles
Company A																																			
Company B																																			
Company C																																			
Company D																																			
Company E																																			

| Figure 5.3 Date | WEIGHTED SERVICES AND PERFORMANCE | | | | | | | | | | | | | | | | | | Prepared by |

Company	Price	Technical specification	Delivery services	Packaging	Supporting services	Company reputation	Product reputation	Reciprocal trade agreements	Captive markets	Personal relationships	Outside influences	Product performance	Finish design	Length of service	Advertising and public relations	Merchandising	Sales strength	Sales ability	Channels of distribution	Total assessment
Own company																				
	Sales				£$															
	Sales				£$			% total sales							Market share					
	Sales				£$			% total sales							Market share					
	Sales				£$			% total sales							Market share					
	Sales				£$			% total sales							Market share					
	Sales				£$			% total sales							Market share					
Comments																				

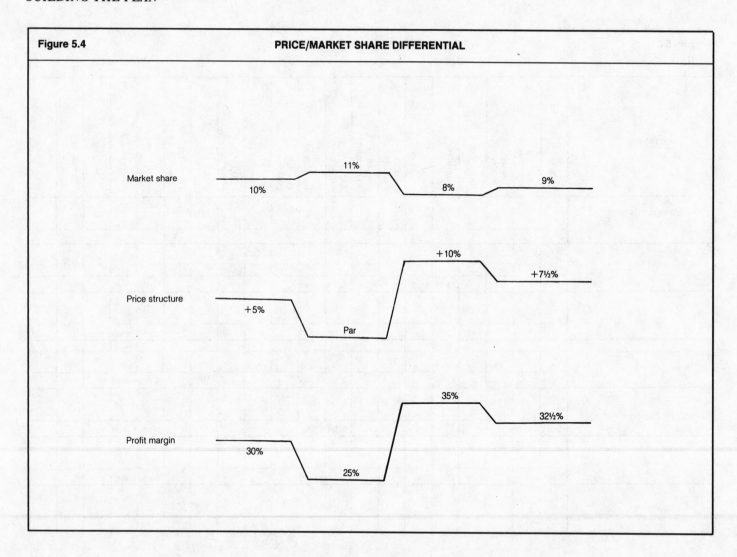

Figure 5.4   PRICE/MARKET SHARE DIFFERENTIAL

Market share

11%

10%

8%

9%

Price structure

+10%

+5%

Par

+7½%

Profit margin

35%

30%

25%

32½%

Figure 5.5 Date		Northern	Yorkshire and Humberside	East Anglia	South East	Greater London	South West	Wales	North West	Scotland	Northern Ireland	Total home market	Overseas area A	Overseas area B	Overseas area C	Total overseas	Total sales
GEOGRAPHICAL SALES DISTRIBUTION Prepared by																	
Company (by product group)	£$000s sales																
	% total																
	£$000s sales																
	% total																
	£$000s sales																
	% total																
	£$000s sales																
	% total																
	£$000s sales																
	% total																
	£$000s sales																
	% total																

Figure 5.6 Market analysis

Breaking down a total geographical area into significant regions ensures that the company can vet performance and provide monitoring systems. Thus adverse performance in any one region can be remedied at the earliest possible time. Certainly, where performances vary from one period to the next within certain regions, the cause can be isolated and positive action taken to counteract it.

Figure 5.7 Penetration of sales outlets

In any one area at any one time the total number of outlets can vary. Some large companies can, over a period of time, develop a near monopoly situation in a region or town and force the closure of many smaller outlets. The significance of this development tends to restrict the number of opportunities which a company has available, for, if there are a large number of outlets, a salesman should be able to convert a number of prospects whereas, with one large outlet, the opportunity is severely limited. Sometimes industries go through a period of considerable rationalization and the total number of outlets diminishes substantially. Once such a trend becomes apparent, it is vital that the company establishes the extent to which outlets it serves are declining in total compared to the national picture, in case its own outlets are closing at a greater rate than those of competitors.

Figure 5.8 Size of outlets

In this illustration it is possible to use this basic information to note the extent to which each company is increasing its number of outlets by opening new accounts and retaining the business of established accounts. The system can also be used to prepare arbitrarily market shares by region and so have a guide to performance against that of competitors.

Figure 5.9 Competitive pricing chart

Because of the significance of pricing practices in any business environment it is necessary for every business to maintain surveillance over variations in the pricing strategy adopted from time to time by different companies.

In the chart illustrated it is possible to establish the effect of pricing strategy on each company's performance by product group and market share. Used properly, this chart can give indications of the price level at which maximum penetration may be achieved for any given product group.

Figure 5.6   **MARKET ANALYSIS**

AREAS
CODE

Code	Area
1	**NORTH AND SCOTLAND**
11	Cumberland
12	County Durham
13	Northumberland
14	Westmorland
15	Scotland
2	**YORKSHIRE AND LINCOLNSHIRE**
21	Yorkshire
22	Lincolnshire
3	**EAST MIDLANDS**
31	Derbyshire
32	Leicestershire
33	Northamptonshire
34	Rutland
35	Nottinghamshire
4	**EAST ANGLIA**
41	Cambridgeshire
42	Huntingdonshire
43	Norfolk
44	Suffolk
5	**SOUTH EAST**
51	Bedfordshire
52	Berkshire
53	Buckinghamshire
54	Essex
55	Hampshire
56	Hertfordshire
57	Kent
58	Surrey
585	Oxfordshire
59	Sussex
6	**SOUTH WEST**
61	Cornwall
62	Devonshire
63	Dorset
64	Gloucestershire
65	Somerset
66	Wiltshire
7	**WEST MIDLANDS AND WALES**
71	Herefordshire
72	Shropshire
73	Staffordshire
74	Warwickshire
75	Worcestershire
79	Wales
8	**NORTH WEST**
81	Cheshire
82	Lancashire
83	Isle of Man
9	**GREATER LONDON AND MIDDLESEX**
90	Greater London
91	Middlesex
01	**NORTHERN IRELAND**
02	**EIRE**
03	**OVERSEAS**

INDUSTRIES
(Standard Industrial Classifications)
CODE

Code	Industry
A	Agriculture, Forestry, Fishing
B	Mining & Quarrying
C	Food, Drink & Tobacco
D	Coal & Petroleum Products
E	Chemicals & Allied Industries
F	Metal Manufacture
G	Mechanical Engineering
H	Instrument Engineering
I	Electrical Engineering
J	Shipbuilding & Marine Engineering
K	Vehicles
L	Metal Goods not elsewhere specified
M	Textiles
N	Leather, Leather Goods & Fur
O	Clothing & Footwear
P	Bricks, Pottery, Glass, Cement, etc.
Q	Timber, Furniture, etc.
R	Paper, Printing & Publishing
S	Other Manufacturing Industries
T	Construction
U	Gas, Electricity & Water
V	Transport & Communications
W	Distributive Trades
X	Insurance, Banking Finance & Business Services
Y	Professional & Scientific Services
Z	Miscellaneous Services
ZZ	Public Administration & Defence

When planning your programme
use the code letter for easy reference.

MANAGEMENT STATUS
CODE

Code	Status
Admin.	Administration
O & M	O & M/Planning/Development
Prod.	Production
DP	Data Processing/Scientific/Technical
SM	Sales/Marketing
Pur.	Purchasing/Stock Control
Con.	Consultancy
Fin.	Financial
Govt.	Government
LL	Librarians/Lecturers etc.

Source: Business Systems—Equipment Target Mailing Service

Figure 5.7 PENETRATION OF SALES OUTLETS

		Class						Age Groups							Television areas													
		A	B	C₁	C₂	D	E	0 – 15	16 – 25	26 – 35	36 – 45	46 – 55	56 – 65	65+	ITV 1	ITV 2	ITV 3	ITV 4	ITV 5	ITV 6	ITV 7	ITV 8	ITV 9	ITV 10	ITV 11	ITV 12	ITV 13	ITV 14
Total number of outlets																												
Movement prior year %																												
Sales value from outlets																												
Movement prior year %																												
COMPANY A	Active accounts																											
	Percentage total																											
	Value £ $																											
	Percentage total																											
	Penetration																											
COMPANY B																												
COMPANY C																												

Figure 5.8	SIZE OF OUTLETS				
	Establishments	Enterprises	£/$m net output	£/$000's net output per establishment	£/m capital expenditure
Employees 1 – 24					
25 – 99					
100 – 499					
500 – 1999					
2000 – 4999					
5000 – 9999					
10000 – 19999					
20000+ _____ All manufacturing	_____	_____	_____	_____	_____

Figure 5.9 Date		COMPETITIVE PRICING CHART								Prepared by						
	Sales	over +15%	+15%	+12½%	+10%	+7½%	+5%	Par price	−5%	−7½%	−10%	−12½%	−15%	over −15%
Total market sales														
Total market sales %	100													
Company A Product group 1 £/$														
Market share %														
Product group 2 £/$														
Market share %														
Product group 3 £/$														
Market share %														
Product group 4 £/$														
Market share %														
Company B Product group 1 £/$														
Market share %														
Product group 2 £/$														
Market share %														
Product group 3 £/$														
Market share %														
Product group 4 £/$														
Market share %														
Company C Product group 1 £/$														
Market share %														
Product group 2 £/$														
Market share %														
Product group 3 £/$														
Market share %														
Product group 4 £/$														
Market share %														

Part Two
Building the Plan

Introduction to Part Two

Many managers find it difficult to accept some of the principles being used in marketing today. They may acknowledge the logic of segmentation and the concept of brand differentiation but become sceptical about abstract ideas such as transference or positioning theory. They will go along with the unique selling proposition as a competitive advantage provided it is based on aspects of quality or on functional features, but draw the line at themes based on imprinting or psychological drives. They feel comfortable with the traditional form of promotion where a company relied on *putting a proposition* to customers – a reasoned argument emphasizing the benefits of a product.

The more recent approach has been a shift away from this *pure* form of communication. For buyers are now conscious of prestige and have become aware of the intangible benefits that arise out of ownership or consumption. People no longer simply wish to enjoy the utility of a product, but want to attain the status associated with particular life-styles. Their purchasing behaviour therefore reflects what they want to be or the image they wish to project to others. Social acceptance and approval is now so important that people will go out of their way and spend a great deal just to achieve this.

Marketing people are now mass producers of customers, using communication techniques to handle consumer demand; to control its volume, its perception of values, and its preferences. They do this by using basic drives such as social approval, self esteem, or sexual attraction, or the secondary related drives such as reward, recognition, and romance. These drives are coupled with brand images.

These techniques are successful because people are subject to irrational, emotional impulses and blockages, guilt complexes, day dreams, fantasies, and hidden yearnings. They behave impulsively and compulsively.

Marketing professionals set out to condition people and 'buy' customers. This is done by persuasively infiltrating a customer's mind and, as with hypnosis, these individuals then respond automatically to the triggers of action, as used in advertising appeals. In return for the desired emotional security, they become psychologically hooked.

This is no longer just theory. It works. It is practised throughout the industrialized world by the largest and most successful companies.

It also works for commercial buyers. Traditionally regarded as logical and practical in purchasing behaviour they can now be seen to be subject to the same kind of motivation as consumers; behavioural traits, beliefs, and attitudes are common.

Marketing professionals operate within the marketing mix (see Figure B). The variables within the mix are used to produce the firm's marketing strategy. Each variable requires a decision. The resulting strategy represents what has to be done: the marketing plan in action.

Part Two of this book deals with the creation of a marketing plan, the plan of action necessary to win customers, establish a mutual franchise, give continuing satisfaction, and achieve an increasing return on investments made.

A marketing plan based on the guidance of the chapters that follow is not just a reference document; it is an operational manual. Used daily it stimulates positive thinking, fosters experience, and compels action.

The initiative and momentum for planning lies with company chief executives, for it is they who have the authority to sanction the decisions necessary for the future. It is the chief executives who are accountable to the board and that is a full-time job. Planning therefore becomes their chief responsibility. Their functional heads of department provide them with necessary expertise and submit plans for their own department's performance. Plans may be prepared in detail for the next accounting year, in outline for a further five years, and in principle for the next twenty years. Chief executives have ultimate responsibility for the company strategic plan while their chiefs of staff are held responsible for operational plans. So chief executives with the approval of their board decide the direction and route for the company while implementation is in the hands of their subordinates.

The maximum benefit of planning comes from its input and development, that is the gathering of knowledge, the accumulation of experience, the tackling of problems, the discussion of ideas, and the accountability for goals well in advance. It is therefore important that all managers and executives are involved in this process. Initially time has to be found but once the plans become operational day-to-day problems diminish for they will have been anticipated, policies agreed, and solutions provided all in advance.

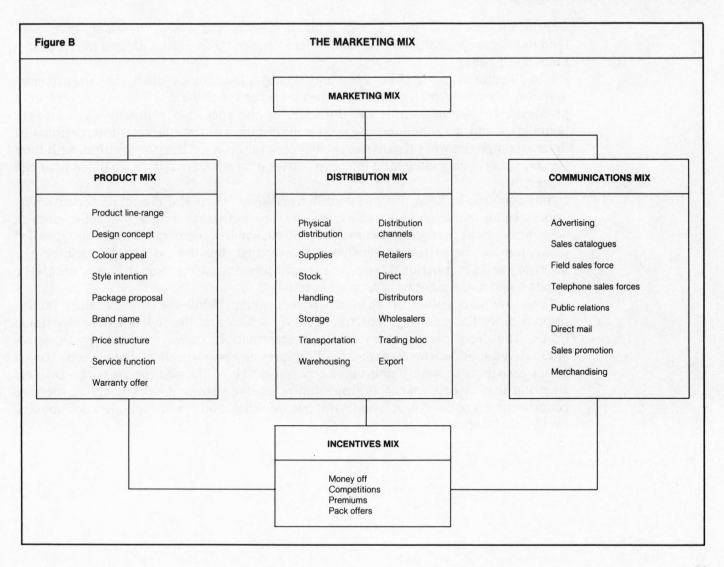

Figure B — THE MARKETING MIX

MARKETING MIX

PRODUCT MIX

Product line-range

Design concept

Colour appeal

Style intention

Package proposal

Brand name

Price structure

Service function

Warranty offer

DISTRIBUTION MIX

Physical distribution	Distribution channels
Supplies	Retailers
Stock	Direct
Handling	Distributors
Storage	Wholesalers
Transportation	Trading bloc
Warehousing	Export

COMMUNICATIONS MIX

Advertising

Sales catalogues

Field sales force

Telephone sales forces

Public relations

Direct mail

Sales promotion

Merchandising

INCENTIVES MIX

Money off
Competitions
Premiums
Pack offers

Contingency plans can even be made for the unexpected. Decisions made in advance tend to be more logical, practical, and objective than those dealt with in a hurry, or in a moment of panic.

Not all companies are alike. They may be large, medium or small; they may operate domestically or internationally or may be diverse or specialist. Each has a different set of problems. In planning terms the domestic or the specialist company has narrower boundaries and may therefore be in closer contact with its markets. International or diverse companies will prepare marketing plans for each territory or division, with their separate plans being integrated into one master plan which may be a qualified financial document.

Small companies keep closer to their markets than others and the chief executive may undertake all of the planning alone, except for discussions with a few colleagues, an accountant, bank manger or a consultant. In the small company, activities and detailed plans may not be so comprehensively documented, but the essence of planning, the necessary skills in functional tasks, and the strategy emanating from due reasoning – the inputs – still make planning a profitable activity.

Large companies often have a planning department. While the chief executive retains responsibility the planning department services him and his functional or divisional heads. The department gathers data and information, carries out analyses, assesses alternatives, monitors performance, and explores new opportunities. Planning personnel act as assistants to senior staff and carry out much of the routine work. In an ideal situation they release managers from dull repetitive planning work enabling them to concentrate on policy formulation, strategic thinking, and operational decision-making for the next decade.

Developing Objectives

6

Company objectives must not only be realistic and achievable but with short, medium and long-term goals shown separately. They should also be sufficiently challenging to stretch the capacity and capabilities of the executives responsible for their achievement. All objectives included in the marketing plan must be definable and therefore quantifiable and comparable for planning purposes.

Money is the common language of business and is, therefore, the most suitable medium for expressing company objectives. The prime objective of any business must be the profit required. Although many companies are well known for pursuing other objectives, either of a political or social nature, they should be pursued only while they continue to cause an increase in profitability. They are, therefore, secondary objectives and no more than a means to an end, although the means may well be considered laudable in its own right.

In planning a future profit requirement it will be essential to predict the sales volume required to achieve that profit. Sales are the direct results of orders and orders themselves are a result of quotations or tenders. Enquiries have to be obtained before the company can implement the chain of events which lead to the transaction being recorded in the sales ledger. By investigating historical performance, the marketing executive should be able to establish conversion ratios for each step in the chain. Once the actual amount of planned profit is agreed, the conversion ratios can be applied to indicate the sales volume needed to achieve that profit and the enquiries, quotations and orders which must be obtained before the sales can be achieved.

In determining such objectives, forecasts of likely events must be made. Every possible factor which could, conceivably, affect the business in a significant way should be considered, whether favourable or otherwise, and over which, in the short term, there can be little or no control. In listing these basic assumptions many operating problems soon become apparent to management.

All companies have their problems, for problems are the reason for the existence of decision-making managers. The difficulty facing the modern manager is not so much solving the problem as discovering its nature and cause. Often managers confuse cause with effect. Lack of sales does not necessarily mean poor selling. It could be the result of poor management planning. In overcoming business problems the company has to develop marketing strategy.

There is still much confusion between marketing strategy and marketing tactics. Strategy is the art of preparing the company's resources to ensure maximum sales penetration upon which company profitability is so dependent. It means understanding the buying habits, attitudes and characteristics of potential customers. It is capitalizing on the strength and weakness of competitors. Tactics, however, are the methods employed in face-to-face dealings with customers and prospective customers.

One contributory cause of confusion between strategy and tactics is the interdependence of certain activities. In pricing, for example, the company may decide to slot into a particular price level – the level it decides is the most vulnerable for exploitation. This is strategy. Once the price level has been established, necessary variations in the unit price from day-to-day are tactical.

Other marketing objectives are included within the appropriate chapters. In the company marketing plan they will appear in this section and cross-references made to the functional activity concerned.

Furthermore, ratio objectives shown in Chapter 12 (Administrative Controls) and Chapter 23 (Realizing Plans) are supporting objectives and, again, cross-references are necessary in the company marketing plan.

Figure 6.1(a) and (b)   Corporate policy objectives
Policy objectives are best divided into two groups: the resources used (Figure 6.1(a)) and the trading resulting from those resources (Figure 6.1(b)). Clearly the resources are the result of earlier trading and this is how the business is seen objectively, as a continuing entity. Objectives are expressed in relative terms, historically, currently, and futuristically. Once tabulated it is possible to see, at a glance, trends in both strengths and weaknesses. Necessary action is highlighted immediately and may take the form of cost control, manpower planning or marketing action.

Figure 6.1 (a)   **CORPORATE POLICY OBJECTIVES**

Measure	Unit
ASSETS	Ratio
Net profit b/t to total assets	
Net profit b/t to net assets	
Current assets to current liabilities	
Liquid assets to current liabilities	
Working capital to sales	
Debtors to sales	
Creditors to purchasers	
Fixed assets to sales	
Fixed assets to working capital	
CAPITAL	%
Net profit a/t to ordinary shares	
Price/earnings	
Interest to borrowed capital	
Interest to total profit	
Borrowings to equity	
Share earnings	
Dividends to share price	
EMPLOYEES	
Management to labour costs	%
Administrative to labour costs	%
Average number of employees	
Employee turnover	%
Average age of employees	
Output per employee	$/£
Hours worked to hours budgeted	%
Average wage cost/employee	$/£
Average total cost/employee	$/£
Profit per employee	$/£
Sales per employee	$/£

Figure 6.1 (b)   **CORPORATE POLICY OBJECTIVES**

Objective	Unit
TRADING	
Sales revenue growth	%
Sales volume growth	%
Market share growth	%
Order turnover	
Debtors to sales revenue	%
Gross profit to sales revenue	%
Net profit to sales revenue	%
Stock turnover to cost of sales	
Materials to manufacturing costs	%
Labour to manufacturing costs	%
Market share actual	
Sales force cost to sales revenue	%
Return on sales revenue	%
Return on working capital	%
Return on p/t profits	%
Number of customer returns	
Number of customer complaints	
Number of actual enquiries	
Profit growth rate	%
Debtors to sales revenue	%
Creditors to sales revenue	%
Debtors credit days	
Shrinkage margin	%
Maximum tolerable staff turnover	
Total cost reduction goal	%
Research and development charge	$/£
Stock level valuation	$/£
Short-term credit needed	$/£
Average cash turnover	$/£

Figure 6.2   Financial objectives

This is in essence a rudimentary planned profit statement. It is the basis upon which the company's future plans are to be established and should be used as a trigger document for the development of company policy in future years. It is a dynamic document which compels discipline on the total marketing operation both in philosophy and in operation.

The insertion of objectives for year one beside objectives for year five is a deliberate attempt to divorce long-term objectives from those which are developed for the immediate future. In looking ahead it is too easy to build upon historical information and simply extend an established trend forward. In the development of objectives it is advisable for management to consider the future without being hindered by current ideas, philosophies, operations and systems. At this early stage in the development of the company's marketing plan it is suggested that executives should establish for themselves, without preconceived doctrines, the position that they would like to see the company adopt five years hence, then start to consider the ways in which the financial objectives can be achieved.

The illustration necessarily is expressed in purely monetary terms but will normally be the result of much deliberation and discussion between senior executives. A full report will be prepared before the actual objectives, in terms of action, are put into financial terms. Actual objectives will vary from company to company, but certain aims or goals are shown here as a guide.

Figure 6.3   Analysis of profit improvements

Every business must plan to improve its profitability by increased productivity and it should make a positive effort to improve its performance in expenditure, of fixed and variable costs, and by revenue by higher prices and sales expansion. It is only by recording and implementing profit improvement efforts that a company is able to investigate and analyse the present operation in the search for profit improvement and potential.

Figure 6.4   Planned changes, profit performance

Many events will affect future profit performance and those shown in this illustration are typical of many businesses. By recognizing the likely effect of these changes on the business, the company is able to actively pursue remedial action.

Although the factors which affect changes in profit performance are numerous, for most businesses the more usual influences and certainly the most significant can be isolated. The major items shown in this illustration are the usual elements affecting profitability; forecasts of their likely effects when made will prepare management for changes in the ratios encountered among operating costs.

Figure 6.5   Marketing objectives

A selection of marketing objectives is shown in this chart. They are primary objectives and apply to most companies. Nominal changes can be avoided if the action section is completed by a cross-reference to an action identified elsewhere in the plan. How to bring about a favourable change is far more important than the amount of the change targeted. Planning is more concerned with how to achieve aims than it is with what to achieve.

Figure 6.6   Sales objectives

This is not a conventional set of sales objectives. It is intended to correlate historical figures with external forces in an attempt to discover how much sales revenue is allied to external forces and therefore not attributable to management performance.

A number of the objectives are tied specifically to management or salesman performance and may again be correlated historically and currently against outside forces. They should reveal an indication of possible relationships.

Figure 6.7   Selling objectives

These objectives are more conventional, for they will indicate the ability of each salesman, subject to management direction, relative to other salesmen. The section on customers within each sales territory should reveal how well the salesman is doing, and the extent to which he is able to do well. It should, as a chart, indicate whether a salesman's territory is too large or too small.

In markets where substantial accounts are tied to competitors and where the salesman has no realistic chance of securing business, an appropriate category should be included in the analysis.

Figure 6.2 Date						**FINANCIAL OBJECTIVES**							Prepared by		
Prior year actual			Current year budget			Activity	Current year forecast			Objectives year 1			Objectives year 5		
£/$ value	% total	% growth	£/$ value	% total	% growth		£/$ value	% total	% growth	£/$ value	% total	% growth	£/$ value	% total	% growth
						Sales product Group A									
						Group B									
						Group C									
						Group D									
						Total sales									
						Gross margin									
						Marketing expense									
						1 Salaries and wages									
						2 Vehicles									
						3 Publicity									
						4 Rent and rates									
						5 Commissions									
						6 Depreciation									
						7 Government charges									
						8 Taxes									
						9 Interest charges									
						10 Other expense									
						Net profit									
						Employees:									
						Management and supervision									
						Salesmen									
						Administration									
						Clerical									
						Other									
						Order input									
						Total assets									
						Return on assets									

Figure 6.3
Date

ANALYSIS OF PROFIT IMPROVEMENTS

Prepared by

Income and expense Analysis	Prior year Actual	Current year		Prior year actual = 100									
		Budget	Forecast	Selling price changes	Purchase price changes	Wage rate changes	Productivity agreements	Sales expansion products	Sales expansion by SIC	Stock valuation	Depreciation	Currency exchange	Total changes
Year 1													
Purchases													
Works costs													
Sales group A													
Sales group B													
Sales group C													
Sales group D													
Gross margin													
Marketing expense													
Stock													
Work in progress													
Value													
Year 5													
Purchases													
Works costs													
Sales group A													
Sales group B													
Sales group C													
Sales group D													
Gross margin													
Marketing expense													
Stock													
Work in progress													
Value													

Figure 6.4	PLANNED CHANGES, PROFIT PERFORMANCE		
ACTIVITY	Change prior year		
	Year 1	Year 5	
	£/$	£/$	
Selling price increases			
Selling price decreases			
Purchase price changes			
Wage rate changes			
Salary, overheads			
Taxation and duties			
Changes in distribution mix			
Changes in product mix			
Changes in investment			
Changes in working capital			
Changes in sales volume			
Productivity agreements			
Stock valuation			
Depreciation			
Currency exchange			
Other			
Changes in profit performance			

Figure 6.5	MARKETING OBJECTIVES		
OBJECTIVE	TARGET		ACTION
Secure new customers	+	%	
Consolidate casual customers	+	%	
Retain existing customers	+	%	
Increase sales of existing customers	+	%	
Expand existing market	+	%	
Move customers up market	+	%	
Increase actual market share	+	%	
Balance product-mix sales		R	
Establish price position	±	%	
Introduce new products	+	N	
Serve more markets	+	N	
Reduce seasonal sales	±	%	
Improve distribution network	+	N	
Increase number of outlets	+	N	
Improve rate of stock turn	+	N	
Reduce stock-out periods	−	N	
Improve rate of quality rejects	−	N	
Improve credit control	−	$/£	
Increase market awareness	+	%	
Increase sales productivity	+	%	
Increase advertising responses	+	%	
Increase media coverage	+	%	

Figure 6.6	SALES OBJECTIVES			
Sales revenue, measured against		FOR EACH SALESMAN	FOR EACH BRAND	FOR EACH MARKET SEGMENT
Historical trends				
National trends				
Market potential				
Index of retail prices = 100				
Unemployment rate				
Industry price index				
Inflation rate				
GNP rate				
Oil price rate				
Wage rates				
Competitive sales				
Gross profit margins				
Population trends				
Interest rates				
Imports				
Established products				
New products				
Established accounts				
New accounts				
Stock value				

Figure 6.7

SELLING OBJECTIVES

THE SALESMAN	Quota Trend % 19XX = 100	Prior Year Actual %
Total territory sales		
Density brand sales		
Other brand sales		
Selling expenses		
Marketing overhead		
Profit contribution		
Profit variance		
Competitive sales		
Selling expenses per order		
Number of calls made		
Ratio orders/calls		
Average order value	£/$	£/$
New business accounts		
Lost business accounts		
New product business		
THE CUSTOMER		
Total purchases	£/$	£/$
Company purchases	£/$	£/$
Profit contributions	%	%
Credit days taken	D	D
Average order value	£/$	£/$
Average order frequency	N	N
Returns and credits	£/$	£/$
Order lead time	D	D
New product business	£/$	£/$
Priority rating	54321	54321

Preparing the Sales Forecast

7

The sales forecast is the basis of the total marketing plan. Preparing a sales forecast is not just a matter of looking at historical sales and attempting to establish trends, but an effort to look into the future and to estimate market sales potential. In assessing the future and endeavouring to predict what products the market will demand and what new modern products, or product innovations, will be required to satisfy that demand, a company has begun to be objective about its future. Obviously many of the techniques used are purely subjective in nature, but by establishing targets which are realistic and obtainable, and which will show an acceptable profit return, the company will be eliminating many of the numerous variables which face every business, and, if properly organized, will tend to reduce the risk element.

A forecast based on market sales potential is based on future customer requirements and is a measurement of the needs of the market for a definite period into the future. Every effort is made to predict changes in pattern of demand and on recent events of the immediate past which have not yet been sufficiently significant in total or over an adequate period of time for a trend to become clearly established. It will make full allowance for new applications in established markets and for innovations in new markets. In looking into the future it is necessary to dissociate the mind from traditional product concepts and to think more specifically about the product or service which the company can provide and which is consistent with the determined business activity.

The period which companies choose for their sales forecast may vary from five to twenty years. For most companies five years is the most appropriate time span and, as many products which will be sold in five years' time are already established within the present product range, it is normally possible to use historical sales performance on which projections into the future can be *based*. Such a projection is dependent on future events being similar to those which have occurred in the past. Due allowance must be made for changes in general economic conditions and for changes in competitive forces within the industry which serves the company's market.

The projections need to be subjected to detailed evaluation of why the trends have appeared and how relevant they will be in the future. Published economic data can be used to compare movements, either short-term fluctuations or medium to long-term trends within the total market. Sometimes acceptable degrees of correlation can be traced. These tied indicators become useful parameters in forecasting. If a company is able to correlate industry sales to a published statistic and that statistic is subjected to medium to long-term forecasting techniques from a reliable source, any forecast based upon such figures can become significant to the company's planning.

The sales forecast may be as sophisticated or as simple as is justified by the business. The techniques borrowed from other disciplines such as operational research are complex in themselves, but may be used to simplify forecasting. These techniques are more often used by larger organizations with diverse products and markets. The small to medium-sized business is better able to maintain close contact with its markets and, as such, is able to monitor immediately any likely changes in demand. For this reason the smaller business may use elementary forecasting methods which can often produce better results than those employed by the larger company where contact with customers has become distanced by longer lines of communication.

Because of the expense involved, and the considerable skill required in preparing sales forecasts, the larger company will carry out its own research using its own specially-recruited personnel. The smaller business cannot economically justify such recruitment and will usually commission elementary research from specialist agencies.

In recent years multi-client projects have become particularly significant and there is every indication that their growing acceptance will continue. In spreading the cost of research over a number of sponsors it is possible for the research company to employ highly-skilled people and to carry out projects in considerable depth across a broad front. In addition, many of these agencies will prepare a report that will be confidential to the sponsor concerned. Such a report will indicate to management, in a detailed and unbiased manner, the image that their company has developed. It will show how they are regarded as manufacturers, in the eyes of present customers and potential customers, as a future investment and even, perhaps, as an employer. The sponsor firm will be able to discover why a company is winning business and under what circumstances business is lost. Management is given the opportunity to assess product acceptability and the effectiveness of its marketing activities when compared to major competitors.

These multi-client projects are proving to be of increasing value to users and are a sure sign of the recognition by companies of the need for research into such areas as market size, market growth rates, the factors affecting market change, market shares broken down by application and type of product, and the decision-making process leading to purchase. Usually these research projects will identify the normal sources of supply, market shares held by individual suppliers, the various product specifications, and, frequently, the most suitable means of communication by publicity and the sales force.

While more and more people are becoming convinced of the need to produce forecasts, few feel competent to tackle forecasts of the volume likely to be achieved in overseas territories. Marketing practitioners no longer use the expression 'export markets' because the word 'market' means one segment of a total market open to penetration, irrespective of geographical boundaries. In principle, there is no difference between home and overseas areas, and it is only the application of research techniques and the implementation of those techniques which distinguish one geographical area from another. In preparing the market sales potential for an overseas territory the executive must make allowances for an increased number of variables likely to be encountered. A distinction should be drawn in each territory between expatriate salesmen and performance achieved by natives, that achieved by competitors at home and that achieved by others.

Any investigation must also include details of the vested interests which the country concerned has to protect, and any possible political interference. Frequently the durability of forecasts will vary from country to country, for forecasts by para-governmental bodies in industrially-advanced nations have more stability than those by countries undergoing rapid economic and social change. Certainly allowances should be made for the degree of sophistication of the national statistics produced by each country.

Whatever the market segment or geographical area to be investigated, for which forecasts are to be prepared, the major benefits accruing to the company follow the detailed consideration of sales opportunities which should produce clear indications of its future prospects.

The object of sales forecasting must be clearly defined at the outset. The objectives must take the form of a clear brief on the extent and detail of the forecast and the amount of time and money which can be justified in development. By defining objectives it is possible to avoid the natural tendency to break down the forecast within predetermined limits based upon traditional or conventional parameters.

Sales forecasts must be prepared in such a form as to show how the company's marketing strategy can be used to increase sales and volume and at what cost in terms of time, money and effort, and the profitability which will accrue at various levels of sales performance.

Any sales forecast is subject to numerous influential factors which must be isolated and capable of measurement according to some predetermined standard. While the variables facing the forecaster can be related almost to infinity, certain influential factors have considerably more effect than others. The forecaster must endeavour to isolate the factors and grade them according to their significance in such a way that weightings can be applied and an acceptable forecast be determined within tolerable limits.

Many people confuse a forecast of market sales potential with their own company forecast or targets. They should appreciate that every company recognizes the fundamental need for growth, and is struggling to increase its markets. This happens even in a declining or static market and, inevitably, leads to some company failure. In forecasting there is nearly always a bias towards one's own company and this tendency must be avoided, otherwise operating budgets, which are based on sales forecasts, will be overestimated and profitability will suffer.

In the struggle to increase market shares some of the competing companies may resort to pricing tactics in order to overcome their marketing deficiency, and this will, inevitably, lead to an industry profits decline. Companies which remain strong during this situation are those which have planned their strategy on customer benefits which can be provided economically and for which the customer is willing to pay a premium. Forecasters will normally avoid bias towards their own company and products if they apply the same standard of measurement for any element of strategy to be used against those of competitive companies and their products.

In preparing a forecast it is necessary to predict market sales potential based not only on general economic conditions, but also on the interplay of total competitive activity, which often causes an expansion of the total market, before deciding the individual strengths and weaknesses of the main competitors in the market-place.

Forecasts must also be made of trends in related industries which provide indirect competition to the company's own products and which may be an influential factor in the growth rate of the industry concerned. To do this forecasters must concentrate initially upon total demand and the various applications which will satisfy that demand. They should then simplify that demand into those products which are directly competitive to their own, not only at the present but also during the period of the forecast. It is at this stage that the forecaster should be able to discover opportunities for product innovation or for new product development.

Figure 7.1   Forecasting techniques
Although many companies avoid the use of quantitative techniques, it is now possible to buy sophisticated calculators or desk-top computers that will handle the data and produce trends without the user needing to know the intricacies involved. A selection of statistical techniques, with full workings, is given in the Appendix.

Figure 7.2   Sales and gross margin analysis by product and market segment
In developing a forecast it is necessary to provide a base year on which an industry can be projected. In using a full year of actual sales performance achieved two years ago, and by using prices which were current at that time, it is possible to develop forecasts which are related year by year and which are exactly comparable over the full period of the forecast. At this stage of the forecast it is not necessary to think in terms of sales volume as opposed to value, for price increases are discounted, leaving growth margin percentages consistent for each year of the forecast period.

It is necessary to include gross margin percentages as a control measure against anticipated sales. In this illustration sales performance is divided into product groups as a first step towards production programming. In addition, forecasts are shown in market segments which will be in groups or categories appropriate to the company concerned but ideally should be some combination of groupings within the standard industrial classification. Predicted sales for five years hence can be tabulated in outline for each product group to be recorded.

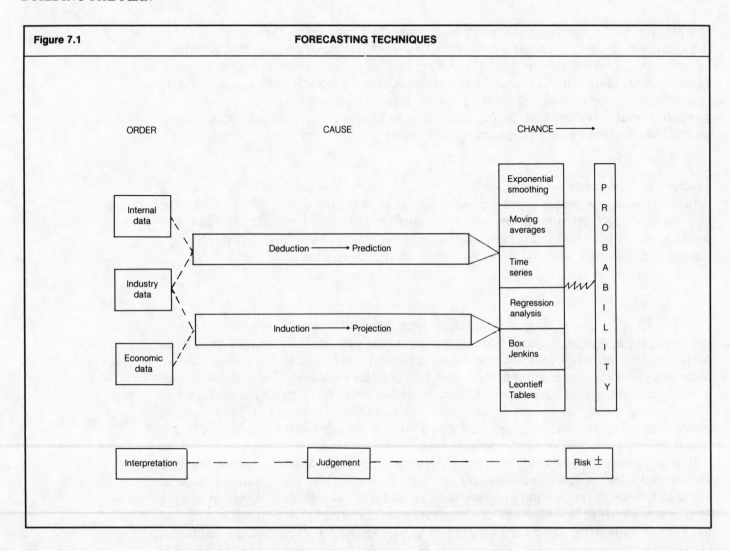

Figure 7.1   **FORECASTING TECHNIQUES**

Figure 7.2
Date

SALES AND GROSS MARGIN ANALYSIS BY PRODUCT AND MARKET SEGMENT

A = Sales and value   B = Gross margin %   C = Growth prior year 2 = 100

Prepared by

Prior year 2 actual			Prior year 1 actual			Current year forecast			Activity	Plan year 1			Plan year 2			Plan year 3			Plan year 4			Plan year 5		
A	B	C	A	B	C	A	B	C	Product group	A	B	C	A	B	C	A	B	C	A	B	C	A	B	C
									Total sales															
									Market segment															
									Total sales															

Figure 7.3   Sales and gross margin year forecast
This forecast shows historical sales for each of two full years in the past and apportions sales performance for the next full year by quarterly periods. Once again the sales value is shown with the appropriate gross margins. Market segments are also clearly indicated, as these are a necessary source of information for sales planning and promotional activities. This one-year forecast should be shown in considerable detail, not only for production planning purposes but also to enable the financial controller to arrange a realistic cash flow.

Figure 7.4   Sales barometer
Frequently, companies with an adverse actual sales performance against forecast find that remedial action, no matter how successful, is too late to bring the company back on a profitable course and worthwhile sales opportunities are subsequently lost. This chart is a control document which can indicate performance only after sales have appeared on the sales ledger.

In order to avoid such consequences the company must develop early warning signals. As enquiries, quotations and orders have been set as part of company objectives it is necessary only to split the objectives into equal periods, for the year sales are forecast, and programme them according to the established ratios, making full allowance for the time-lag between each element in the conversion of enquiry into sales, for early warning signals to be established.

The sales barometer must not only include the past performance of the company by months, but must also indicate the general trend established month by month cumulatively throughout the sales year. In this way it is possible to establish clear trends within one sales year. It is often not appreciated that growth in sales does not happen in one year but goes on, day by day, week by week and month by month. By establishing trends in this way it is possible to make revised forecasts for the following period and a cumulative revised forecast for the year-end. Obviously, if the revised year-end forecast shows a decline compared to budget, the marketing contingency plan must be brought into operation.

Figure 7.3 Date					SALES AND GROSS MARGIN YEAR FORECAST					Prepared by									
Prior year 2 actual		Prior year 1 actual		Current year forecast		Activity		Quarter 1		Quarter 2		Quarter 3		Quarter 4		Full plan year 1	
Value	GM	Value	GM	Value	GM	Product		Value	GM	Value	GM	Value	GM	Value	GM	Value	GM
						Market segment											

Figure 7.4 Date			SALES BAROMETER						Month					Prepared by	

Prior year same period	Prior year same period cumulative	Product	Budget month	Budget month cumulative	Current month actual	Current month actual cumulative	Variance current/budget	Variance current/ budget cumulative	Next month budget	Next month budget cumulative	Next month revised forecast	Next month revised forecast cumulative	Variance budget/forecast	Variance budget/ forecast cumulative	Full year budget	Full year forecast

Figure 7.5   Elasticity of demand

Products and product groups have different demand schedules and their elasticity varies according to the circumstances of the industry concerned. Tracking these elasticities is essential to short-term forecasting. Demand for meat tends to be inelastic as it is consumed daily and almost universally. It is considered essential to everyday living. Yet demand for different types of meat may be elastic. The price of beef may rise to the point where consumers consider it out of proportion to its value *to them* and so will buy an alternative which *for them* has a better relative value. Similarly, where low-priced cuts of meat climb in price they may reach a point where the consumer considers the price excessive *for what it is* and is prepared to pay a little more in order to get better value from a more expensive cut. In both these cases the demand may be elastic.

However, in the short term, demand for meat will not vary much, but the demand mix may change drastically after a price change.

In Figure 7.5, part (a) shows inelastic demand for meat while part (c) shows elastic demand for beef. Part (b) shows a change in the supply position and price of meat – the price rises and the quantity made available begins to increase. In part (d) a shortage of beef may increase price to a much lesser extent than the decrease in quantity purchased. In parts (b) and (d) the two rectangles together are equal to total income (price $\times$ quantity = total income); the shaded areas indicate the changes in total income.

Figure 7.6   Economic indicators

No company operates in complete isolation. Effects of the national economy and world trade in general have to be considered in the development of detailed forecasts of market sales potential and market share which the investigating company plans to achieve. This illustration lists many of the usual indicators.

The use of the statistical technique known as 'moving annual totals' is of particular value in controlling the factors referred to in this chapter.

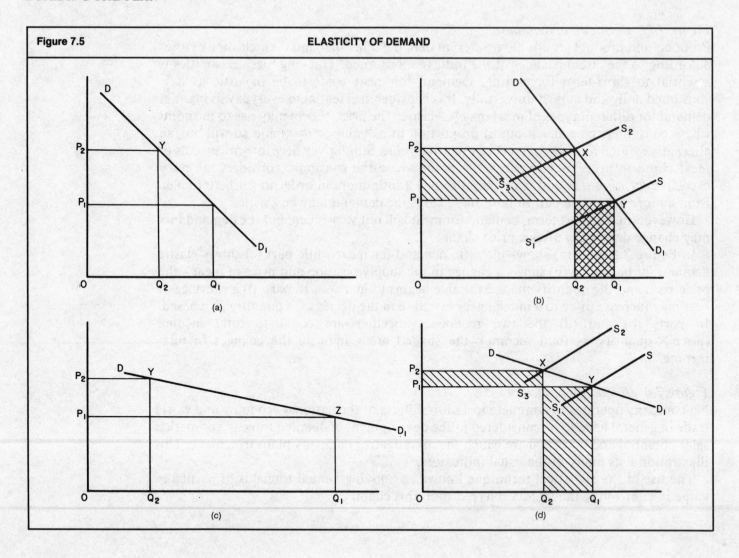

Figure 7.5

ELASTICITY OF DEMAND

Figure 7.6			ECONOMIC INDICATORS			
Price year 2	Price year 1	Current year	Activity	Plan year 1	Plan year 2	Plan year 3
			Company sales			
			Industry sales			
			Gross national product			
			Gross national product per capita			
			Population			
			Working population			
			Index of hours worked			
			Index of wages			
			Index of raw materials			
			Cost of living index			
			Index of wholesale prices			
			Balance of trade			
			Balance of payments			
			Investment			
			1 Manufacturing			
			2 Other private industry			
			3 Nationalized industries			
			4 Stock building			
			5 Housing			
			6 Roads			
			7 Other public services			
			8 Transfer costs land and buildings			
			Defence			
			Consumption – personal			
			Social and public services			
			Exports			
			Imports			
			Oil prices			
			Other energy prices			
			Inflation rate			
			Credit balance			

8 Constructing the Budgets

Budgetary control, properly developed, planned and implemented, portrays the entire business operation in a common unequivocable language. Company resources are allocated in predetermined amounts to specific business activities. The expected return is predicted for each of these activities, to provide the maximum possible profit for the enterprise.

Because all forecasts are based on considered judgement, the system enables executives to assess the likely alternative courses of action and spotlight the best opportunities. As all alternatives have been considered in advance, any change in operating conditions requiring remedial action therefore becomes a matter of logical decision. Deviations from budget can be investigated and the cause isolated. At the time the budgets were set, certain environmental conditions must have been anticipated; investigations into actual conditions should highlight the cause of deviations.

Though the actual implementation of a budgetary control system is essentially an accounting function, it is necessary for marketing executives to understand fully its workings, functions and practical value. Not only will they be preparing the information fed in but they will also be responsible for its control and for reporting and recommending alternative courses of action should they become necessary.

Because of the complexity of present-day responsibilities of marketing executives it is essential that senior marketing executives should be specialists in general marketing operation. In this way they become businessmen in the widest sense of the word with a full understanding and appreciation of the financial control of the marketing function.

As senior executives, marketing managers must be profit-orientated and, in order to implement profit-making plans, must understand the nature and the implications of financial accounting. As they are normally responsible for pricing, they will need to be conversant with cost-accounting principles and the allocation of company resources towards achieving the required profit on sales irrespective of sales volume or sales growth.

In developing company marketing strategy it is necessary to recognize that the first charge to the business – that is, the first essential cost – is the profit that must be achieved in order to repay shareholders for their investment in the company and for the confidence they have placed in its executives. In preparing detailed marketing budgets executives are stating the financial resources the company will need to achieve the sales volume necessary to produce the profit being charged to the business. The marketing function is thus being prepared according to financial investment principles and should be subjected to the monitoring and measuring of performance according to standards adopted for all other forms of investment. The marketing function is not a separate activity capable of measurement in isolation, but is a part of the total company operation within which it must be fully co-ordinated and measured within total performance of the company.

The essence of budgeting is as a control system. By setting budgets the company is establishing high standards, against which actual performance can be measured. Where deviations come to light, explanations can be sought and contingency plans brought into operation to ensure that the profit level is maintained. Until recently, the financial performance of a company could not be measured – extracting, tabulating and presenting the information was a long drawn-out process. The information obtained in this way referred to long-passed accounting periods. The causes and counter-measures necessary came too late to be effective.

Today, large firms use computers to give them almost instantaneous management information, while small to medium-sized businesses make use of computer bureaux or, even more effectively, computer terminals. The use of electronic data processing equipment makes it easier to employ management information systems and to prepare budgets for control purposes. In future years more companies will make use of computer power to program alternative sets of operating conditions to assess the effects of marketing strategy and marketing tactics on the company's profitability. Effectively, this is a form of trial and error using simulation instead of actual business environment. This minimizes the consequences of inappropriate decisions to nothing more than the expenditure on stationery used by the computer's printing equipment.

The actual deployment of resources adopted by the marketing executive to achieve the objectives of the business is commonly known among marketing staff as the marketing mix. It is the total blend of resources expressed in purely financial terms, incorporating the elements, manpower, time and energy devoted to exploiting a current and anticipated market situation. It is on the assessment and realization of prevailing conditions that marketing prosperity depends. By choosing the most vulnerable area for penetration, and devoting the company's resources to that point, the market-orientated company ensures its own prosperity.

It is in the use of budgeting operations that the term management by objectives has come into common usage. The use of management information systems in the modern business environment has resulted in the creation of a volume of paperwork which would prove a full-time job for the ordinary executive to process. Using properly controlled budget systems, responsible executives should receive only information on activities which show a significant deviation from budget and for which corrective action is required. Where actual results prove better than those budgeted, the executive concerned will also be advised of the situation so that a favourable situation can be further exploited.

The financial liquidity of any company is dependent on an adequate flow of revenue to cover all outgoings. Frequently, new product launches or the recruitment of additional staff requires an initial investment which can only be recovered at some time in the distant future. In order to retain a positive cash flow situation the financial controller will need to have advance warning of such investments in order to obtain the necessary funds. When the entire business operation is properly planned and all activities are subjected to budgetary control, the financial controller should be able to utilize fully the company's assets so as to avoid unnecessary borrowing at high interest rates to finance investments.

Figure 8.1 Marketing budget
This illustration shows in outline the standard categories of expense for marketing activities – the marketing mix. It shows expenditure for each month of the budgeted year and provides useful control ratios, as a guide to marketing productivity.

The total marketing expense is related to budgeted sales both for the prior and actual periods and for the full year ahead. The percentage indicator against each pound spent is used to indicate the interrelationship between individual items. There is provision for showing the average remuneration of management and staff for each month of the year. It also shows the marketing expense per employee as an indication of pressures on recruitment.

Figure 8.2   Analysis of marketing expense

This form shows marketing expense within the full period of the marketing plan and isolates in detail the various expenses incurred in the administration and implementation of marketing policies. Actual expenditure for each year during the course of the plan is plotted and the percentage increase or decrease year by year is featured.

Figure 8.3   Allocation of expense

It is a principle of budgeting that those people responsible for controlling a budget should also be responsible for working out the expenditure they will need to incur to achieve the tasks they have been allocated. In giving them this responsibility the company's management will expect them to carry out a detailed investigation into the resources they will require and to provide justification for their recommendations.

In operating successfully, every company needs to make maximum use of the limited resources it has available. Allowing executives to develop their own budgets ensures that the responsible manager has every confidence in his staff achieving the performance required. However, the most responsible of executives tend to overestimate as they allow psychologically for the unexpected. There is, almost always, room for some pruning, although this should be done in the presence, and with the general approval, of the executive responsible.

Senior management is responsible for co-ordinating the activities of its executives. To allow each ambitious manager to develop plans in complete isolation from other departments is fundamentally wrong to business planning principles. Each manager must be given an adequate briefing on the tasks expected, in the period under review, and must submit budgets to achieve these tasks. When all budgets have been submitted, all activities should be co-ordinated by senior management and available funds allocated accordingly. Some activities will require greater priority than others and the spread of funds will be determined according to priorities.

In this illustration provision has been made for the manager's own assessment of the maximum and minimum performance which he would expect to achieve if his full budget were approved.

Figure 8.4   Cost centres
In making individual managers fully responsible for the control of their own department operations, it is necessary for budgets to be prepared for each department, and for actual performance against budget to be reported against each budget period.

In departmentalizing budgets the company is creating cost centres which, though an integral part of the total company operation, have been given almost autonomous control, but subject to policy and financial dictation laid down by the company. Not all of these cost centres will be revenue raising, but their performances will be measured against the specific objectives set for their achievement at the time the plan was produced.

The cost centres shown in this illustration are for the normal marketing activity groupings, typical of many businesses. Companies may develop their own categories and, hence, cost centres, according to the requirements of their own operations. Apart from the head count that is recorded on the form, there is provision for month-by-month expenditure and for cumulative expenditure with variances against each period. In the final column the 'red flag' action feature should be provided and, where necessary, an indication of remedial action can be itemized.

Figure 8.5   Budget control
Many companies prefer to budget their expenditure according to product groups, particularly where they have introduced the product group manager as part of the implementation of marketing principles. Product group managers, under these circumstances, are usually responsible for the profitability of the products within their group, and will draw on the services of the sales force and marketing services department in order to promote their products and achieve their profit forecast.

Some companies may use the same basic format shown but delegate profit responsibility to an area or branch manager who has responsibility for a given geographical area and whose performance is measured by achievement against budget according to a given percentage for that area. Other companies allocate this responsibility to marketing managers who have a similar function to product group managers but provide a full range of the company's products to specific market segments.

Figure 8.6   Decision budgets

A company may delay making a decision involving the contraction of a particular activity in the hope that it will right itself after a given period of time. Frequently this means that the financial consequences resulting from that activity are much more pronounced because of a delayed decision. Once the deterioration has become apparent, every effort should be made to rectify the situation. If at the time of planning a contingency programme has been drawn up, at a given point of decline the activity can either be abandoned or completely restructured. The subsequent developments are then more likely to be soundly conceived. It is difficult to make a rational decision when under considerable stress, and the best time to make a decision affecting the jobs of colleagues or the activities of a department or of a product is when, in possession of all the facts, it can be arrived at calmly and without emotion.

Figure 8.1 Date			MARKETING BUDGET													Prepared by	
Prior year actual		Activity	Jan	Feb	Mar	Apr	May	Jun	Jul	Aug	Sep	Oct	Nov	Dec	Full year	
£/$	%		£/$	£/$	£/$	£/$	£/$	£/$	£/$	£/$	£/$	£/$	£/$	£/$	£/$	%
		Budgeted sales														
		Total expense														
		Ratios														
		Salaries and wages														
		Management and supervision														
		Administration														
		Salesmen														
		Clerical														
		Other														
		Total														
		Total head count														
		Average remuneration														
		Other expense														
		Assisted labour benefits														
		Rent and rates														
		Communications														
		Travel and entertaining														
		External commissions														
		Media advertising														
		Sales and literature														
		Public relations														
		Exhibitions														
		Samples														
		Sales force commission														
		Miscellaneous expense														
		Total other														
		Grand total														
		Expenses per head														

Figure 8.2 Date				**ANALYSIS OF MARKETING EXPENSE**												Prepared by	
Prior year 2		Prior year		Activity	Current year		Plan year 1		Plan year 2		Plan year 3		Plan year 4		Plan year 5		
£/$	+ − %	£/$	+ − %		£/$	+ − %	£/$	+ − %	£/$	+ − %	£/$	+ − %	£/$	+ − %	£/$	+ − %	
				Labour													
				Salaries													
				Entertaining													
				Travelling													
				Car expenses													
				Subscriptions													
				Recruitment													
				Training													
				Telephone, telex, fax													
				Stationery													
				Postage													
				Office equipment													
				Professional fees													
				Rent													
				Rates													
				Insurance													
				Lighting													
				Heating													
				Repairs													
				Commercial vehicles													
				Hire charges													
				Catering													
				Depreciation													
				Warehousing													
				Carriage													
				Public relations													
				Press advertising													
				Sales promotion													
				Total													

Figure 8.3 Date							ALLOCATION OF EXPENSE					Prepared by		
							Total budget sought							
Activity	Performance last year 19XX = 100	Total assets last year	Return on assets last year	Variance – last year budget ± %	Total assets forecast	Return on assets forecast	Amount	Minimum % performance	Maximum % performance	% ± last year	Management rating	Priority weighting total = 100%	Allocation approved

Head count			Cost centre	Expense						
Budget	Actual	Variance		Current month budget	Current month actual	Current month variance	Cumulative budget	Cumulative actual	Cumulative variance	Red flag action
			Marketing research							
			Publicity							
			Planning							
			Administration							
			Distribution							
			Sales force							
			Totals							

Figure 8.4
Date
COST CENTRES
Prepared by

Figure 8.5 Date		BUDGET CONTROL													Prepared by
Prior year actual	Product group	Jan	Feb	Mar	Apr	May	Jun	Jul	Aug	Sep	Oct	Nov	Dec	Full year
	Budget													
	Actual													
	% achievement													
	% performance													
	Budget													
	Actual													
	% achievement													
	% performance													
	Budget													
	Actual													
	% achievement													
	% performance													
	Budget													
	Actual													
	% achievement													
	% performance													
	Budget													
	Actual													
	% achievement													
	% performance													
	Budget													
	Actual													
	% achievement													
	% performance													
Total	Budget													
	Actual													
	% achievement													
	% performance													

Figure 8.6
Date

DECISION BUDGETS

Prepared by

Activity	Jan	Feb	Mar	First quarter review	Apr	May	Jun	Second quarter review	Jul	Aug	Sep	Third quarter review	Oct	Nov	Dec	Fourth quarter review	Annual review
Annual budget																	
Annual actual																	
Annual variance																	
Decreasing contingency																	
Annual budget																	
Annual actual																	
Annual variance																	
Decreasing contingency																	
Annual budget																	
Annual actual																	
Annual variance																	
Decreasing contingency																	
Annual budget																	
Annual actual																	
Annual variance																	
Decreasing contingency																	
Annual budget																	
Annual actual																	
Annual variance																	
Decreasing contingency																	
Annual budget																	
Annual actual																	
Annual variance																	
Decreasing contingency																	
Total annual budget																	
Annual actual																	
Annual variance																	
Decreasing contingency																	

9   Establishing Customer Service

Customer service forms the nerve centre of a business enterprise. It co-ordinates all other functions, provides a steady flow of vital information in all directions, maintains records for operational and control purposes, and supplies a supporting role in many activities either behind the scenes or in the forefront of the business organization. Companies credited with marketing strength often owe this reputation to the fortitude of the customer service department, and it is almost invariably true that a company with a reliable customer service section is prosperous.

Customer service has failed to earn itself a fashionable image because it covers a broad activity front and there is little opportunity for individuals to earn a reputation in a short period of time. It is not a glamorous profession, but it does provide ideal opportunities for career advancement. Working within the department provides the ambitious with an opportunity to study the wider aspects of the business and so gain a full command of its intricacies. Under the watchful eye of management it enables the career-minded to win confidence, and because operational results are left to the operating divisions, service departments will be judged qualitatively, which means subjectively. This is the ideal environment for a young manager to formulate ideas.

Because the department provides career opportunities it also provides a refuge for the work-shy, so opportunities for improvements in productivity are abundant. Apart from providing excellent potential for improvement in business efficiency itself, the department, as the central intelligence unit, is in a position to influence the extent to which operating departments are cost-effective. Clearly, the scope in customer service is considerable.

While many companies fail through over-trading, others dissipate their effort over a broad area of activity to avoid missing any opportunities, thereby never really grasping and exploiting any of the real potential that appears. Far more companies would profit if they turned away business to which they are not really suited and concentrated on providing the level of service required in one or two segments of their particular industry. In this way the company becomes customer-orientated and the basis for future prosperity is laid. There are six categories of business strategy available to a company.

1 *Full customer service.* In this category a company attempts to provide a group of customers with all their needs within a given product area. Perhaps the best example is in banking where banks try to provide for clients all financial needs, while recognizing that a number of the services provided are, in themselves, unprofitable. Another example is the mail order house that attempts to offer the equivalent of a department store in the home.

2 *Limited product line specialist.* This type of concern selects a particular product group and then concentrates in that field. Typical is the small firm that makes a successful product and then finds it dominates the whole of its production capacity, and growth becomes a consequence. Good examples would be IBM or Rank Xerox. Both companies have grown largely in one product group area.

3 *Specific product specialist.* Firms in this category have one general-purpose product, that is one that serves a wide range of uses but remains basically the same. For example, coal, electricity and gas, and also such products as newspapers, or self-adhesive materials.

4 *Market specialist.* Here, the company chooses a particular market and then tries to offer a comprehensive service. Dixons offers a comprehensive range of electronics goods, Mothercare caters for the expectant parent, and subsequent needs of offspring.

5 *'Specialist' producer.* These companies usually operate some general-purpose machine that can be used to provide custom-built or specified work. Examples are engineers, jobbing printers, or plastics moulders. The bespoke tailor is the nearest example at retail level although it is then a question of a particular skill rather than a machine.

6 *Product line specialist.* Companies in this group offer a wide range of commodities within one general category; for example, companies such as Heinz, Cadbury-Schweppes, Prestige, and Ladbroke Leisure.

Companies falling within these categories have all resolved the problem of their business activity and have decided what business they are in. They operate, usually with success, within their chosen field of operation and are customer-orientated because they have decided what service to provide. They have identified their customers, established likely benefits, and sell the product accordingly. Even where the companies are product or even production-orientated because of the nature of their product they have still contrived to establish marketing-orientated policies by segmenting markets and offering the appropriate customer service.

Customer service

Formulating the necessary service presents the first problem, because it is difficult to define exactly what customer service is. To some companies, it is establishing appropriate delivery and distribution services, whilst to others it is offering credit or hire-purchase facilities. In many cases it is ensuring the friendly co-operation of sales assistants in a store. The reason for the various interpretations is the provision of what is possible. Figures 9.1 to 9.7 illustrate many customer service activities. No firm could possibly provide all of the services listed, and so some selectivity must be made. Simply, the procedure is to identify the services needed by customers, ideally things that are being missed by present suppliers, and to incorporate them into the company policy. This is another ramification of the 'gap analysis' method of identifying business opportunities.

Figure 9.1   Credit control record card

Credit collection is often regarded as the function of the accounts department, headed by people with a striking resemblance to the bailiffs. Properly used, however, credit control provides an efficient company with a valuable promotional tool. Clearly, this principle has been well established in the consumer goods field but has yet to migrate to other marketing areas. Customers identified as sound security risks and operating a growing business will always need money for expansion. Often they will take credit as a means of financing their expansion. Shrewd suppliers recognize this fact and operate their supply position as part banker. They make sure their pricing policy covers the costs of the system and provides for cover against risks of bad debts. Suitably armed they supply customers with their needs, providing reasonable credit under control – and that means constant contact with the customer's accounts department. The customer should be in a position to acknowledge what is happening and recognize the benefit of an understanding supplier, even if the prices are a little higher than those of other suppliers. The essence of this business is proper control. Suppliers understand that they are making what amounts to an investment in a customer. It should be treated as an investment not as a debt.

Figure 9.2   Trade discount reckoner
Discounts are incentives and should not be used to placate buyers. Developed to achieve specific policies, they may often provide invaluable growth opportunities. Most people realize the value of these special incentives. What can be tedious is working out the real cost of a discount when more than one party is involved. Offering discounts to particular classes of retailer may prove expensive if the wholesaler concerned is to be similarly motivated.

This chart shows combined discounts for two or three parties. For example, if discounts of 10 per cent retail, 5 per cent wholesale, and 2½ per cent distributor are to be offered they add up to 16⅔ per cent on the collective amounts.

Figure 9.3   Benefits of telephone selling
Personal calls on customers by salesmen are costly in terms of both time and money. In a typical business 80 per cent of trade comes from 20 per cent of the customers. It follows that these customers should get all the service from salesmen that their purchases warrant. The majority of customers, however, which account for the minor part of the trade, do not warrant the attention they get. Some may be worth time and effort because of potential, but most do not justify a salesman calling regularly; an occasional visit should be sufficient. To ensure that this business is maintained, and as a total it is obviously significant, contact can be maintained quite successfully by telephone. In fact many businesses serving small outlets with low average-order value may not be able to justify maintaining a sales force. Telephone selling has many benefits and provides advantages that personal selling cannot match. The benefits shown in this chart suggest many opportunities to companies with a real need to improve the productivity of their selling effort.

Figure 9.1	CREDIT CONTROL RECORD CARD		

Name of firm	Limited ☐	Proprietorship ☐	Partnership ☐

Address

Previous address

Year established	SIC	Products	
Estimated value of stock £	Condition 100% 80% 70% 60% 50%	Insurance £/$	F☐ T☐
Freehold ☐ Leasehold ☐	Rateable value £/$	Rent £/$	Monthly

Number of employees: Management	Supervisory	Clerical and administration	Operatives

Nature of business	Cash ☐	Credit ☐	Cash and credit ☐	Leasing ☐

Estimated growth rate	19_____	19_____	19_____	19_____	19_____

Competitors

	Customers Yes/No ref
	Customers Yes/No ref
	Customers Yes/No ref

Business location

Owner/Buyer/Manager

Condition of premises	Good ☐ Poor ☐	Fixtures and fittings	Good ☐ Poor ☐	Vehicles	Good ☐ Poor ☐

Date of last inventory	Value of last year's sales £

Bank

References

Principal suppliers

Control: Average credit taken	1st qtr_____(days)	2nd qtr_____(days)	3rd qtr_____(days)	4th qtr_____(days)

D & B report

Figure 9.2								TRADE DISCOUNT RECKONER								
%	0	2½	5	10	15	20	25	27½	30	32½	35	37½	40	45	50
2½	.025	.049	.074	.123	.171	.220	.269	.293	.318	.342	.366	.391	.415	.464	.513
5	.050	.074	.098	.145	.193	.240	.288	.311	.335	.359	.383	.406	.430	.478	.515
10	.100	.123	.145	.190	.235	.280	.325	.348	.370	.393	.415	.438	.460	.505	.550
2½ + 5	.074	.097	.120	.167	.213	.259	.305	.329	.352	.375	.398	.421	.444	.491	.537
2½ + 10	.123	.144	.166	.210	.254	.298	.342	.364	.386	.408	.430	.452	.474	.517	.561
5 + 5	.098	.120	.143	.188	.233	.278	.323	.346	.368	.391	.413	.436	.459	.504	.549
5 + 10	.145	.166	.188	.231	.273	.316	.359	.380	.402	.423	.444	.466	.487	.530	.573

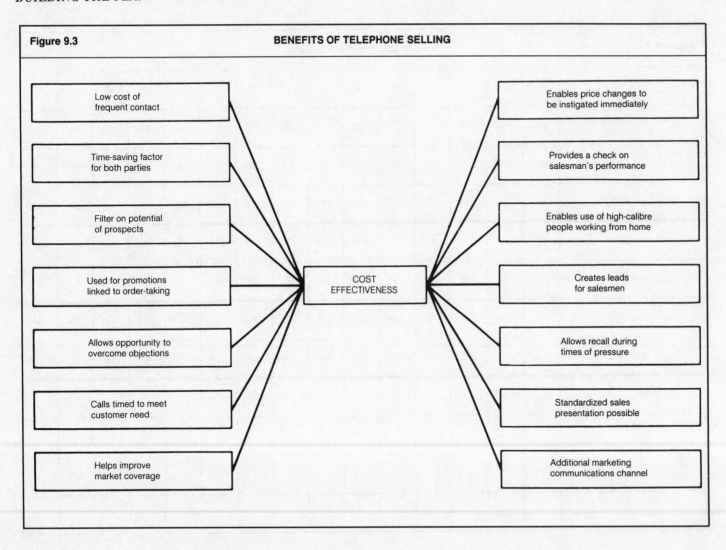

Figure 9.3　　　　　　　　　**BENEFITS OF TELEPHONE SELLING**

Low cost of
frequent contact

Time-saving factor
for both parties

Filter on potential
of prospects

Used for promotions
linked to order-taking

Allows opportunity to
overcome objections

Calls timed to meet
customer need

Helps improve
market coverage

COST
EFFECTIVENESS

Enables price changes to
be instigated immediately

Provides a check on
salesman's performance

Enables use of high-calibre
people working from home

Creates leads
for salesmen

Allows recall during
times of pressure

Standardized sales
presentation possible

Additional marketing
communications channel

Figure 9.4   Franchise marketing

Franchising is both a channel of distribution and the financial arrangement for the granting of a commercial privilege. Although considered a new system the method has been practised for many years. Petrol stations and public houses operate on franchise, although in recent years there has been a tendency towards managers rather than tenants. Perhaps the best known franchise is the Coca Cola bottling agreement that enables mineral water manufacturers around the world to bottle Coca Cola according to an agreed formula using an essence supplied by the Coca Cola Company. In recent years, however, Coca Cola Companies have become regional autonomies.

At one time this form of marketing came into some disrepute because some franchisors awarded franchises indiscriminately and many people lost their savings. The Department of Trade has on occasions forced companies to stop trading because of their methods of operation. Franchise marketing, however, has much to commend it as a system. It is thought to be one of the ever-increasing methods by which individuals can set up in business on their own account.

Figure 9.5   Present value analysis

Many of the ingredients of customer service demand an investment of funds. Providing a branch office, new delivery vans, mechanical handling equipment, or even an extension to a warehouse all require investment. Too often the company will make arbitrary decisions based on what amounts to guesswork, when a more realistic approach may be possible. Assuming that the firm makes a capital investment in order to improve profitability, two items of information will be required:

1 The expenditure involved. This will normally be in one outlay.
2 The subsequent inflows of cash as a direct result of the outlay. The inflows will normally be a series of returns spread over a number of years. Sometimes this return will remain constant over the years concerned, and in other investments the return will either increase or decrease.

Where the annual return is constant the 'present value of 1 per annum' table is used, but where the annual return is likely to increase or decrease the 'present value of 1' table is chosen.

In the second table the figure in the top left-hand column is 0.990099 and is the current value of 1 received in one year's time where the discount rate is 1 per cent. Similarly, the figure 0.148644, shown in the bottom right-hand corner of the same table, shows the value of 1 to be received in 10 years' time at a discount rate of 10 per cent. In the first table it can be seen that £1 per year received for each of the past five years at a discount rate of 5 per cent has a current value of £4.32948. £100 per year received for each of five years at a discount rate of 5 per cent is worth £432.948.

Figure 9.6   Consumer customer profile
No book on marketing is complete without an analysis of the classifications of customers. Several such classifications will be found elsewhere in this book, but this illustration provides a formal grouping for which published figures are available or are being made available. In many cases the published information is linked to the mass media and so provides the marketing person with the means to calculate the likelihood of cost-effective communication to specific target audiences.

In general, socio-economic groups are a feature of the 1960s, and psychographics of the 1970s, while Acorn is the hope for the future.

Figure 9.7   Industrial customer profile
Because industrial or commercial customers are measured in hundreds or thousands rather than the millions in consumer goods, each customer is relatively more important. Developing an individual profile is therefore essential. This illustration provides the foundations. In practice, customer record cards will include purchasing records, accounting details and product-mix growth.

Figure 9.4	FRANCHISE MARKETING
Advantages: The franchisee 1 Has the vested interest of the entrepreneur 2 Benefits of full association with large operation 3 Managerial advice and guidance 4 Joint promotion and reputation 5 A tried and proved system of operation	Advantages: The franchisor 1 Enjoys the self-motivation of the franchisee 2 Expands total distribution 3 Limits capital involvement 4 Limits administrative problems involved

CHECK-LIST FOR POTENTIAL FRANCHISEE
(Compiled by the Institute of Marketing, UK)

A statement of the support that is offered to you in the way of training, supervision, advertising, promotion and other services.

If you are to operate from premises other than your home, a statement of the responsibilities of each party in determining the location of the premises to be used and in financing their purchase.

A statement of the geographical area in which you are to have permanent exclusive rights. (You don't want to build up a business and then have part of it taken away by a newcomer in that area.)

A statement of the franchise fee to be charged, and the purpose to which such fee will be put by the franchisor, together with a statement of total investment to be made by you. A statement should also be obtained of any other payments or fees that you will be required to pay of whatever kind in relation to the franchise business.

A statement of any goods, fixtures or services you may be required to buy at the direction of the franchisor.

A statement of the terms and conditions of any finance arrangements to be provided by the franchisor.

A statement of any restrictions on the goods or services you may offer your customers.

The name and address of the franchisor and the name of any parent or affiliated company that will engage in business with you.

The names and addresses of the directors, partners or proprietors of the franchisor together with a statement:

1 of any criminal conviction or civil liability involving fraud, embezzlement, fraudulent conversion or misappropriation of property;

2 of any bankruptcy with which any of them has been concerned, whether as private individuals or as managers of a company.

3 of the results of any enquiry conducted into the business by any court or government body.

The length of time the franchisor has operated the franchise in question, the number of franchisees currently operating, and the number sold but not yet operating. Additionally, a full list of names of current operators should be made available so that you can check experiences of a sample.

A statement of the franchise earnings you can expect to make together with a statement of the date upon which the forecast is based. This statement should also indicate the results on which payment will be based, and if a significant proportion depends on recruitment by you of further franchisees, rather than on selling the product, we strongly advise you to have nothing to do with the organization.

A recent balance sheet and profit and loss account audited by a chartered accountant together with a statement of any material changes that have occurred since the date of the statement.

When the person selling the franchise is a sub-franchisor, all the above information should be required in respect of him as well as the franchisor.

A statement of the terms on which the franchise can be terminated by either side. In particular the terms on which goods will be bought back by the franchisor. If more than 10 per cent is deducted from the sales price to you it is unreasonable. If a period much in excess of six months must elapse before the refund is made, that too is unreasonable.

A general description of the business which is the subject of the franchise together with the details of the trade names and trade marks involved, plus a description of the goods or services involved.

Figure 9.5 — PRESENT VALUE ANALYSIS

Present value of 1 per annum (used where the annual return is constant)

Year	1	2	3	4	5 (Percentage)	6	7	8	9	10
1	0 99099	0 980392	0 970874	0 961538	0 952381	0 943396	0 934579	0 925926	0 917431	0 909091
2	1 97040	1 94156	1 91347	1 88609	1 85941	1 83339	1 80802	1 78326	1 75911	1 73554
3	2 94099	2 88388	2 82861	2 77509	2 72325	2 67301	2 62432	2 57710	2 53129	2 48685
4	3 90197	3 80773	3 71710	3 62990	3 54595	3 46511	3 38721	3 31213	3 23972	3 16987
5	4 85343	4 71346	4 57971	4 45182	4 32948	4 21236	4 10020	3 99271	3 88965	3 79079
6	5 79548	5 60143	5 41719	5 24214	5 07569	4 91732	4 76654	4 62288	4 48592	4 35526
7	6 72819	6 47199	6 23028	6 00205	5 78637	5 58238	5 38929	5 20637	5 03295	4 86842
8	7 65168	7 32548	7 01969	6 73274	6 46321	6 20979	5 97130	5 74664	5 53482	5 33493
9	8 56602	8 16224	7 78611	7 43533	7 10782	6 80169	6 51523	6 24689	5 99525	5 75902
10	9 47130	8 98259	8 53020	8 11090	7 72173	7 36009	7 02358	6 71008	6 41766	6 14457
11	10 3676	9 78685	9 25262	8 76048	8 30641	7 88687	7 49867	7 13896	6 80519	6 49506
12	11 2551	10 5753	9 95400	9 38507	8 86325	8 38384	7 94269	7 53608	7 16073	6 81369
13	12 1337	11 3484	10 6350	9 98565	9 39357	8 85268	8 35765	7 90378	7 48690	7 10336
14	13 0037	12 1062	11 2961	10 5631	9 89864	9 29498	8 74547	8 24424	7 78615	7 36669
15	13 8651	12 8493	11 9379	11 1184	10 3797	9 71225	9 10791	8 55948	8 06069	7 60608
16	14 7179	13 5777	12 5611	11 6523	10 8378	10 1059	9 44665	8 85137	8 31256	7 82371
17	15 5623	14 2919	13 1661	12 1657	11 2741	10 4773	9 76322	9 12164	8 54363	8 02155
18	16 3983	14 9920	13 7535	12 6593	11 6896	10 8276	10 0591	9 37189	8 75563	8 20141
19	17 2260	15 6785	14 3238	13 1339	12 0853	11 1581	10 3356	9 60360	8 95011	8 36492
20	18 0456	16 3514	14 8775	13 5903	12 4622	11 4699	10 5940	9 81815	9 12855	8 51356

Present value of 1 (used where the annual return increases or decreases)

Year	1	2	3	4	5 (Percentage)	6	7	8	9	10
1	0 990099	0 980392	0 970874	0 961538	0 952381	0 943396	0 934579	0 925926	0 917431	0 909091
2	0 980296	0 961169	0 942596	0 942556	0 907029	0 889996	0 873439	0 857339	0 841680	0 826446
3	0 970590	0 942322	0 915142	0 888996	0 863838	0 839619	0 816298	0 793832	0 772183	0 751315
4	0 960980	0 923845	0 888487	0 854804	0 822702	0 792094	0 762895	0 735030	0 708425	0 683013
5	0 951466	0 905731	0 862609	0 821927	0 783526	0 747258	0 712986	0 680583	0 649931	0 620921
6	0 942045	0 887971	0 837484	0 790315	0 746215	0 704961	0 666342	0 630170	0 596267	0 564474
7	0 932718	0 870560	0 813092	0 759918	0 710681	0 665057	0 622750	0 583490	0 547034	0 513158
8	0 923483	0 853490	0 789409	0 730690	0 676839	0 627412	0 582009	0 540269	0 501866	0 466507
9	0 914340	0 386755	0 766417	0 702587	0 644609	0 591898	0 543934	0 500249	0 460428	0 424098
10	0 905287	0 820348	0 744094	0 675564	0 613913	0 558395	0 508349	0 463193	0 422411	0 385543
11	0 896324	0 804263	0 722421	0 649581	0 584679	0 526788	0 475093	0 428883	0 387533	0 350494
12	0 887449	0 788493	0 701380	0 624597	0 556837	0 496969	0 444012	0 397114	0 355535	0 318631
13	0 878663	0 773033	0 680951	0 600574	0 530321	0 468839	0 414964	0 367698	0 326179	0 289664
14	0 869963	0 757857	0 661118	0 577475	0 505068	0 442301	0 387817	0 340461	0 299246	0 263331
15	0 861349	0 743015	0 641862	0 555265	0 481017	0 417265	0 362446	0 315242	0 274538	0 239392
16	0 852821	0 728446	0 623167	0 533908	0 458112	0 393646	0 338735	0 291890	0 251870	0 217629
17	0 844377	0 714163	0 605016	0 513373	0 436297	0 371364	0 316574	0 270269	0 231073	0 197845
18	0 836017	0 700159	0 587395	0 493628	0 415521	0 350344	0 295834	0 250249	0 211994	0 179859
19	0 827740	0 686431	0 570286	0 474642	0 395734	0 330513	0 276508	0 231712	0 194490	0 163508
20	0 819544	0 672971	0 553676	0 456387	0 376889	0 311805	0 258419	0 214548	0 178431	0 148644

Figure 9.6　　　　　　　　　　　　**CONSUMER CUSTOMER PROFILE**

Socio-economic group	Age group	Television region	
A	0–15	1	11
B	16–25	2	12
C₁	26–35	3	13
C₂	36–45	4	14
D	46–55	5	15
E	56–65	6	16
	65+	7	17
		8	18
		9	19
		10	20

TARGET GROUP INDEX	PSYCHOGRAPHICS MALES		ACORN CENSUS ENUMERATION DISTRICTS	
Sex	Quiet family man		A	Modern family housing for manual workers
Age	Traditionalists		B	Modern family housing for higher income groups
Class	Discontented man		C	Older housing of intermediate status
Standard region	Ethical highbrow		D	Very poor quality older terraced housing
TV region	Pleasure orientated		E	Rural areas
Household income	Achiever		F	Urban local authority housing
Psychographics	He-man		G	Housing with most overcrowding
Terminal education age	Sophisticated		H	Low income areas with immigrants
Marital status	Product use	all users	I	Student and high-status, non-family areas
Years married		heavy users	J	Traditional high status Suburbia
Number of children		medium users	K	Areas of elderly people
Readership publications		light users		Key variables: 1 Level of unemployment; 2 Proportion
Television viewing		non-users		of students; 3 Number of two-car households;
Cinema going	Brand use	all users		4 Proportion working in particular sectors;
Underground usage		solus users		5 Social class; 6 Age; 7 Five-year migrancy;
Poster viewing propensity		major users		8 Tenure type; 9 Proportion of immigrants from
		minor users		Commonwealth; 10 Level of overcrowding; 11 Level
		non-users		of basic housing amenities.

Figure 9.7   INDUSTRIAL CUSTOMER PROFILE

SIC   1–26   Size of firm: index employees; index operatives; index others; index square footage; index manufacturing; index others. Trade unions: % penetration

Methods of distribution	a)	b)	c)	d)

Market segment 1–26 industrial production

1–26 advertising expenditure

Index changes in output	Index changes in manpower	Index changes output per head
Index fixed investment	Index working capital	Index distribution costs
Index imports		Index exports

Index ROI (%)	19 . . .	19 . . .	19 . . .	19 . . .	19 . . .	19 . . .

Index oil consumption

Index of growth	Index of prices	Index of advertising

Associated companies	Bankers
Public/subsidiary/private/partnership/other	Estimated market share
Floor space office	other

Rating of management

Known applications	Likely applications
Present purchasing power, per annum	Seasonal pattern

Prospect rating	A	B	C	D	E	F	G	H

Sales	Profit

Comments on management	Decision-taker/maker	Comments on consumption
	Managing director	
	Board	
	Committee	
	Secretary	
	Office manager	
	Buyer	
	Parent company	

Name ....   Folio ....

Organizing the Marketing Team 10

In the modern business environment a company's most valuable asset is its management and staff. To establish and maintain a lead in the battle for increasing prosperity any successful company develops a sound recruitment policy. Although this is true of all departments, it is particularly true of the marketing department for it provides the main source of contact between the company and its customers. A sound recruitment policy must be continuous, practical and, at times, experimental. By adopting such a policy the company will always be looking for recruits and will encourage colleagues and employees to report on promising material. Although employment may not be immediately available, suitable candidates should be interviewed and told that they will be advised as soon as a suitable vacancy arises. It is advisable to contact any prospective employees from time to time to reassure them that they have not been forgotten.

To ensure that the recruitment policy remains economic it is not necessary to automatically select the national media for recruitment. If a continuous recruitment policy is maintained there will be a steady stream of applicants who can be vetted as necessary. After a period of time a company will be able to devise the most economic method of attracting suitable applicants to ensure an appropriate selection. Each method and each medium should be kept under constant surveillance and measurement of responses, both in quantity and quality, should be recorded. A practical recruitment policy is an integral part of the total marketing plan and the required type of employee can be documented well in advance even to the full period of the marketing plan. It is only by building these short, medium and long-term recruitments into the overall marketing plan that a company will be able to recruit in a practical and realistic manner.

In recruiting salesmen, allowances must be made for a certain type of person who may eventually become a supervisor. It now seems apparent that good supervisors are not necessarily brilliant salesmen. They are usually good but will not always appear at the top of the sales performance league. Often top salesmen are ambitious and will go their own brilliant way, rejecting responsibility for control systems and the like, but still bringing in a phenomenal amount of business. These are not the characteristics of supervisors and such people are not always successful in this role. In the recruitment programme it is important to ensure that as many top salesmen as possible are recruited and that qualities are sought which eventually lead to a supervisory post.

To satisfy all future needs the company should be seeking different types of people who, initially, will be doing the same kind of job. Many companies have established routines when recruiting. This practice is restrictive and many good people will be missed unless the executives responsible for the recruitment use their imagination and experiment with different types and methods of recruitment. Provided the type of people the company require actually exists, it is only a question of contacting them. This, basically, is the recruitment problem. The company should try every method and different media in an effort to obtain the best results. Any advertisement for staff should include details of the type of job being offered, the type of person to fill the job, salary and future prospects. The company recruitment policy should be aimed at a wide enough field to ensure suitable applicants; the purpose of screening is to select those suitable applicants and to narrow the field to the point where managers will be able to distinguish applicants in their own mind by the career records provided, prior to the interview. Interviews should be designed to produce a shortlist of three or four candidates from which it should be possible to select one who shows the greatest likelihood of early compatibility.

The screening standards are a list of the minimum requirements for the job. The applicant who falls below these standards in any way whatsoever should be rejected. The list should not include items which the company might allow if a candidate meets standards in all other respects. When advertising, it will be necessary to maintain a balance between the need to attract applicants and the screening standards, not only because of the cost but because of the need to preserve confidential information. Sometimes it may be necessary to exclude certain screening standards from the advertisement, but these must be applied when the applications are received. Using screening standards helps by reducing the time senior managers need to reserve for interviewing. It also aids in establishing standards for the job itself.

In practice, marketing is part art and part science. Skill in marketing comes from knowledge and the practice of that knowledge. By adopting a realistic training programme a company will give its staff opportunities that will develop the skills necessary to achieve company objectives. Training is now considered a necessity at all levels, and any person in the organization who is in contact with customers and prospective customers needs to learn how to deal with these people, upon which the future prosperity of the firm will depend. This includes telephone operators, correspondence clerks, receptionists, messengers, delivery drivers, advertising copywriters, public relations staff, typists, accounts clerks and in particular, installation and maintenance mechanics and salesmen. Salesmen are most frequently in contact with customers; in the minds of most customers the salesman is, in fact, the company.

Historically, sales teams have mainly been recruited in the traditional image of the firm's representatives. Many customers seem, on the surface, to prefer this type of individual because they usually have technical prominence and interest in their product and its uses, and gain considerable job satisfaction in developing confidence and amicability with contacts. Many of these salesmen have only a relatively low degree of selling skill and little appreciation of the need to improve sales performance, and reject the need for the application of selling processes. A training course for salesmen is therefore vital, and should be continuous to maintain enthusiasm. After the main introductory course, training should be given by the field sales manager, whose coaching and day-to-day leadership control is necessary if selling theories are to be translated into practice on the job.

The salesman of today must fulfil two essential communication functions: find customers and potential customers and feed back basic information to the company for management use.

Figure 10.1   The marketing team
The organization structure of the marketing department is often the most revealing aspect of a company's marketing orientation. It suggests the marketing spectrum within a company and how it views its marketing responsibilities. The organization chart shown in this illustration is intended to remind all members of the team and their staff of collective responsibilities, of the outside agencies involved in the marketing programme, whom the company serves, and of the essential ingredients of the marketing philosophy.

Such an organization chart is intended to help to break down functional barriers and to establish common goals and procedures, so establishing the basis for total co-ordination of effort.

Figure 10.2   Job specification – marketing manager
Unless all employees know the exact extent of their responsibilities and the scope of their authority, they will be unable to act with confidence. In the absence of a specification for their job they will not be able to assess their own progress or develop knowledge or skills relevant to their activities.

   The writing of job specifications, particularly for management functions, is a task to be undertaken directly by the company's senior executive and, once introduced, periodically reviewed and amended where necessary. This must be done if the company wants to avoid the tendency for individuals to isolate themselves from other executives and to operate independently within the confines of their job specification. As the management team operates in unity, it is the responsibility of the senior executive to direct the day-to-day interpretation of each manager's responsibilities and authorities.

Figure 10.3   Staff profile
Job specifications and related staff profiles define the job and the person most likely to succeed on the job, thus enabling selection, recruitment, supervision, delegation, training and promotional policies to be effective.

Figure 10.4   Field sales performance controls
In measuring the performance of each salesman it is usual to compare actual sales results with a quota set for the territory. The quota for each salesman's territory may be allocated according to product group, by value, or by market segment by value. In many companies individual salesmen's quotas are allocated according to historical performance. Although this is frequently the simplest means of deciding, it makes no allowance for variations in territories which can differ by industrial concentration or market segmentation, availability and effectiveness of local advertising media, regional strength of competitors, whether or not it is a development region, or on the company's past record.

   So, although the actual performance of salesmen must be recorded and evaluated, it is by itself only a partial measurement.

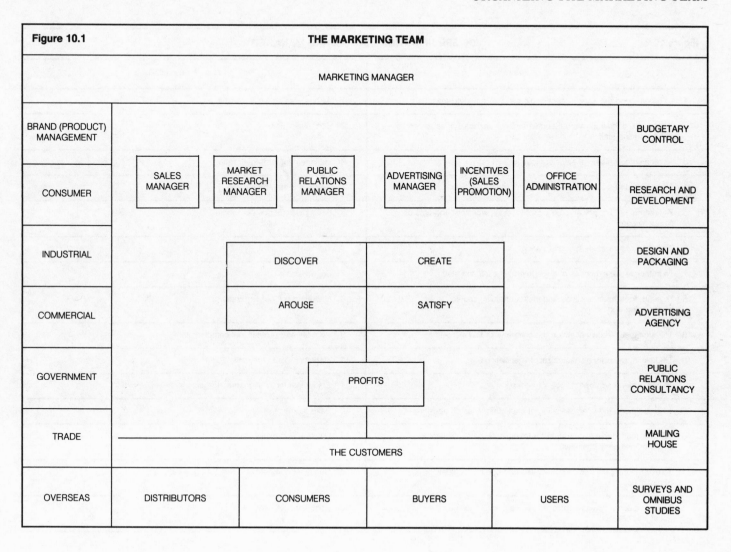

Figure 10.1 **THE MARKETING TEAM**

MARKETING MANAGER

BRAND (PRODUCT) MANAGEMENT

CONSUMER

INDUSTRIAL

COMMERCIAL

GOVERNMENT

TRADE

OVERSEAS

SALES MANAGER

MARKET RESEARCH MANAGER

PUBLIC RELATIONS MANAGER

ADVERTISING MANAGER

INCENTIVES (SALES PROMOTION)

OFFICE ADMINISTRATION

DISCOVER

CREATE

AROUSE

SATISFY

PROFITS

THE CUSTOMERS

DISTRIBUTORS

CONSUMERS

BUYERS

USERS

BUDGETARY CONTROL

RESEARCH AND DEVELOPMENT

DESIGN AND PACKAGING

ADVERTISING AGENCY

PUBLIC RELATIONS CONSULTANCY

MAILING HOUSE

SURVEYS AND OMNIBUS STUDIES

Figure 10.2	JOB SPECIFICATION – MARKETING MANAGER	
Authorities		**Responsibilities**
1 To recommend the appointment or dismissal of reporting managers		1 All business activities of staff
2 To approve or disapprove the appointment or dismissal of salesmen and marketing staff		2 Communications
3 To recommend plans for sales campaigns		3 Management staff merit rating
4 To recommend the introduction of new products		4 All sales value and volume
5 To recommend the policy to be adopted for replacement and type of company cars		5 Sales performance decisions
6 To call on technical staff for assistance		6 Training
7 To authorize the expenses of departmental heads and staff		7 Supervision
8 To send departmental heads and staff on training courses where warranted		8 Marketing budget expenditure
9 To recommend shows at which the company should exhibit		9 Publicity and promotional campaigns
10 To develop publicity plans and recommendations		10 Marketing control reports
11 To recommend appropriate sales forecasts		11 Equipment used by marketing personnel
12 To recommend the commissioning of marketing research activities		12 Sales literature
13 To incur reasonable expenditure for travel, hotel and entertaining whilst on company business		13 Displays and exhibitions
14 To use the car provided as considered appropriate, including personal use		14 Customer complaints
15 To use working time as appropriate subject to direction by the managing director		15 Long-term planning

Figure 10.3		STAFF PROFILE		
Date				Prepared by
Characteristics	Yes	No	Interviewer's notes	
Physical make-up				
1 Appearance				
2 Dress				
3 Health				
Attainments				
4 Education				
5 Technical qualifications				
6 Experience in own industry				
7 Experience				
8 Knowledge of marketing technique				
9 Ease of manner				
Motivation				
10 Initiative				
11 Ambition				
12 Interest in peace and team work				
13 Administration and delegation				
14 Job/home relationship				
Intelligence				
15 Analytical ability				
16 Judgement				
17 Evaluation of new ideas				
18 Leadership				
19 Energy level				
20 Emotional maturity				
21 Loyalty				
22 Decisiveness				
23 Hours of work				
Circumstances				
24 Financial stability				

Figure 10.4 Date	FIELD SALES PERFORMANCE CONTROLS												Prepared by		
	Product group A			Product group B			Product group C			Product group D			Total product groups		
Salesman	Budget	Actual	Variance	Budget	Actual	Variance	Budget	Actual	Variance	Budget	Actual	Variance	Budget	Actual	Variance

Figure 10.5   Field sales activity controls

By introducing activity controls it is possible to measure individuals by market sales potential rather than by actual historical sales turnover. In addition, it is possible to measure the effort and expense that will be required to decide upon local expansion plans, revised delivery facilities and local marketing strategy. Such policy decisions will thus be based on likely profit return rather than on the powers of persuasion of local salesmen or their managers.

Sales revenue achieved in each territory depends upon potential and opportunities open to the person on the spot. While potential can be measured within tolerable limits, opportunity is subject to rapid change. Frequently, due to factors outside the company's immediate control, performance can fluctuate without warning and remedial action is delayed. Effective monitoring can be achieved by analysing, at regular intervals in each territory, the effort devoted by each salesman to achieving sales turnover. The efforts to be measured are the activities of the salesmen and not necessarily the value of the orders they manage to obtain.

Figure 10.6   Merit rating form (sales representative)

In measuring the total effectiveness of the sales force it is necessary to build up an assessment of each individual member. Although the sales performance of the company may be on target, it is likely that some salesmen will be exceeding their targets and others are lagging behind. While it is accepted that this situation is typical, it will, nevertheless, not meet the standards necessary in the future. Many such sales forces lack the purpose, enthusiasm and method which can only be provided by lengthy periods of resolute and skilled leadership. One of the basic tasks of such field leadership is to prepare job specifications and related staff profiles for a sales function, to define sales territories based on sales potential, to introduce planned selling and, more specifically, selective selling. Field sales managers also act as a communicating force between company and salesmen, and salesmen and company, particularly in establishing the need for targets, quotas and budgets. Above all, a measure of organizational stability must be established in the individual sales task so that salesmen, when taught the techniques of planned selling, will see the advantages to them as individuals, and will then co-operate in providing self-motivation.

The merit rating form illustrated is the evaluation by the field sales manager of each salesman for whom he is responsible. When completing this form it should be discussed in detail with the salesman concerned, giving reasons why the judgement recorded has been made and the means by which weaknesses can be overcome and strengths exploited.

Figure 10.7   Time planning analysis sheet
All salesmen face a problem with the organization of their time. Under normal circumstances the only possibility of increasing sales is when salesmen are face to face with their customers. In certain circumstances telephone calls and letters result in orders, but normal practice is to sell personally to a customer. In increasing the face-to-face time with buyers it is necessary to reduce the amount of time spent on other activities. By using a time and control sheet, salesmen should be able to vet their performance day by day and decide where time is not being used to best advantage. They will then be able to work out ways in which actual time spent with customers can be increased and non-productive time minimized.

Few companies make the necessary effort to improve the productivity of salesmen by journey planning. Such planning involves the development of low and high-frequency calls, establishing priorities in terms of customer value and customer potential value, so minimizing travelling time, evolving a call pattern, assessing the work-load, and combining programming flexibility. As salesmen will have accounts of varying sizes, large accounts justify more time than smaller accounts. It is important that management recognizes the cost per minute of selling time. Often salesmen will spend much time with potential customers who could be substantial buyers. Usually such customers not only buy big but also buy well, but the profitability of such orders, when obtained, does not always justify the effort in winning the order. Often the medium-sized potential customer buying at list price is getting indifferent service from competitors, and is more receptive to a proposition.

Figure 10.8   Organization chart – line functions
In any organization there will always be some confusion among the staff about who is responsible for certain activities. This is particularly true of telephone operators and

receptionists. Frequently, members of the sales force are unaware, because of their isolation, of the individuals who hold actual responsibilities for different aspects of company activities. By publishing an organization chart a company ensures that the significant responsibilities for each of its senior executives are known to all staff. This eases the means of communication and reduces much time and effort expended by employees and, in particular, by customers who may wish to obtain further information or wish to discuss a particular problem with the company.

Figure 10.9(a) and 10.9(b)   Selection of an advertising agency
Advertising agencies, or practitioners as they are more accurately called, provide necessary time, organization, experience, contacts, and personnel. They are people-orientated and markets are people. Almost always they supply the mass communication between buyer and supplier where widespread communication is essential. For buyers the practitioner's work should be seen as representing the company, and the company should see the practitioner as a department within the company, but the department as the voice of the market connection.

Figure 10.5 Date	FIELD SALES ACTIVITY CONTROLS		
			Prepared by
Territorial variations	Weighting	Salesmen activities	
1 Size		1 Growth compared with national average	
2 Industrial concentration		2 Selling costs/enquiries	
3 Market segments		3 Selling costs/orders	
4 Road facilities		4 Selling costs/sales	
5 Delivery service		5 Sales costs to marketing costs	
6 Local branch support		6 Number of calls made	
7 Local advertising media		7 Number of interviews obtained	
8 Strength of competitors		8 Number of enquiries received	
9 Development region		9 Number of quotations submitted	
10 Company's past reputation		10 Number of orders obtained	
11 Political influences		11 Cost per call	
12 Decentralized buying		12 Cost per interview	
13 Reciprocal trading		13 Average value of orders	
14 Strength of local economy		14 Number of orders per clock mileage	
15 Pricing policies		15 Average gross margin per order	
16		16 Local advertising against competitors	
17		17 Number of canvassing calls made	
18		18 Average mileage per journey cycle	
19		19 Number of accounts to service	
20		20 Average value of accounts	
21		21 Ratio of customers to prospects	
22		22 Number of new accounts opened	
23		23 Number of accounts lost	
24		24	
25		25	
26		26	
27		27	

Figure 10.6 Date	**MERIT RATING FORM (SALES REPRESENTATIVE)**				Prepared by
Performance	Specification				Remarks
	Above	Par	Under	Well Under	
Customer relations					
General					
Prospects					
Complaints					
Objections					
Selling skill					
Approach					
Presentation					
Closing the sale					
Product demonstration					
Technical and product knowledge					
General					
Industry					
Product					
Pricing					
Awareness					
Benefits					
Personal organization					
Reporting and paperwork					
Maintenance of records					
Catalogues, brochures					
Planning of time					
Customer records					
Journey planning					
Personal					
Appearance					
Manner					
Health					

BUILDING THE PLAN

Figure 10.7	TIME PLANNING ANALYSIS SHEET					
	Week 1	Week 2	Week 3	Week 4	Week 5	Week 6
Travelling						
Meals						
Entertaining						
Waiting time						
Preparing demonstration						
Preparing sales aids						
Paperwork						
Total non-selling time						
Total selling time						
Total time						

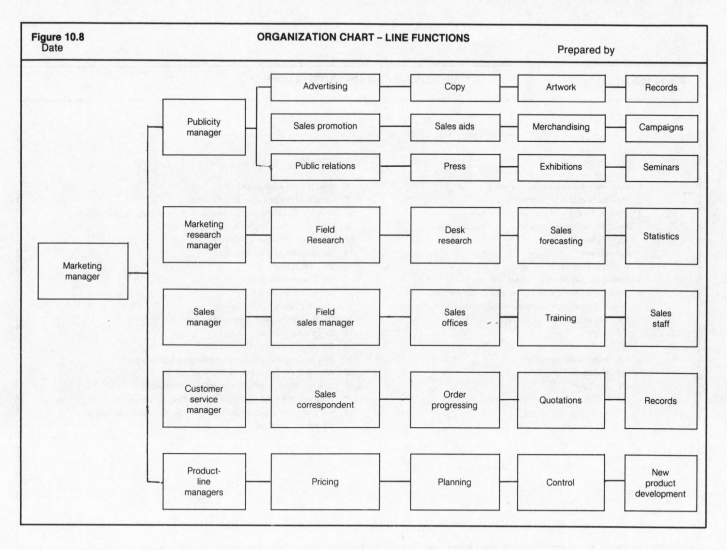

Figure 10.8
Date

ORGANIZATION CHART – LINE FUNCTIONS

Prepared by

Advertising	Copy	Artwork	Records
Sales promotion	Sales aids	Merchandising	Campaigns
Public relations	Press	Exhibitions	Seminars

Publicity manager

Field Research	Desk research	Sales forecasting	Statistics

Marketing research manager

Field sales manager	Sales offices	Training	Sales staff

Sales manager

Sales correspondent	Order progressing	Quotations	Records

Customer service manager

Pricing	Planning	Control	New product development

Product-line managers

Marketing manager

Figure 10.9 (a)   **SELECTION OF AN ADVERTISING AGENCY**

AGENCY QUESTIONNAIRE

1 How many employees in the agency?
2 How many clients at present?
3 What is the range of the clients total billing?
4 What accounts are similar to ours in the following:
   (a) Markets?
   (b) Outlets?
   (c) Sales appeal?
5 How long have the clients been with you?
6 What pertinent experience has your personnel?
7 Who in your agency would perform the following functions:
   (a) Contact?
   (b) Copy?
   (c) Art?
   (d) Merchandising?
   (e) Research?
   (f) Media?
   (g) Traffic?

8 What is their experience?
9 What are their positions in the agency?
10 What media executives are familiar with the work of your agency?
11 What executives of clients may we contact?
12 Who sits on the plans board?
13 What is your policy regarding:
   (a) Direct mail?
   (b) Sales promotion?
   (c) Merchandising?
   (d) Packaging?
14 Do you work for any of our competitors?
15 Do you sub-contract?
16 If so do you invite competitive bids?
17 Do you carry out research into advertising effectiveness?
18 What is the organization of your agency?
19 Who would be responsible for policy formulation?
20 What would be the procedure for handling our account?
21 Will you make a presentation, after initial discussion, on how you will sell our product?

Figure 10.9 (b)   **SELECTION OF AN ADVERTISING AGENCY**

COMPANY QUESTIONNAIRE

1   How long has the agency been in business?
2   How many accounts does the agency have?
3   In what industries are they?
4   What companies are they?
5   What is the agency's record of growth?
6   How many new accounts has the agency acquired in the last two years?
7   How much agency growth represents new business, and how much is due to increased billing from present clients?

3   Does it approach problems intelligently?
4   Has the agency developed any particularly effective business-publication campaigns?
5   Has the agency had experience in our field?
6   Does the agency have a proved formula for effective advertising?
7   Does the agency experiment with new communication techniques?
8   Is the agency 'arty', or is it marketing oriented?
9   Does it show a good basic grasp of desirable busienss practices?

ORGANIZATION

1   Does the agency seem well organized?
2   What is the general experience of the group with whom we talked?
3   What type of personnel does the agency have?
4   Is the agency staffed to handle our business?
5   Who would work on our account? On how many other accounts would these people work?

ADDITIONAL SERVICES

1   Is the agency equipped to handle our public relations?
2   Market research?
3   Solve our marketing problems?
4   Product publicity?
5   Dealer displays?
6   Our sales meeting?
7   Package design?
8   Make market tests?

RELEVANT EXPERIENCE

1   Has the agency solved problems similar to ours?
2   Can it identify problem areas?

141

11 Controlling Distribution

The deliberate selection of customers and the means by which they are served is an essential part of marketing strategy. In a marketing-orientated company, products have been developed for which sufficient market demand has been established. In measuring the market demand the company should ideally have developed a profile of a typical customer; all outlets which are close to matching that profile will be the target for the company's sales force, and for all other promotional activity. The manufacturer is concerned with ensuring that these customers are supplied with each product, either by the development of appropriate channels of distribution or by delivering the product direct from his own warehouse or factory.

The distributive process has two essential elements. The *channels of distribution* are the means by which a product is promoted and sales progressed from manufacturer to ultimate consumer. *Physical distribution* is the actual transportation of goods from the point of origin to the point of actual consumption.

Channels of distribution in the consumer field have undergone considerable change in recent years. Apart from an immense increase in the number of supermarkets and self-service stores, some companies have achieved rapid growth by the provision of mail order facilities, while others have increased their market share by party plan selling methods.

Direct selling continues to grow and the use of franchise marketing methods is still considered to be a new concept with high growth potential. In the industrial field, changes in distributive channels have not yet been significant but some have already become well-established, leasing for factories and capital equipment and, more specifically, the use of computer bureaux for data processing. It is not only in the service field that progress can be made; the opportunities for alternatives are immense.

The cost to the nation of distribution became fully recognized when the Government of the day introduced a tax on services of which the distribution process is perhaps the most significant. Certainly the cost to industry of distributing a product may range from 15 to 60 per cent of the ultimate selling price, according to the nature of the product and the distribution channels chosen. Active control of distribution can reduce these costs and allow a substantial increase in profitability.

Apart from the actual direct costs incurred, many related functions can be improved in effectiveness following the improvement of actual distribution. For example, a study of the levels of geographical market demand and of purchasing patterns, by day of the week or time of the year, enables a supplier to arrange effective stock control at each warehouse point and then to plan entire production schedules according to forecast demand. Distribution is a critical part of marketing management and is the means by which a company can increase its sales volume and its own profitability. The distribution process is essential to provide for customers' needs with the right product at the right time at the right place at the right price.

Marketing executives must endeavour to reconcile the needs of customers for a full service with the needs of their own company to provide a minimum level of service cost. If they should decide that the most appropriate means by which their company can win sales, at the expense of competitors, is to provide a superior distribution service then the cost of that service is a deliberate expense incurred in the marketing budget as an alternative to other marketing activities and expenditure.

Often, however, the manufacturer will endeavour to supply the maximum service at minimum cost. This usually means providing immediate delivery, relatively speaking, for products in frequent demand but an extended delivery for less popular products. In the consumer goods field, supermarket chains measure the performance of an individual outlet by comparing its performance in growth against the average for a previous period of sales per square foot of floor space or per employee or even per customer. A ratio of scales of different operating costs is kept in addition to staff lists and details of absenteeism. These are additional to the traditional measurements of retail effectiveness, such as rate of stock turnover and net profit as percentage of capital employed.

Because of the forces of competition, the demand for any one product from any one source and any one particular type can vary substantially. It is the distributive function to provide a contingency against such wide variations in demand, and the manager's responsibility to develop a distributive pattern which will cater for these deviations from the norm. Some are predictable, and the product mix from the factory must be adjusted to meet demand. By developing a replenishment mean time, and progressing stocks through the channels of distribution while still maintaining a constant delivery pattern, it is possible to design a distributive system which will operate not only effectively but also economically. It must be remembered that carrying stocks is not only for the benefit of customers, it also serves the purpose of allowing the factory production to continue without frequent changes, according to day-to-day pressure on production facilities. Properly controlled, the distributive system can protect a company against giving customer dissatisfaction and will enable it to achieve a high level of productivity by ensuring economical production runs according to predetermined programming.

Realizing and justifying the need for new branch offices or warehouses is a project which is worth considerable time and effort when the costs, both direct and indirect, are considered. An example is the continued use of a centralized office or warehouse when demand in another area is such that valuable profits are being lost because the company does not have the appropriate information on which to base a decision on the need for a new branch. Opening a new office and allowing the local salesman to work from that office does not normally require a substantial investment, but it does justify the appointment of a branch manager who will need to carry the full responsibility for the area's profitability. The new branch manager responsible for performance which has never previously been measured is faced with the possibility of failure. No one has yet discovered a means of measuring something that does not exist. Simply believing that demand exists is insufficient.

Opening a new warehouse will always involve considerable expense and it is important to ensure that this is justified by a requirement for service at a sufficiently high volume which cannot be catered for adequately by the transportation of goods from the factory or by a reduction in transport charges using bulk transport facilities. Before considering a new warehouse the company should first evaluate every other means of providing the required facilities. Is it possible that service from the factory can be improved by an overhaul of the present system, perhaps by giving priority to the region under pressure, particularly if in other regions delivery is not quite so critical? There may also be faster means of transport which, though more expensive when compared with the regular means of distribution, may well be considerably less than the cost of opening a new warehouse. It may also be possible for a new warehouse to be opened as a satellite to a main warehouse which is closer than the factory and from which buffer stocks can be drawn as required. The location of branch offices and warehouses, and the selection and appointment of appropriately sited salesmen to ensure adequate distribution of the company's products are a vital part of the marketing process.

Figure 11.1 Physical distribution costs

Few companies appreciate fully the true extent to which physical distribution has grown as a proportion of the selling cost of a product. In this chart, likely costs have been divided into those incurred internally within an organization, and those which will be incurred in the actual carriage of the goods. Allowance is made for those goods which may be shipped overseas and for which the distribution costs will be greater than those sold on the home market.

On this chart all costs are compared by product as the costs of distribution per product often vary according to the value of the goods, their bulk or shape, or the container used. Often, in analysing distribution costs in this way, it is discovered that some of the bestselling lines yield little or no profit but do make substantial contributions to overheads. By establishing this fact it is possible to concentrate priorities should an opportunity arise for a bulk order which may fill up production capacity at the expense of more profitable opportunities.

Figure 11.2 Distribution costs comparison

This illustration is a guide on how best to fulfil customer requirements for urgent delivery and the cost of providing the service demanded. With a chart of this description readily available, the decision whether a particular consignment should be dispatched urgently by passenger train or by air parcel is a simple one. Often there is little to choose in terms of time in sending goods by passenger train or by air because of the comparative inflexibility of UK airports.

Of particular importance is the guide shown in this document on whether the manufacturer wishes to be in the transport business, as well as being a manufacturer, or whether it is best for the specialist distributors to provide an adequate service to meet all needs. In practice very few companies can afford their own transport fleets although, for those that do, the volume that they handle would seem to justify the expense incurred. Certainly no individual company could possibly afford to offer the full range of facilities which is available from specialist transport companies and services.

Figure 11.3   Distribution services and charges

Some manufacturers find it worthwhile to send a major proportion of their exported goods by air. Usually these commodities are small in size but high in value, for example jewellery, works of art, drugs and essential oils. Many of these manufacturers use shipping or forwarding agents rather than setting up their own specialist department to handle the documentation and the administration involved. These agents may use scheduled airlines or may charter flights at periodic intervals. There can be considerable variation in their charges and the facilities they are able to offer.

Using this illustration the exporter is able to weigh the cost of different agents against the urgency of a particular consignment. Some agents offer first-class facilities for certain areas of the world in which they have built up a considerable volume of business and their charges may compare favourably with other agents for those areas. In other parts of the world they may suffer in comparison, their charges and facilities not being competitive. This illustration show exporters how to control their use of agents for certain areas and they are able to choose whichever agent provides the best service at the most competitive rates for a particular destination.

Figure 11.4   Stock record card

Different methods of stock valuation may have a favourable or adverse effect on a company's annual profit statement. A high valuation of stock will appear to inflate the net profit of the business, whereas a low valuation will produce a less than realistic net profit. It is essential that the actual value of stock held by the company is a realistic one and full control procedures must be introduced.

The stock which a company carries is a buffer against fluctuations in demand and is a pliable part of company marketing strategy. Stocks of slow-moving goods must be carried at the minimum level according to needs and it is usually better to manufacture in small quantities at a high unit cost rather than manufacture at normally economic levels and carry too high a stock. Stock ties up the company's working capital and uncontrolled stock levels can cause a serious deterioration in the company's cash flow; a frequent cause of bankruptcy. Values in a proper stock control record with maximum, minimum and reorder stock levels, each determined as part of marketing policy, will help to ensure that the needs of customers are met, production programming is efficient and the company's resources are adequately employed.

Figure 11.5 Stock control objectives
Stock indemnifies the company against seasonal demand. In a number of companies, available stock to meet all contingencies becomes their major marketing strategy. Spare parts readily available are essential to the prosperity of the automobile industry while at the other extreme a corner shop open late at night survives by making stock immediately available.

Holding stock represents a cost, so matching changing demand with economic production runs is both a marketing opportunity and a marketing cost. In inflationary times stock can also be an asset. Marketing planning provides the input for effective stock control.

Figure 11.6 Branch organization – fixed and variable expenses
A branch organization must be viewed as an almost autonomous profit-making operation in its own right. There is no justification for any branch which does not perform its company function in producing maximum profits for the capital invested. The fixed expenses shown in (a) are those items of expenditure which have to be recovered irrespective of sales handled by that branch. If accounted for in the manner shown, this chart will give the basic information for the branch break-even point in sales volume. It will also be a guide to the expense which will be incurred should a new branch be opened in another region, and will also indicate the volume of sales to be obtained over and above those already being serviced direct from the factory. In opening a new branch, managers tend to think only of the sales volume already being obtained and that it alone will justify the opening of a branch. What is not realized is that the present sales volume in a particular area is already contributing to present overheads at the factory and by opening a branch in the area additional costs are incurred which can only be paid for out of increased volume.

Although the expenditure shown in (b) is subject to considerable variation, according to the volume of business and the administrative procedures necessary in obtaining and monitoring business, it is essential that every part is a budgeted expense and is subject to the control which becomes an integral part of branch organization. Necessarily, every item is considered to be justified in practice in order to achieve branch objectives. All items listed are those which would normally be incurred in business; individual companies will be able to add those items which are peculiar to their own systems or procedures.

Figure 11.7   Overseas country profile
Formalizing the details of particular overseas territories and developing a comprehensive file on trading conditions, credit restrictions, legal details, and prohibited substances helps to ensure co-operative trade. Establishing a detailed list of valuable contacts should be part of the procedure.

Figure 11.1 Date	Internal							External							Overseas	Control	
Product	Transfer charges	Salaries and wages	Interest	Movement	Warehousing	Wastage	Total	Vehicles	Interest	Wages	Wastage	Charges	Total	Other costs	Shipping insurance and carriage	Total costs	Costs per unit

PHYSICAL DISTRIBUTION COSTS — Prepared by

Figure 11.2   **DISTRIBUTION COSTS COMPARISON**

Date   Prepared by

Product	Road				Rail			Sea					Air			Post				Waterways	Other
	Own transport	Contract hire	Carriers	Other	Passenger	Freight	Other	In bond	On deck	Hold	Hovercraft	Other	Parcel	Freight	Other	1st Class	2nd Class	Parcel post	Other		

Figure 11.3 Date	DISTRIBUTION SERVICES AND CHARGES																Prepared by		
	Airline		Air agent A			Air agent B			Air agent C			Air agent D			Air agent E		
Destination	Kilo rates	Minimum charge	Kilo rates	Minimum charge	Departure days	Kilo rates	Minimum charge	Departure days	Kilo rates	Minimum charge	Departure days	Kilo rates	Minimum charge	Departure days	Kilo rates	Minimum charge	Departure days

BUILDING THE PLAN

Figure 11.4 Date							STOCK RECORD CARD						Prepared by
Item	Reference number	Price	Maximum stock	Minimum stock	Reorder level	Date received	Order number	Received from or issued to	Quantity received	Quantity issued	Quantity missing	Balance remaining	Value

Figure 11.5	STOCK CONTROL OBJECTIVES
\ MARKETING STRATEGY TO IMPROVE CUSTOMER SERVICE, REDUCE COSTS, AND IMPROVE PRODUCTIVITY	
Absence of production hold-ups	More economic order quantities
Better inventory records	Reduced inventory level
Better records of stock movements	Reduced stocklevel of parts mix
Better utilization of production machinery	Reduction in number of machines
Greater diversity of products	Reduction in losses
Improved feed of parts to assembly	Reduction in cyclical affects
Improved servicing to production	Shorter deliveries
Increased throughput	Shorter leadtimes
Less storage space	Smooth work flow
Less work in progress	Variable order quantities
Lower material handling costs	Variable order times
Lower stock/issue rate	Win bulk order discounts
Lower stock/sales rate	Withdraw obsolescent parts

Figure 11.6

(a) BRANCH ORGANIZATION – FIXED EXPENSES

Rent	Rates	Insurance	Depreciation	Interest charges	Assisted labour benefits	Paid holidays	Management head count	Management salaries	Sales force head count	Sales force salaries	Clerical head count	Clerical wages	Miscellaneous	Total manpower	Total fixed expense	Transfer charges	Budget allocation

(b) BRANCH ORGANIZATION – VARIABLE EXPENSES

Commissions	Labour wages	Assisted labour benefits	Overtime	Welfare	Training	Heating	Lighting	Repairs and maintenance	Stationery	Postage	Telephone	Publicity	Recruitment	Discounts	Miscellaneous	Cleaning	Total variable expense

Figure 11.7 **OVERSEAS COUNTRY PROFILE**

Country _____ Population _____

Capital city _____ Political stability [A | B | C]

Principal products or commodities _____

Gross national product 1980 = 100 _____

Per capita income 1980 = 100 _____

Currency _____ Reserve currency _____

Conversion rate £ _____ $ _____ DM _____

International trade

	Country	Country	Country
	Imports exports balance	Imports exports balance	Imports exports balance
1988			
1989			
1990			
1991			
1992			

Trading bloc _____

Source _____

Climate _____ Hottest _____ °C _____ Coldest _____ °C _____

Seaports _____

Airports _____

Major competitors Native _____ Sales

Foreign owned _____ Sales

Foreign _____ Sales

Imports of competitive goods £ _____ Exports of competitive goods £ _____

Taxes/duties/tariffs

Bilateral agreements _____

Unilateral agreements _____

Prospect rating [A | B | C | D | E]

12 Administering Controls

Effective marketing control is based on the establishment of firm objectives for each function, activity, and executive. It means, therefore, the planning, organization, direction, and monitoring of resources so that they may be effectively and efficiently used to achieve marketing objectives. In effect, control is based on information and action.

There are five critical factors in control: objectives, measurement, interpretation, selectivity, and accountability. Establishing objectives requires the formulation of standards of performance and these must be attainable and specific. Therefore objectives will have particular elements such as time, quantity, cost, and quality. Stipulating a particular time limit for completion imposes a discipline on all executives concerned. They all have a time period during which they work towards their objectives. It enables a formal co-ordination of executive activity.

Each objective has to be stated in exact form, so that quantification of objectives is a necessary factor. Unless they are suitably quantified, objectives and achievements against them cannot be measured. The quantification may be relative, in percentage or ratio form, or absolute, in volume or monetary units. Objectives expressed in other than quantitative terms are not goals but simply aims, and are therefore not capable of measurement or comparison. Most qualitative factors can be expressed in numerical form; if not then they are unlikely to be satisfactory objectives.

Furthermore, all objectives have to be costed, for they are the purpose of all investment. Return on investment becomes an objective in its own right as a road to profitability. Every business decision has a cost element, either direct or indirect. Knowing the likely cost of these, including those that are hidden, and comparable costs against alternatives provides for investment appraisal, cost-benefit analysis, and for measures of managerial competence. The quality of any objective is a reflection of its origination. If it is measurable, realistic, and obtainable, specific in purpose, results orientated, and established within time parameters it is likely to have the necessary quality to stretch management to the utmost efficiency.

Effective control becomes possible once the time period between actual results and their publication, and between variations from budget and remedial action and between necessary corrective action and performance adjustments, are virtually eliminated. Control, however, is not a function to be delegated to a computer. While it is desirable to operate a control system which functions automatically, with remedial action or contingency plans brought into action at preconceived or predetermined levels, most commercial or industrial activity results require interpretation. A decline in brand sales may be the result of the malfunction of any part of the marketing mix, or of unexpected competitive or Government action; knowing what remedial action to take requires an understanding of what has caused deviations from budget.

Frequently, the human factor is the cause of many business problems. People are not machines, and performance may be continually variable. Personality and temperament, pressure, tension, and ill-health are significant elements in many failures to reach a required standard of performance. Planning for corrective action and providing for these instances which result in substandard performance enable management to give support to key executives for necessary periods of time rather than incurring the cost of the consequences. In this way, executives operating within a known and accepted field of responsibility with a recognized need for periodic cover are provided with regular servicing and maintenance facilities. When planning is organized and prior decisions made to meet all possible obstacles, operating decisions may be taken by subordinates.

In this sense control is taken to include the preservation of the capability of all key executives. If half of all management time is devoted to planning, and planning will necessarily mean learning from seniors and teaching juniors, and one-quarter to controlling the business, it is possible to allocate the remaining time to executives so that they may recharge themselves. It is accepted that although many men and women are adequately qualified to perform at senior level, very few are truly capable. Normally, these exceptions are the ones able to absorb the responsibilities thrust upon them, or taken by them. To arrange for a week's compulsory relaxation period in each month will enable all executives to assume greater responsibility yet remain fresh. A dynamic executive weighed down from 60 hours' weekly work-load, and 48 hours at weekends to worry about the work still to be done, is not capable of matching the output and sharpness of a contemporary who is making the bulk of decisions a year before the need arises, has delegated implementation to assistants, and is troubled only when deviations from target beyond pre-selected levels are recorded. The latter has learned the secret of personal restraint. There is no doubt which of the two will survive the longest.

Control is therefore the main manifestation of planning. It is concerned with forecasts, strategies, and tactics, and also machines, communications, and personnel. They all have potential and limitations. Control is the equation between the two.

Figure 12.1   Establishing criteria for control
Effective control is dependent on the formalization of roles within the business organization. Top management forms the framework, the chief executive decides the priorities for improving profitability, and the marketing team establishes the business philosophy. As these areas form the basis for planning, so they provide the criteria for control.

Figure 12.2 (a) and (b)   Budget control quotas
Permutating the mix for optimum profitability is almost a logistics exercise. Each of the factors of enterprise is the equivalent of a cylinder in an automobile. Finely tuned, they all pull together, but without tuning they pull at different speeds, so that fuel is wasted and road performance is adversely affected. The quotas suggested in the two parts of this illustration are indicative of those affecting many companies, and will provide the foundations for subsequent development according to individual company needs.

Figures 12.3 and 12.4   Increases in volume/selling price and *Decreases in variable/non-variable costs.*
These illustrations are based on break-even analysis and show the effects on profits of increases in volume or selling price, and of decreases in variable and non-variable costs. These charts will normally be produced during the early planning stage, and may be incorporated into the company's contingency plans documents. The value of the charts to management lies in control of profit performance.

Figure 12.1	ESTABLISHING CRITERIA FOR CONTROL		
MEANS BY WHICH PROFITABILITY MAY BE IMPROVED		ESTABLISHING THE BUSINESS PHILOSOPHY	
1	Increase prices	1	What business are we in?
2	Change product mix	2	What markets will we serve?
3	Reduce investment	3	Who are our potential customers?
4	Reduce costs	4	What gaps do we expect to fill?
5	Increase sales volume	5	What will they buy from us?
6	Change channels of distribution	6	How do we reach them?
		7	What marketing organization do we need?

ROLE OF TOP MANAGEMENT IN PLANNING	
1	Setting levels of risk
2	Selecting alternatives
3	Deciding opportunities
4	Providing resources
5	Taking ultimate responsibility

Figure 12.2 (a)		BUDGET CONTROL QUOTAS
A		MARKETING
	1	Overall market volume (forecast)
	2	Intended market share
	3	Sales volume
	4	Product mix
	5	Sales prices
	6	Revenue
	7	Marketing manpower and expenses
	8	Measurements of productivity
	9	Contribution to profit
B		PRODUCTION
	1	Volume of output required
	2	Yields and losses
	3	Capacity required
	4	Utilization of capacity
	5	Additions to production capacity
	6	Materials, fuel and manpower required
	7	Production costs
	8	Measurements of productivity
	9	Contribution to profit
C		TECHNICAL – PLANNED IMPROVEMENTS IN PRODUCTION METHODS
	1	Throughput rates
	2	Yields
	3	Qualities

Figure 12.2 (b)		BUDGET CONTROL QUOTAS
D	DISTRIBUTION	
	1	Volumes to be shipped by alternative methods
	2	Distribution facilities required
	3	Manpower required
	4	Distribution required
	5	Measurements of productivity
	6	Contribution to profit
E	ADMINISTRATION	
	1	Timetable for development of services
	2	Manpower
	3	Expenditure
	4	Measurements of productivity
	5	Contribution to profit
F	MANPOWER	
	1	Overall manpower strength
	2	Overall productivity measurements
	3	Management requirements
G	FINANCIAL RESULTS	
	1	Sales values
	2	Costs
	3	Profits and profit margins
	4	Capital employed
	5	Sales and profits on capital employed
	6	Cash flow

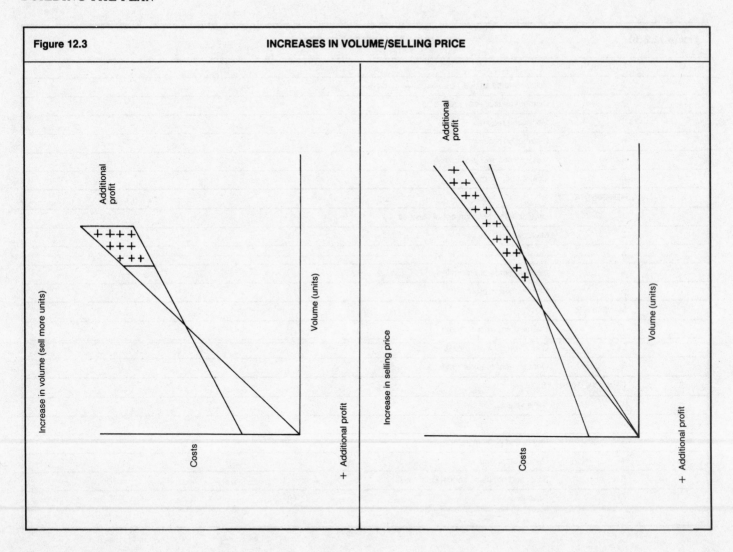

Figure 12.3   **INCREASES IN VOLUME/SELLING PRICE**

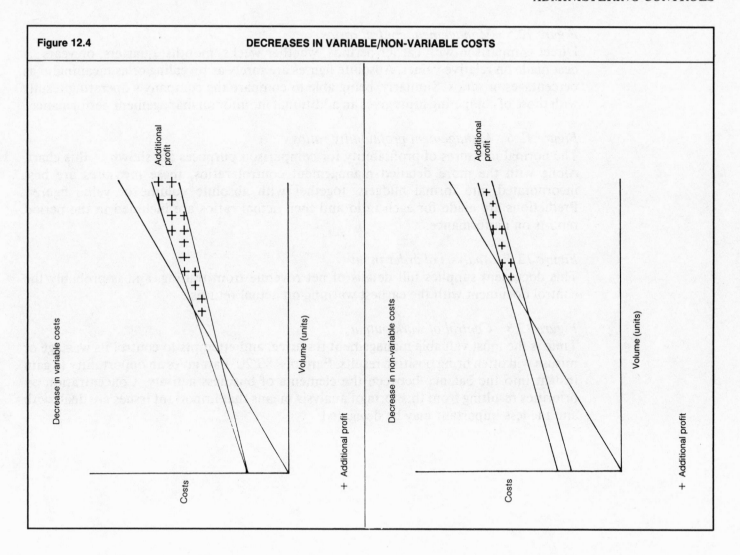

Figure 12.4   **DECREASES IN VARIABLE/NON-VARIABLE COSTS**

Figure 12.5   Management control ratios
Direct comparison with earlier periods, whether weeks, months, quarters, or years, is best made on relative values. Absolute figures are rarely as revealing or as meaningful as percentages or ratios. Similarly, being able to compare the company's operating results with those of competing firms gives an additional monitor on management performance.

Figure 12.6   Management profitability ratios
The normal measures of profitability for comparison purposes are shown in this chart. Along with the more detailed management control ratios, these measures are best incorporated into formal budgets, together with absolute volume or value figures. Predictions are made for each ratio and then actual ratios are included in the period reports on performance.

Figure 12.7   Analysis of order input
This document supplies full details of net revenue from trading, and is probably the control document with the earliest warning on actual returns.

Figure 12.8   Control of work output
Time is the most valuable management resource, and attempts to control its wastage or misuse will often bring positive results. Pareto's '80/20' Law gives an opportunity to gain insight into the balance between the elements of business activity. Concentration on priorities resulting from this form of analysis means that important issues are dealt with and the less important may be delegated.

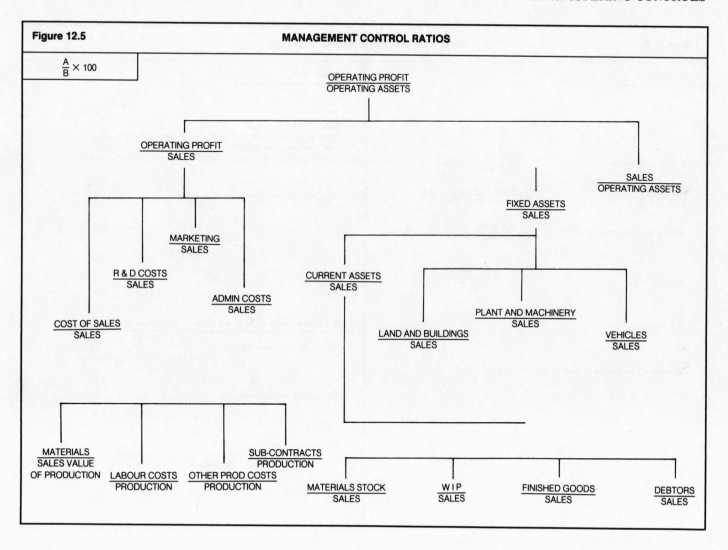

Figure 12.5 MANAGEMENT CONTROL RATIOS

$\frac{A}{B} \times 100$

$\frac{\text{OPERATING PROFIT}}{\text{OPERATING ASSETS}}$

$\frac{\text{OPERATING PROFIT}}{\text{SALES}}$

$\frac{\text{SALES}}{\text{OPERATING ASSETS}}$

$\frac{\text{FIXED ASSETS}}{\text{SALES}}$

$\frac{\text{MARKETING}}{\text{SALES}}$

$\frac{\text{R \& D COSTS}}{\text{SALES}}$

$\frac{\text{ADMIN COSTS}}{\text{SALES}}$

$\frac{\text{CURRENT ASSETS}}{\text{SALES}}$

$\frac{\text{COST OF SALES}}{\text{SALES}}$

$\frac{\text{PLANT AND MACHINERY}}{\text{SALES}}$

$\frac{\text{LAND AND BUILDINGS}}{\text{SALES}}$

$\frac{\text{VEHICLES}}{\text{SALES}}$

$\frac{\text{MATERIALS}}{\text{SALES VALUE OF PRODUCTION}}$

$\frac{\text{SUB-CONTRACTS}}{\text{PRODUCTION}}$

$\frac{\text{LABOUR COSTS}}{\text{PRODUCTION}}$

$\frac{\text{OTHER PROD COSTS}}{\text{PRODUCTION}}$

$\frac{\text{MATERIALS STOCK}}{\text{SALES}}$

$\frac{\text{W I P}}{\text{SALES}}$

$\frac{\text{FINISHED GOODS}}{\text{SALES}}$

$\frac{\text{DEBTORS}}{\text{SALES}}$

Figure 12.6   **MANAGEMENT PROFITABILITY RATIOS**

Profitability

Return on investment $\dfrac{\text{PROFIT}}{\text{INVESTMENT}} \times 100\%$

Return on incremental investment $\dfrac{\text{Incremental profit}}{\text{Incremental investment}} \times 100\%$

Return on manageable assets $\dfrac{\text{Assigned profits}}{\text{Controllable investment}} \times 100\%$

$$\text{Residual income} = \text{profit} - \dfrac{\dfrac{\text{Minimum acceptable return}}{} \times \text{investment}}{100}$$

$$\text{Net present value} = \sum \dfrac{\text{Cash flow }\sigma}{\left(1 + \dfrac{\text{return}}{100}\right)\sigma}$$

Investment = assets or capital employed

Break-even

Profit = revenue − total costs
Revenue (for a single market segment) = sales volume × price
Total costs = variable costs + fixed costs
Variable costs (for a single product) = sales volume × unit cost

$$\text{Break-even volume (minimum)} = \dfrac{\text{Fixed cost}}{(\text{price}-\text{unit cost})}$$

Break-even volume (to give a minimum acceptable profit)

(a) Capital intensive industry

$$\text{BEVol} = \dfrac{\text{fixed cost} + \text{minimum cash profit}}{(\text{price}-\text{unit cost})}$$

(b) Labour intensive industry

$$\text{BEVol} = \dfrac{\text{fixed costs}}{(\text{price}-\text{unit cost}-\text{profit/unit})}$$

(c) General formula

$$\text{BECol} = \dfrac{\text{fixed cost} + \text{minimum cash profit}}{(\text{price}-\text{unit cost}-\text{profit/unit})}$$

Figure 12.7			ANALYSIS OF ORDER INPUT						
	Type	Description	Number	Cost of goods	VAT	Net charges	Discount	Selling	
Purchases	55	**Invoices at selling**							
	56	Invoices at cost and selling							
	57	Order/invoices							
	58	Special invoices							
	59	Cancel appd invoices							
	60	Returns							
	61	Credit adjustments							
	62	Debit adjustments							
	63	Manual payments							
	64	Cancel payments							
		Total purchases							
Transfers	73	Stock transfers							
	74	Cost transfers							
		Total transfers							
Expenses	45	Expense invoices							
	46	**Credit expenses**							
	47	Expense dockets							
		Total expenses							
Sales	80	Sales							
	81	Total sales							
	82	**Class sales**							
		Total sales							
Adjustments	95	Opening stock adjustments							
	96	Stock adjustments							
		Total adjustments							
Orders		Write up commitments:							
	41	Orders							
	46	Input commitment							
	46	Special input commitment							
	47	Cancel commitments							
	47	Special cancel commitments							
	48	Transfer commitments							
	48	Special transfer commitments							
		Total orders							
Unapproved	50	Registration invoices							
	51	Invoices at cost							
		Total unapproved							

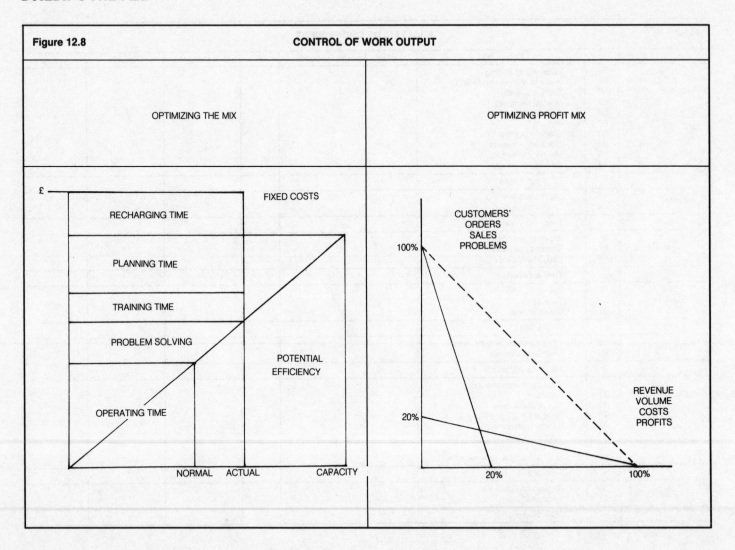

Figure 12.8   **CONTROL OF WORK OUTPUT**

OPTIMIZING THE MIX

OPTIMIZING PROFIT MIX

£

FIXED COSTS

RECHARGING TIME

PLANNING TIME

TRAINING TIME

PROBLEM SOLVING

POTENTIAL EFFICIENCY

OPERATING TIME

NORMAL   ACTUAL   CAPACITY

CUSTOMERS' ORDERS SALES PROBLEMS

100%

20%

REVENUE VOLUME COSTS PROFITS

20%   100%

Rationalizing the Product Portfolio 13

Almost every company suffers from product clutter – a number of products achieving little or no sales volume, making at best a small positive contribution to profit and at worst a large negative contribution. Whatever the history of such products, they are now almost certainly causing a disproportionate cost in terms of both time and effort. These sleeper products often cause a bottleneck in the company's overall efficiency and a decision to eliminate them, despite protests from their supporters, will invariably improve prospects for the future. Rarely have any of them come prematurely to a market not yet ready for them.

Eliminating the product clutter is the first step towards creating a realistic product portfolio. Rationalizing the product mix to the point where procurement, production, distribution, and sales of the entire range, at predetermined levels for each product line and for each brand, produces the optimum profit is the ultimate product portfolio. It requires a balance in pricing strategy, promotional expenditure, and distribution logistics. Brands have to be positioned in the market-place, demand effectively managed, and a continuing innovation policy implemented. In the modern marketing environment genuine unique product advantages soon disappear. Competitors will soon copy successful innovations, and perhaps make further improvements. So a successful launch and skilful marketing is necessary for rapid penetration into a market. If the net profit growth rate for a company is to be maintained, particularly when confronted with escalating marketing costs for established products, constant new product development is essential. Even those companies which have development programmes need to improve further the ratio of success in new product development as part of the total investment programmes.

There are basically three different methods by which new products can be introduced into the company: members of the sales force are constantly reporting comments from customers and prospects; the company's own production and research executives frequently suggest new product possibilities; and outside the company recommendations may come from independent inventors, distributors, suppliers, advertising agents, the trade press, and even competitors.

The ideas emanating from internal or external sources may be spontaneous thoughts which may or may not have validity in terms of market sales potential. This is often the main level of ideas for many companies and the system usually brings a high failure rate. Less frequently, but possibly more effectively, a company may make a conscious effort to study systematically the markets it satisfies in an endeavour to establish new needs, or rediscover old needs that have never been properly satisfied. It is also possible that gaps in supply could be exploited if a satisfactory product was made available and its benefits emphasized. Logically this approach could be adopted by all companies – its use takes advantage of present market knowledge, it is within the company's own business activity, and is in an area where marketing skills have been developed.

In evaluating such needs a company may often find that a small company has been specializing in the satisfaction of a current need but does not have the resources or, perhaps, the inclination to develop the market to the full potential. The acquisition of such a company may prove a sound investment as established business can be obtained, with much of the development costs written-off, together with personnel having experience and knowledge of product uses and applications. This method of marketing development could well become the principal means by which new products are introduced, for the larger organization rarely embarks on pioneering programmes.

In setting up a new development programme it is necessary to define carefully the objectives, the means by which they are to be achieved, the resources immediately available, and the additional resources that can be called on, if necessary, to achieve the objectives. Ideally, new product ideas will come from the marketing research team, although occasionally suggestions from research and development will provide a stimulus to new thinking, providing any ideas that do arise are subjected to market acceptability before any attempt is made to commercialize them.

Once a steady stream of suggestions has been developed, the company needs to introduce a filtering process to improve on the quality of ideas and to reduce research and development costs on propositions that ultimately prove impractical. All successful new products have one thing in common – they satisfy a basic need, whether it be physical, emotional, or psychological. So although the actual development programme will vary from one industry to another, and from one company to another, there are several basic considerations that are necessary, irrespective of the particular environment or circumstances of the company concerned. Each development project is allotted a budget, allowing time for full consideration of each operating step. Clear responsibility and authority is allocated to each individual member of the team according to the task to be undertaken. At all times the objectives and priorities must be supervised, with a regular monitoring schedule to keep management informed of progress. Each product is developed according to specifications laid down and agreed and, where necessary, collective agreement is obtained. At all times the development team must be advised of the commercial needs of each product to ensure that individual scientists do not pursue personal satisfaction rather than company objectives.

Product life cycle
The product life cycle is divided into four stages: *introduction*, *growth*, *maturity* and *decline*. During market development, the introduction stage, sales are slow because marketing effort, in its fullest sense, is still ponderous. Initially buyers will be among the more affluent members of society, willing to pay the higher introductory price and more likely to have learned about and have judged the product through the columns of the serious press. Mass markets are best created by pictures, selective markets by words. So initially, with limited distribution, little advertising and sales promotion, and a high price, sales growth is slow.

The second stage, market growth, is where rapid acceleration occurs and sales 'take off'. This growth may, in fact, be a series of steps each of which appears to be the platform at which maturity is reached. However, new applications and new markets for the product may prolong this period. So the total market size is extended.

Once it reaches the market maturity stage, demand levels off and sales volume is dependent on replacement purchases and population growth. Clearly, this stage in the product life cycle may be prolonged if the company markets its products internationally, each geographical area being at a different stage of development.

Eventually the product reaches the decline stage where it has lost its appeal to the purchasing public. Products decline for different reasons; for example, natural fibres lost a lot of ground – the decline stage – after the discovery of man-made fibres. Consequently, natural fibres were remarketed with emphasis on their particular qualities. As a result they retained a share of the textile market but at a lower level than before. Equally, there are some products which go through two or more of these stages so rapidly that distinguishing one step from another is clearly impossible. Some food products launched nationally, heavily promoted through the trade prior to the launch, and given full television advertising support may be examples.

As marketing is concerned with profitability and not just with sales volume, it is worthwhile considering how closely profits conform to the curve of the product life cycle. Certainly, little profit would be earned during the development stage because R & D expenses have to be recovered, and because initial production costs tend to be subsidized, particularly in so far as overhead absorption is concerned. During the growth stage advertising and sales promotion, together with additional distribution costs, also prohibit profit achievement. So it is during the period of maturity that profits are mainly earned, although actual profit margins will tend to decline as maturity gives way to decline. It is in this period that over-capacity will have been built up, with the industry anticipating further growth. As inflation pushes up costs, suppliers find it difficult to pass on these increases through higher prices, despite continuing increases in sales volume.

The product life concept applies at three levels. Firstly, it can be a product class, such as cars, secondly it can be a product type such as a sports car or saloon and thirdly it may be a brand such as the Jaguar XK40. Each of these levels or dimensions has a distinct life cycle. Cars will probably exist as a growth segment, internationally, for a number of generations while sports cars could reach their maturity stage much earlier if they lose their 'aura of excitement' and the 'ultimate sex symbol' becomes fairly commonplace. Equally, the XK40 will, inevitably, become a historical phenomenon.

To use the principle of the product life cycle for strategic purposes one needs to understand how it happens. When a new product is launched its makers first must overcome the usual resistance to change. They must gain *attention*, stimulate *interest*, create *desire*, and persuade *action*. The process begins with the imitators and eventually declines at the saturation point because there is an insufficient number of new buyers to carry on the momentum. By this time the innovators will have discovered some new, that is, less common, replacement product and a new life cycle is begun.

Understanding the workings of the product life cycle gives the marketing professional an insight into the potential for the exploitation of a product's history. At regular intervals, usually during the preparation of the annual marketing plan where five-year forecasts are made, it is necessary to predict the possible remaining length of each product's normal life span, making full allowances for new applications and uses. Clearly, knowing the point in the product's life enables the company to reformulate strategy where necessary. The management may, for example, decide to accelerate a product's decline by increasing its price. In this way a higher unit profit is obtained in the shorter term. Furthermore, a product going through its early growth stage may be helped to develop rapidly, because management decides that expansion is more important in the short term than waiting for a profit-based expansion. Manipulating such elements in the marketing mix is a normal strategic ploy.

Figure 13.1   Maximizing the product life cycle
In Figure 13.1 the company marketing product B has chosen to compromise between the extremes of high volume and low margin and low volume and high margin. It has aimed at a selective part of the market to begin with and then varied its marketing expenditure in order to control the path of the life cycle. It allows slow growth, holding its own against competition through strong marketing, then maintains a high price with full marketing support until the end of the maturity stage. The price is then raised and all aggressive marketing stopped. That way it expects to yield the highest return on capital employed.

Figure 13.2   Assessing product marketability
Most of the criteria are value judgements but used in conjunction with the audit data in Chapter 1 it is possible to arrive at an assessment. The value of making this assessment is the insight into how, and under what circumstances, a product may be marketed. If the decision taken is positive it is because a marketing opportunity has been discovered, the product being the vehicle for satisfying that opportunity.

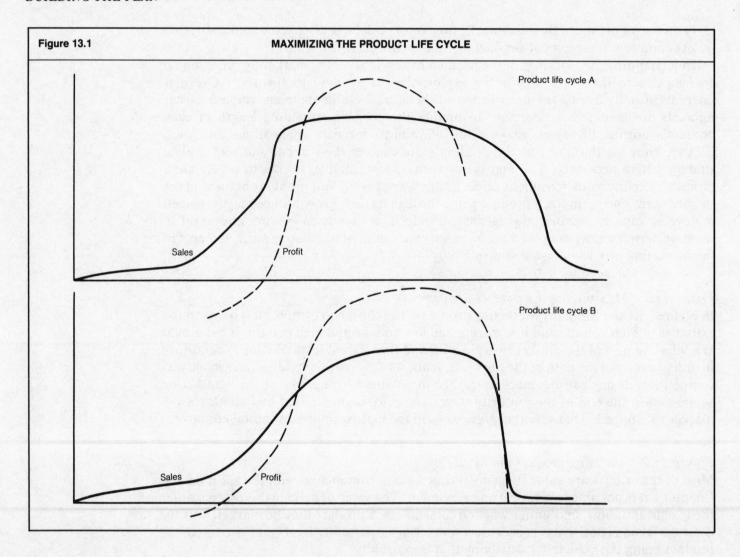

Figure 13.1   **MAXIMIZING THE PRODUCT LIFE CYCLE**

Product life cycle A

Sales   Profit

Product life cycle B

Sales   Profit

Figure 13.2 ASSESSING PRODUCT MARKETABILITY

COMPETITIVE AUDIT

See
Chapter 1

DEMAND WEIGHTING

Stability
Durability
Breadth
Growth

PROFIT RETURN

Margins
Stability
Potential
Incremental

MARKET SEGMENT

Demographic
Psychographic
Functional
Price
Non-differential
Unit size
Trade supply
Overseas

MARKET POSITION

Captive
Volatile
Static
Innovative
New entry
Horizontal
Vertical

PRICING/VOLUME

Upper decile
Penetration
Lower decile

DISTRIBUTION COSTING

Stock holding
Channel discounts
Transport
Warehousing
Penetration

PUBLICITY WEIGHTING

Impact
Frequency
Coverage
Duration

SALES ANALYSIS

Channel
Region
Unit
Season
Order size

Figure 13.3 — **DEFENSIVE PRODUCT STRATEGY**

STRATEGY	EXAMPLE
Appearance	Can the aesthetic quality be improved
Performance	Can the function be improved
Durability	Can the product life be extended
Style	Can the style be improved
Finish	Can the initial impact be prolonged
Environment	Can the user location be changed
Dispensing	Can the application be improved
Packaging	Can the package improve the product
Unit size	Could a different size be preferred
Duality	Is there an additional use for the product
Range	Would a wider range increase consumption
Feature	What additional features can be added
Value	Can the price be revised
Economy	Can user economy be improved
Revaluation	Can the quality be diminished
Services	Can additional services be provided
Promotions	Can incentives be included
Troublefree	Can product-fault be overcome
Credit	Can easier terms be provided
Availability	Can new outlets be found
Seasonality	Can limited seasons be overcome
Merchandising	Can the 'pos' effort be improved
Trade sales	What about another sales channel
Lease/Rental	Are there alternatives to selling
Segmentation	Can one part of the market be used

Figure 13.3   Defensive product strategy
Sleeper products and density products under attack can be revitalized. This chart lists
the most common workable remarketing ideas. They are not exhaustive but in the
absence of a truly imaginative idea they can be employed with more than a little
confidence.

Figure 13.4   Brand name check-list
The value of a company is its market connection and that connection is most often
retained through a brand name. It therefore follows that the brand and how it is named is
one of the most important decisions a company makes.

Figure 13.5   Tracking new product fall-out costs
The two charts in Figure 13.5 show each step in the product development programme
and the proportionate cost of failure at each stage. Clearly, the earlier products are
identified as potential failures, the sooner they are rejected the lower are the resultant
costs of the failure. Without doubt any procedure that enables the company to reduce its
rate of failures will prove invaluable. For immediate economies, however, it makes sense
to find the means by which likely failures are quickly identified, before it becomes
somebody's vested interest and is forced through the vetting machinery as an unreasoned
gamble.

Figure 13.6   Evolution of new product successes
Before finalizing a development programme it is advisable to carry out a preliminary
appraisal of the commercial feasibility of each project. This study should include desk
research in an effort to compile as much information as possible relevant to the product's
development, production, promotion, and acceptance. At the same time the researcher
will consult all known qualified opinion from within the company and, so far as possible,
outside the company. Attempts will be made to test the likely market sales potential and
the sales volume which may be achieved at each stage after the product's launch. The
product's expected design and specification is clearly identified and recorded, while
packaging considerations are listed. A programme of timing for launch and related
promotional activities is then prepared with pricing proposals clearly shown and the

anticipated costs of capital development. Additional labour requirements are specified and other marketing costs budgeted. The whole development programme in fact should be set up in much the same way as the company marketing plan; aims and goals are specified together with the means by which they are to be realized.

If after a thorough screening process the new product idea is considered satisfactory, a full development programme may be continued with some confidence. In making this feasibility study and formulating a development programme it is apparent that the company is launching a product following a perceived and measured market need.

The development programme should contain a clear policy statement. This will indicate whether the new product is intended to bring a higher sales volume and provide more profitable sales to replace, ultimately, products which have a declining profitability. It will specify whether an expansion or concentrated effort is intended into established markets or whether an entrée is required into new markets that may offer better profit potential. The development programme will also include a detailed profit statement with supporting budgets for the period during which the product is test-marketed and later launched nationally to the point where it becomes established.

Often new products are developed to enable the company to enter an entirely new market with which it has no previous acquaintance or background knowledge. When this happens executives concerned tend to recognize more readily the limitations of their market knowledge and may even consider the possible inadequacies of their marketing effort in successfully promoting the proposed new product. What many of these executives do not recognize is that with their established market constantly changing the same principles apply to their approach to that market, even though they do have extensive knowledge and experience. So similar attitudes should be adopted with new product development programmes, for they are fundamental to proper planning.

Test marketing a product in a chosen area which statistically and by observation tends to represent the characteristics of the total market may be a vital method of learning operational deficiencies. One of the most acute difficulties however is in the selection of a trial area. Furthermore, it is not easy to reproduce a national launch in one small area. Simulation is difficult because the national media are not available in isolation for the test area. The test area is normally chosen because it contains sufficient purchasers to provide a realistic sample and yet is small enough to be covered economically, with appropriate control possible. When marketing an industrial product, where the order value may differ according to the type of customer, it is necessary to establish the different types of purchasers in the test area and how they compare with national figures.

The area must be one that has an independent advertising medium – regional or local newspapers or perhaps television – and where members of the local sales force are typical of the average performance of the entire sales force. If the new product is intended to fill an existing gap in the range, the competitive strength of the launching company must be compared against that of others in the area and be related to national market shares before worthwhile conclusions may be drawn. Allowance has to be made for the impact of repeat purchases on any sales figures compiled.

Figure 13.7   New product launch
One of the techniques which most companies could usefully borrow from operational research scientists is a network analysis for launching a new product. So many different elements are essential for a successful launch and are dependent upon each being completed at particular times. Some companies have found it expedient to try a network approach to the test market operation.

Figure 13.4	**BRAND NAME CHECK–LIST**	

FUNCTION	PARAMETERS	CHARACTER
	It should be: Short Comprehensible Imprinted	Unique
GUARANTEE		Differentiated
		Distinctive
	It should be easy to: Remember Pronounce Spell	Cognitive
		Personal
IDENTIFICATION		Valuable
		Credible
	No unfavourable: Meanings Associations Restrictions	Friendly
		Stimulant
PROTECTION		Primary
	Capable of: Personality Associations Registration	

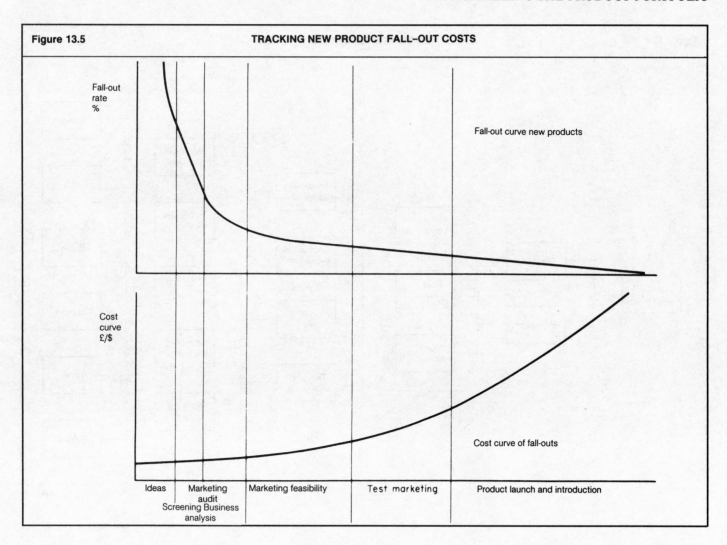

Figure 13.5   **TRACKING NEW PRODUCT FALL–OUT COSTS**

Fall-out rate %

Fall-out curve new products

Cost curve £/$

Cost curve of fall-outs

Ideas   Marketing audit   Marketing feasibility   Test marketing   Product launch and introduction
Screening Business analysis

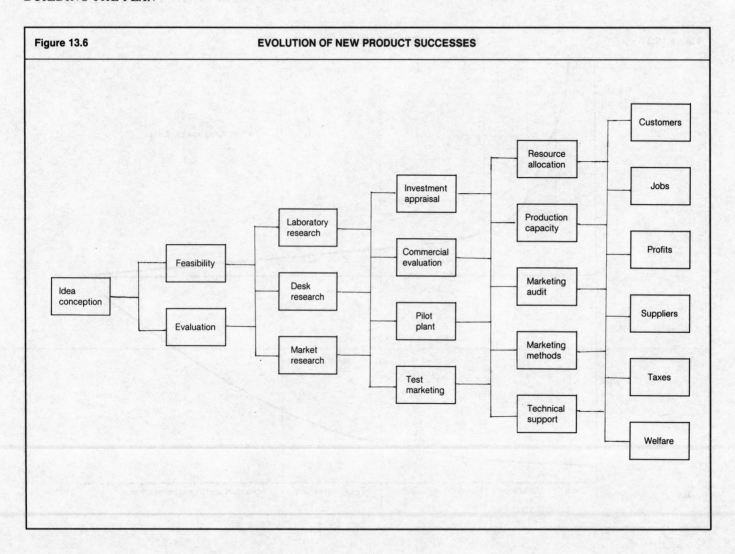

Figure 13.6   **EVOLUTION OF NEW PRODUCT SUCCESSES**

Figure 13.7 **NEW PRODUCT LAUNCH**

Date Prepared by

Packaging	Test launch	Sales conference	National launch
Packs, labels, outers, display, point-of-sale	Research – redesign – costings – final selection – test – final specification		
	Select outlets – collate results – analyse – select		Selling through
The product			
Specification, colour, shape	Actual costings – popular sizes – revise – production trials – acceptability – revision – test – final specification		
Distribution			
Outlets	Wholesalers/distributors/agents – discounts – retail		Significant distribution
Sales force	Merchandising training – test discounts – national preparation		Buyers – merchandising
Sales service	Prepare vehicles – deliver stocks – journey routes		trial discount, trial offers
Publicity			
Consumers	Test launch – develop campaign objectives		National press, TV
Trade	Direct mail – public relations – product potential		Trade – technical
Others	Trade associations – technical press – vested interest		Press releases
Marketing research			
Quantitive	Stock movement – distribution analysis – consumer audits		Distribution studies
Consumer acceptance	Store questioning – analyses of buying groups – repeats		Repeat purchase trends
Desk analysis	Sales penetration – seasonal variation – product awareness		Distribution costings
Marketing decisions	Sales performance – trade – consumer – budgets – approval		Performance against forecast

14   Managing Brands

As more companies grow from repeated successes, it becomes more difficult for one person to control a broad range of products. Furthermore, as marketing has changed from a group of activities confined to a few executives to a management style adopted by an entire management team, top management has become marketing-orientated. The marketing manager is increasingly concerned with policy formulation and planning, making decisions today that will affect the future. A natural development has been the introduction of executives of considerable marketing experience to take control of subsets of the marketing organization. These executives have been appointed brand managers, with a profit accountability for the brand or brands for which they have been given a responsibility. In industrial marketing organizations they have tended to be known as product managers. Although the title is different, the actual responsibilities are similar. However, while the brand manager tends to have extensive advertising and promotions experience and therefore applies that experience to brand development, the product manager is more likely to have selling and sales management experience and uses this knowledge to develop product sales.

The brand manager is a product of organizational need and of business school or college training. The expertise such managers bring to their jobs is a combination of hard experience, often in an advertising agency, and of theoretical learning. While job experience has made them aware of minefields, the studies they have undertaken have also made them aware of gold mines. Many such brand managers have become marketing managers at senior level, and the route to senior positions is now becoming established.

Brand managers are concerned with assessing the balance between sales growth and profit performance for their own brand. They are responsible for discovering market needs, the gap analysis process; they create the appropriate product specification, including pricing strategy; they make sales forecasts at different price levels; and they predict future sales and profit levels. They are also responsible for co-ordinating publicity programmes; and for ensuring effective distribution, so that the brand reaches prominent positions on retailers' shelves and is supported by merchandising at the point of sale.

In large organizations, where specialization by functional management has been necessary to optimize efficiency, a communications gap has developed. In earlier years and in smaller companies such gaps were bridged by the managing director or through regular management meetings. In many cases communication would take place between functional heads at informal levels. In the larger company this is no longer possible, because events move too fast for periodic or intermittent contact. Moreover, in a fully-integrated business operation, where all departments are interdependent, isolated decisions in the name of expediency often concern numerous departments and usually introduce an additional element into policy formulation.

Brand managers undertake responsibility for co-ordinating activities between departments for their brand and fill the communications gap. They therefore fulfil many of the functions of a managing director. They have a profit responsibility but differ from the managing director in that they do not have the authority to control functional departments or to redeploy functional resources. They must secure approval from functional heads in order to carry out changes.

They are therefore the advocate for their brand. They arrive at brand policies and attempt to secure their approval. They must prepare revenue and expenditure budgets and stand responsible for their achievement. It is a competitive task. Brand managers compete within their own organization for opportunities to develop their brand and their own progress. In order to secure the means to develop, they must first provide the foundations, that is an acceptable marketing plan for the brand, and a profit performance warranting the attention and resources that are a premium in any profit-conscious company.

Figure 14.1   Continuing brand life cycles
The brand life cycle is a well-established principle of marketing. The trends shown in this illustration indicate the varying paths of brand sales and profit performance supplemented by new brand introductions. Planned introductions of new or

reformulated products maintain growth and increase profitability. Brand managers carry the responsibility for the progressive introduction of these brands, co-ordinating all the necessary phases and activities.

Figure 14.2   Cosmetic and diagnostic marketing

Too frequently companies introduce only those elements of marketing which are apparent to the world at large and with which the ingredients of success in marketing are associated. This is to misunderstand marketing. To achieve the best results it is necessary to carry out a full diagnosis of the company organization and then to implement those activities of cosmetic marketing appropriate to the results of the diagnostic marketing study. The details shown in this chart identify the areas for diagnostic work and for the establishment of appropriate marketing practice. Brand managers assume the responsibility of the chief executive in ensuring the cosmetic approach is a direct extension of company policy.

Figure 14.3   Brand personality

The ultimate in marketing success is to create a brand 'household name'. These have a personality all of their own – the result of continuing consistent promotion. To reach that stage there are a number of essential steps. For most existing household names the steps were a progression of sound management decisions, either of inspired judgement or intuitive flair. In contemporary marketing it is more likely to be the result of market studies, product planning, and contrived promotional platforms. Whether inspired or contrived, the results are the same: satisfied loyal customers and profitable companies. The contrived attempt is, however, likely to be quicker.

Figure 14.4   Brand management responsibilities

This list is provided as a suggestion to developing companies considering a reorganization of their marketing structure. It will also be beneficial to those companies with established brand management and those needing to revise job specifications.

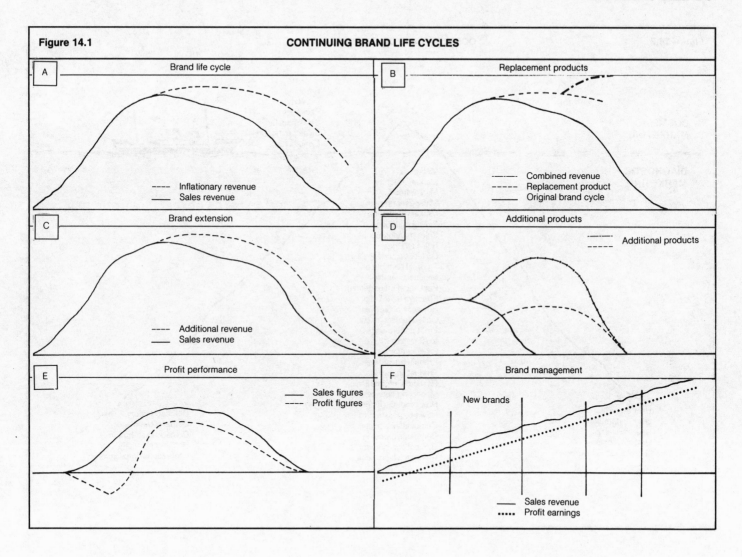

Figure 14.1 CONTINUING BRAND LIFE CYCLES

A — Brand life cycle
- - - - Inflationary revenue
——— Sales revenue

B — Replacement products
-·-·- Combined revenue
- - - - Replacement product
——— Original brand cycle

C — Brand extension
- - - - Additional revenue
——— Sales revenue

D — Additional products
-·-·- Additional products

E — Profit performance
——— Sales figures
- - - - Profit figures

F — Brand management
New brands
——— Sales revenue
······ Profit earnings

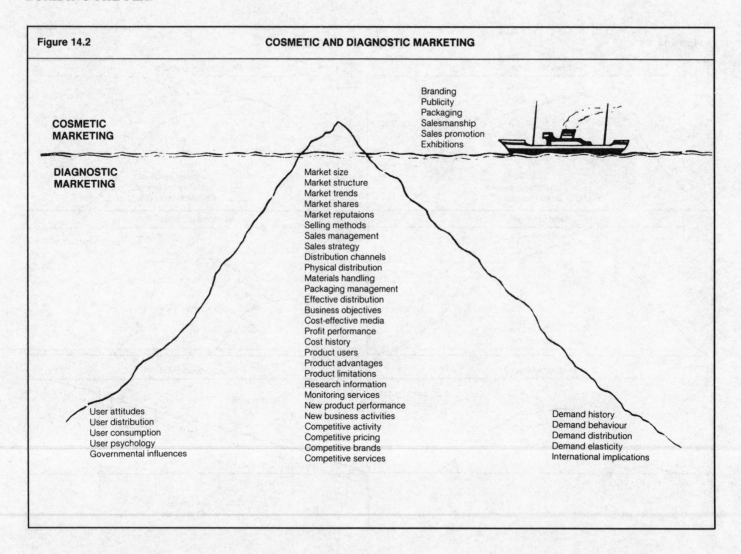

Figure 14.2 **COSMETIC AND DIAGNOSTIC MARKETING**

COSMETIC MARKETING

Branding
Publicity
Packaging
Salesmanship
Sales promotion
Exhibitions

DIAGNOSTIC MARKETING

Market size
Market structure
Market trends
Market shares
Market reputaions
Selling methods
Sales management
Sales strategy
Distribution channels
Physical distribution
Materials handling
Packaging management
Effective distribution
Business objectives
Cost-effective media
Profit performance
Cost history
Product users
Product advantages
Product limitations
Research information
Monitoring services
New product performance
New business activities
Competitive activity
Competitive pricing
Competitive brands
Competitive services

User attitudes
User distribution
User consumption
User psychology
Governmental influences

Demand history
Demand behaviour
Demand distribution
Demand elasticity
International implications

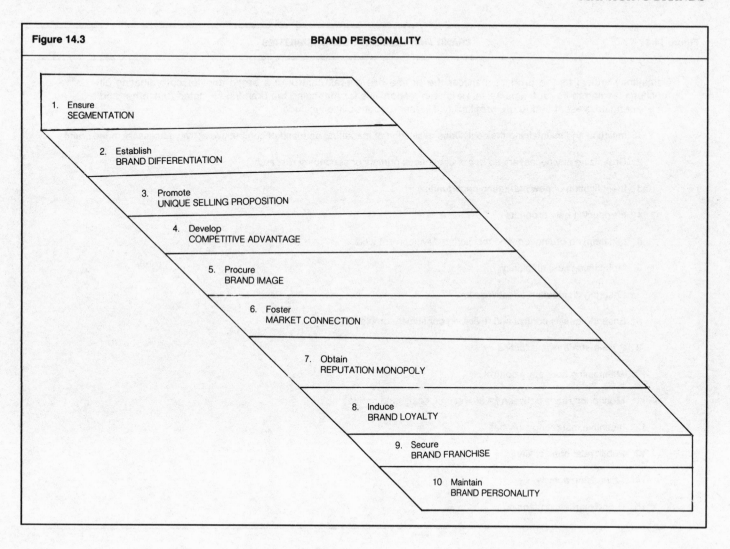

Figure 14.3   **BRAND PERSONALITY**

1. Ensure
    SEGMENTATION

2. Establish
    BRAND DIFFERENTIATION

3. Promote
    UNIQUE SELLING PROPOSITION

4. Develop
    COMPETITIVE ADVANTAGE

5. Procure
    BRAND IMAGE

6. Foster
    MARKET CONNECTION

7. Obtain
    REPUTATION MONOPOLY

8. Induce
    BRAND LOYALTY

9. Secure
    BRAND FRANCHISE

10 Maintain
    BRAND PERSONALITY

Figure 14.4   **BRAND MANAGEMENT RESPONSIBILITIES**

Sometimes known as the product manager, he or she has overall control of a brand and for co-ordinating all functions leading to its profitable sales. He/she is responsible for managing the brand(s) allocated to him/her and for ensuring its present and future profitability. His/her responsibilities include:

1   Initiating and maintaining the continuous evaluation of marketing data and of competitive activity necessary to the brand.

2   Organizing any necessary *ad hoc* or continuous primary or secondary research

3   Identification of new marketing opportunities

4   Introducing new products

5   Initiation, co-ordination, and monitoring development work

6   Maintaining cost efficiency

7   Ensuring distribution effectiveness

8   Ensuring quality control and reviewing consumer complaints

9   Pricing strategy and tactics

10   Maintaining budgetary control

11   Monitoring ratios between sales, volume, costs, and profits

12   Incentive marketing activities

13   Public relations activity

14   Advertising activity

15   Brand marketing planning

Figure 14.5 Information held by brand management
Brand managers need to make decisions, but these decisions must be based on suitable information. The data and information normally held by brand managers for decision-making purposes are listed in this diagram.

Figure 14.6 Launch co-ordination by brand management
This diagram is a flow-chart for the brand manager. It is useful also for distribution by the brand manager to other executives, supported with specific details relevant to a new product launch.

Figure 14.7 Product concept and market strategy
Helping people to buy and therefore finding what it is they buy when making a brand decision provides the theme or scheme for successful brand promotions. The ideas featured in this illustration suggest the underlying buying motives and how they may be treated for each of the fast-moving consumer goods, a consumer capital purchase, and an industrial capital investment.

Figure 14.5   **INFORMATION HELD BY BRAND MANAGEMENT**

Discover		People
Create		Price
Arouse		Promotion
Satisfy		Place

1 DATA ON:	1 INFORMATION ON:
a) Budgets and comparison ratios	a) Company policy
b) Competitor's pricing structures	b) Brand(s) history
c) Competitive data	c) Forward marketing plans
d) Market trends	d) New products schedule
e) Brand specifications	e) Detailed sales forecasts
f) Consumer research	f) Record of brand costings
g) Sales and distribution performance	g) Advertising schedules
h) Advertising media data	h) Product trend data
i) Merchandising and incentive marketing data	i) Competitive advertising
j) Market data	j) Continuous research
k) Published data sources	k) Economic trends

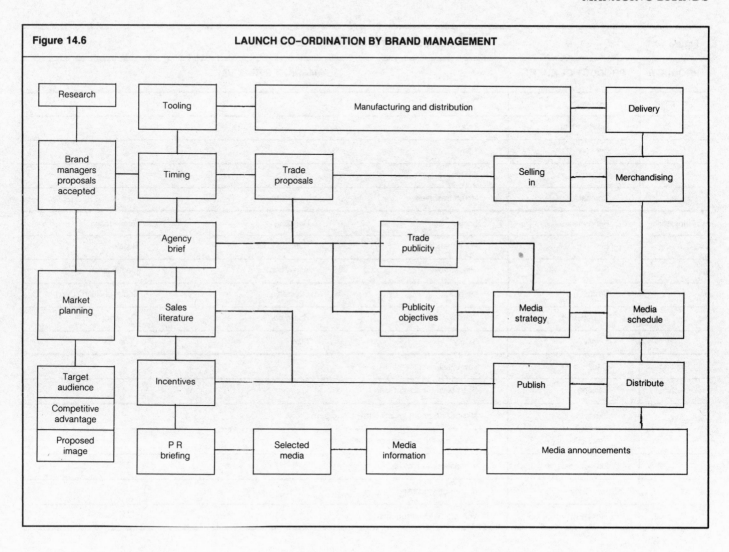

Figure 14.6 **LAUNCH CO-ORDINATION BY BRAND MANAGEMENT**

Figure 14.7		PRODUCT CONCEPT AND MARKET STRATEGY					
PRODUCT	**PRODUCT CONCEPT**	**MARKET STRATEGY**					
Toothpaste	Worrier	Decay					
	Independent	Price					
	Sensory	Taste					
	Sociable	Whiteness					
	Defensive	Mouth freshness					
Automobile	Performance	Speed	- -	Handling	- -	Acceleration	
	Economy	Maintenance	- -	Running costs	- -	Resale	
	Symbol	Substitute	- -	Aspirations	- -	Identification	
	Status	Marque	- -	Executive	- -	Social position	
	Trouble-free	Warranty	- -	Spare parts	- -	Servicing	
	Family	Safety	- -	Size	- -	Price	
Printing	Capital cost	Low initial investment					
machine	Leasing	Short-term tax advantages					
	Expected life	Maximizing return on investment long term					
	Productive capacity	Increasing output economies of scale					
	Labour costs	Increasing productivity					
	Reliability	Output programming					
	Flexibility	Variable batch production					

Operating Pricing Decisions 15

Price management is one of the most vital areas of strategic marketing. Yet rarely is it within the control of the marketing manager. Product pricing tends to be the province of collective agreement among the executive team. A decision to increase price is often taken because inflationary costs are eating into profit margins. An agreed percentage increase across the board is the most common method used. The actual amount is either a matter of industrially-established practice, disregarding the incidence of costs against individual products, or is by implicit agreement among industrial leaders. Conversely, a decision to reduce price is usually an individual company matter, frequently followed however by the rest of the industry concerned, particularly if the price leader has made a significant impact.

In both these cases the pricing decision is made from a position of weakness. Yet pricing decisions made strategically or even tactically from a position of strength can be highly rewarding. Confusion sometimes arises between pricing strategy and pricing tactics. Strategic pricing is the consideration and the implementation of policies involved in deciding the price level at which to enter a market. The decision will be on an assessment of consumer need at different price levels and, therefore, the products demanded. The decision itself will depend on the level showing the greatest potential. Tactics, on the other hand, involve price manipulations from period to period as a promotional device. They include special offers, discounts, and coupons.

Using pricing strategy

Operating pricing decisions from positions of strength demands strong marketing activity. It means a strong sales force, realistic distribution and delivery, and a product (together with its ancillary services) so much in demand that it tends to produce a monopoly situation – attributable to the extent of its brand loyalty. It develops a unique selling proposition. Forceful marketing supports a realistic price. Heavy concentration on price concessions suggests weak marketing.

Marketing people frequently use terms such as marginal pricing, or incremental pricing. These strictly speaking are not pricing policies but costing methods that enable one or more of the pricing policies to be put into operation. One term that does justify some comment is *dumping*. This usually refers to overseas transactions where the selling price is lower than that applicable in the suppliers' home market. By selling overseas the company concerned will be making more economic use of its resources and a higher net profit will often result. This may even apply when prices are lower than the 'cost price' at home. Under these circumstances the home market will normally be making a full contribution to recovery of overheads and only a small contribution becomes applicable from overseas trade.

Figure 15.1   Price elasticity of demand

The economists have long claimed that the operation of the price mechanism is the key determinant of demand. Yet marketing people believe differently. They believe that demand is the sole determinant of price, and that high demand attracts volume and so reduced unit costs of production or supply. Marketing action aids in the stimulation of demand. But it does so firstly by discovering the prices at which different levels of demand may be achieved. Then it selects the most applicable to its own management's aspiration of risk.

What marketing specialists do acknowledge is that some products and some markets respond to marketing stimulus at different tempos or rates of change. Determinants of these tempos involve the significance cost to the customer (how much is the cost of the purchase in relation to overall income) and the consumers' own individual scales of preferences (the significance of the purchase relative to other possible purchases).

Prices are therefore said to be elastic (where demand varies consistently or inconsistently with price) or inelastic (where demand remains consistent irrespective of variations in price). This principle is not necessarily incompatible with that suggested, of making demand a determinant of price. For both price and demand are variable, each subject to sudden change and neither, invariably, forcing the other up or down without resistance.

Between elastic and inelastic extremes there are unit elasticity and zero elasticity. Unit elasticity describes the circumstances involving a change in price, with a change in demand, where the money revenue remains the same. Zero elasticity is the term used to define a change in price where no change in demand results.

Figure 15.2   Volume and revenue changes on price cuts
While most companies recognize that a change in price means a reduction in profit margin and therefore more sales have to be achieved to maintain the same net profit, few seem to appreciate the disproportionate effect this manoeuvre has on handling of volume. To maintain the original profit return it is necessary to increase both volume sold and even more volume actually handled. For example, a 25 per cent profit margin on £100 worth of sales produces £25 profit. If the price is cut by 15 per cent then the profit on the same volume drops to £10. To achieve the same £25 profit it is necessary to increase sales to £212 (that is, £10 on sales of £85 equals £12 on £100 sales or £25 on £212 sales) and at the same time increase the volume handled to 250 per cent (that is, £250 at 10 per cent as it now is) because the lower price means a lower mark-up on each unit of a higher volume of goods.

Figure 15.3   Relationship between price reductions, sales increases, and variable costs
In practice, companies have to assess three variables in pricing policies. These are:

1   price itself
2   sales volume
3   variable costs.

Clearly, price and volume are determinants of variable costs. If a price reduction causes a decrease in the incidence of variable costs, then aiming at increased volume following a price reduction may not produce an increase in net profit. For example, if variable costs are 30 per cent of selling price and the price is reduced by 10 per cent then volume has to be increased by nearly 17 per cent to maintain profit contribution. But if variable costs are 80 per cent of selling price, a price reduction of 10 per cent would require a volume increase of 100 per cent to maintain profit contribution.

As price reductions tend to be the simplest and therefore the commonest means of generating trade they become the significant overall industrial factor. However, as price cuts at any industry level tend to bring in more business, but less than is justified, they weaken an industry and so are undesirable. If, however, price promotions extend the market size and bring in more sales volume than is required to compensate for loss in margin, they strengthen an industry. Using the chart shown in Figure 15.3 enables the marketing manager to calculate the likely effect on margins and to make pricing policy recommendations accordingly.

Figure 15.4 Maximizing profit

Sometimes a company will need to use its pricing flexibility in order to maximize profit. Utilizing the marginal cost theory, the company may work out the price at which additional business is justified. For example, suppose the concern is producing 200 000 units of product X and that at that level the marginal revenue from X production is £1.10 and its marginal cost is 96p only. Additional units of X will therefore each bring 14p and so the firm cannot be maximizing the profits by sticking to the production level of 200 000. It should therefore be prepared to accept additional orders. Any price exceeding 96p for the extra business will bring in additional profits.

The company will be able to derive the marginal cost-equals-marginal revenue proposition from the illustration. At any output OQ total revenue is represented by the area OQPR under the marginal cost curve. Similarly, total cost is represented by the area OQKC immediately below the marginal cost curve. Total profit, which is the difference between total revenue and total cost is, therefore, represented by the difference between the two areas – that is total profits are given by the lightly shaded area TKP minus the small, heavily shaded area RTC. Now it is clear that from point Q a move to the right will increase the profit area TKP. In fact only at point of output OQ_M will this area have reached the maximum size – for profits will encompass the entire area TKHP. But at output OQ_M marginal cost equals marginal revenue; it is the crossing of the marginal cost and marginal revenue curves at this point which prevents further moves to the right (further output increases) from adding still more to the total profit area. Thus maximum profit is being earned.

Figure 15.5 Contract pricing

In this system the company executive will carry out a close examination of the costs involved in a possible contract, and calculate the probability of winning the contract at different price levels. It will then decide the price it will tender according to its own calculation of the risk, depending on the needs of the business at the time. If business is good a high risk may be taken, but in slack times a low price will be tendered. Over a long period the company will select prices intended to bring in the maximum return on a number of contracts – some won and others lost.

Figure 15.6   Transfer pricing

Vertically integrated firms face additional pricing problems. They must decide the level at which one division will charge another, yet recognize that opportunities to sell the output on the open market might show increased profit for the group as a whole.

In this illustration the revenue from increasing sales to outside customers is shown to be falling *per unit sale* in MR_O (section 6 of the chart). Sections illustrating the other divisions likewise show dwindling marginal revenue from expanded sales of the final products of the five other divisions while the two lower lines ($MR_B - MC_B$; $MR_C - MC_C$; $MR_D - MC_D$; $MR_E - MC_E$; $MR_F - MC_F$) show their diminishing net marginal revenues from the conversion of the intermediate, this being the residue of the gross marginal revenues after deducting their marginal costs of conversion. By taking a horizontal sum of the six lines it is possible to construct the line $ANMR_A$ (aggregate net marginal revenue as shown in section 7 of the chart).

Then the line MC_A is drawn showing the supply division's marginal cost of expanding output. The distance from the vertical axis at which these two lines intersect is O_6Q_A. So the supply division will choose to produce a total quantity O_6Q_A of the intermediate, and the distribution of this quantity between the five uses it can be put to (times 20 for each division less the number of interchangeable varieties) is determined by drawing a horizontal line through the intersection and back to intersect the six lines which are aggregated to give $ANMR_A$. In section 6 of the chart the intersection arises vertically above Q_0 and O_5Q_0 is therefore the quantity which, in theory, is to be sold on the outside market. Proceeding similarly back through sections 5, 4, 3, 2, and 1, we arrive at O_4Q_F, O_3Q_E, O_2Q_D, O_1Q_C and OQ_B; as the quantities to be distributed to their respective divisions. All that needs to be done to effect this distribution is for the supply division to fix its transfer price at P_A which is determined by the level of marginal cost at which the intersection takes place in section 7. Faced with this transfer price all divisions will want to take just the quantities indicated leaving O_5Q_A for sale on the open market. The sum of OQ_B, OQ_C, OQ_D, OQ_E, OQ_F and OQ_0 must of course equal O_6Q_A, for the line $ANMR_A$ was constructed by horizontally adding to the abscissae of the points on the other six lines.

Figure 15.7 *Strategic pricing*

Price remains one of the most difficult areas for decision-making in marketing management. It is the final confrontation between buyer and seller. It is tied to perceived image of value, and of rationalization. Consumers will pay premiums on mass-marketed goods because of implied value or because of an association of ideas between price and quality. High prices may be earned by strong marketing action, an investment, while low prices may earn volume. The price, however, is also a reflection of the supplying company and decisions on its chosen image are reflected in pricing policy. The alternative approaches to pricing shown in this illustration suggest the many alternatives open to companies. However, there are two main alternatives. The first is to start at a high price and to aim at a limited market where the need is more important than possible cost and then to reduce price gradually as demand spreads to larger market groups. Subsequently introducing inexpensive alternatives is often the method used in this approach. The second is to introduce at a low price, aim at mass markets and expect a payback in up to three years as volume allows a decrease in average unit cost. Clearly the decision will be determined by the image of the company concerned.

Figure 15.8 *Pricing promotions*

The suggestions contained in this illustration are closely related to incentive marketing (see Chapter 21). The choices shown will enable the company not only to stimulate sales but to do so consistently with image or in such a way as to avoid alienating customers when normal prices are resumed. As a general rule it is better to provide a price incentive from a position of strength, such as in a growth market, than from a position of weakness. Other marketing actions are more appropriate to difficult or highly-competitive conditions. Tactical pricing is best used when the company wants new customers to try the product and is reasonably sure of retaining their custom on merit.

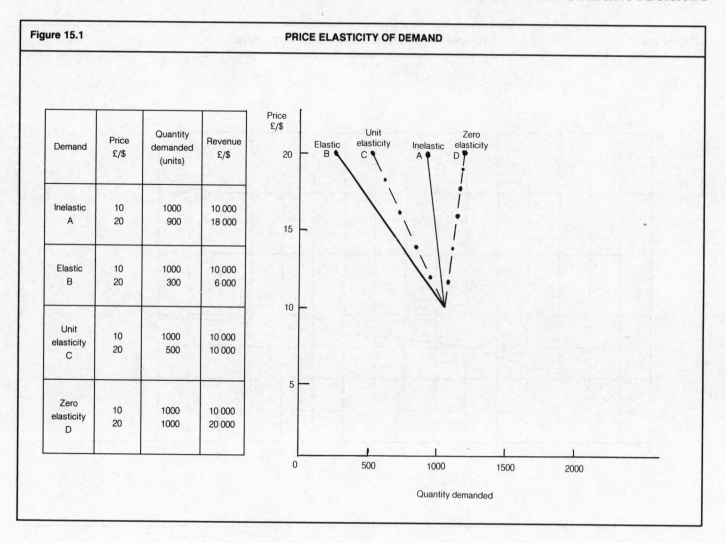

Figure 15.1

PRICE ELASTICITY OF DEMAND

Demand	Price £/$	Quantity demanded (units)	Revenue £/$
Inelastic A	10 20	1000 900	10 000 18 000
Elastic B	10 20	1000 300	10 000 6 000
Unit elasticity C	10 20	1000 500	10 000 10 000
Zero elasticity D	10 20	1000 1000	10 000 20 000

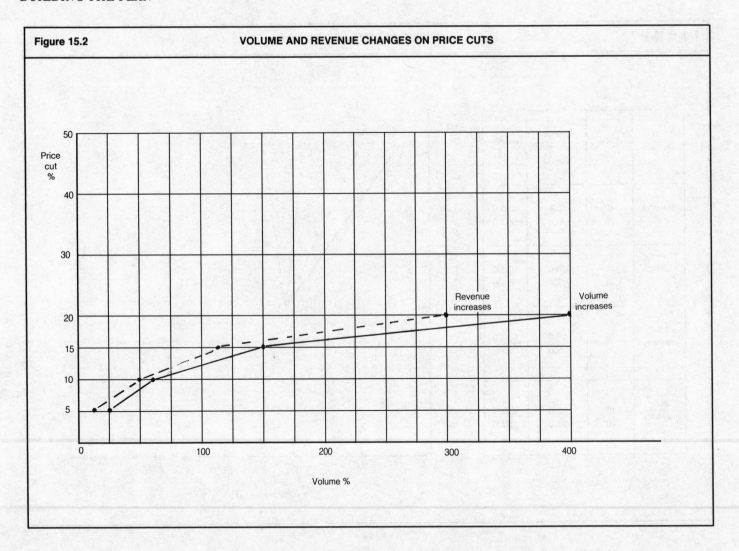

Figure 15.2   **VOLUME AND REVENUE CHANGES ON PRICE CUTS**

Figure 15.3	RELATIONSHIP BETWEEN PRICE REDUCTIONS, SALES INCREASES, AND VARIABLE COSTS									
Variable cost as a % of sales	10	20	30	40	50	60	70	80	90	
Price reductions as a % of sales	Sales volume increase (%) required to maintain profit contribution									
1	1.1	1.3	1.5	2.0	2.1	2.6	3.5	5.3	11.1	
2½	2.9	3.2	3.7	4.3	5.3	6.7	9.1	14.3	33.3	
5	5.9	6.7	7.7	9.1	11.1	14.3	20.0	33.3	100.0	
7½	9.1	10.3	12.0	14.3	17.7	23.1	33.3	60.0	300.0	
10	12.5	14.3	16.7	20.0	25.0	33.3	50.0	100.0		Loss line
12½	16.1	18.5	21.7	26.3	33.3	45.4	71.4	166.7		
15	20.0	23.1	27.2	33.3	42.8	60.0	100.0	300.0		
17½	24.1	28.0	33.3	41.2	53.8	77.8	140.0	700.0		
20	28.6	33.3	40.0	50.0	66.7	100.0	200.0			
25	38.5	45.4	55.5	71.4	100.0	166.7	500.0			
30	50.0	60.0	75.0	100.0	150.0	300.0				
33⅓	58.7	71.2	90.8	125.0	200.0	500.0				
35	63.6	77.7	100.0	140.0	233.3	700.0				
40	80.0	100.0	133.3	200.0	400.0					
45	100.0	128.5	180.0	300.0	900.0					
50	125.0	166.7	250.0	500.0						
				Loss line						
Variable cost as a % of sales	10	20	30	40	50	60	70	80	90	

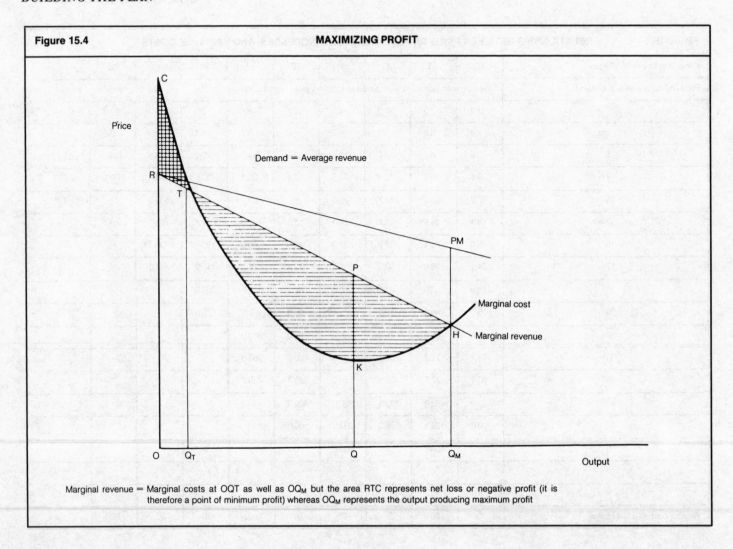

Figure 15.4   **MAXIMIZING PROFIT**

Marginal revenue = Marginal costs at OQT as well as OQ$_M$ but the area RTC represents net loss or negative profit (it is therefore a point of minimum profit) whereas OQ$_M$ represents the output producing maximum profit

Figure 15.5 **CONTRACT PRICING**

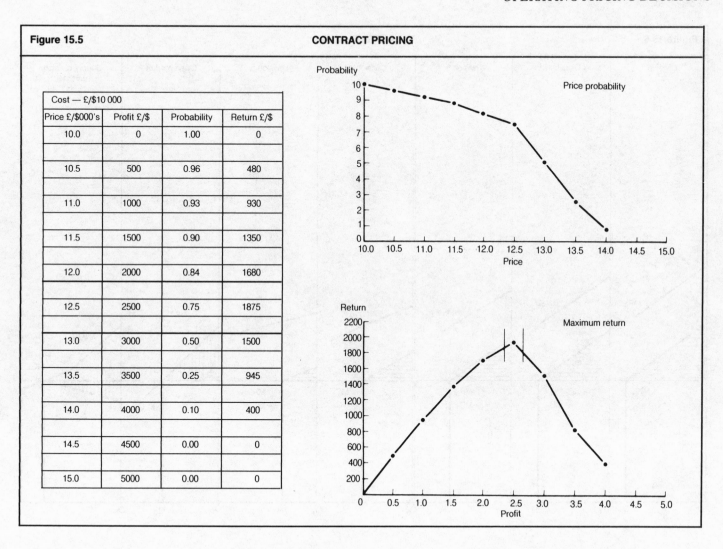

Cost — £/\$10 000			
Price £/\$000's	Profit £/\$	Probability	Return £/\$
10.0	0	1.00	0
10.5	500	0.96	480
11.0	1000	0.93	930
11.5	1500	0.90	1350
12.0	2000	0.84	1680
12.5	2500	0.75	1875
13.0	3000	0.50	1500
13.5	3500	0.25	945
14.0	4000	0.10	400
14.5	4500	0.00	0
15.0	5000	0.00	0

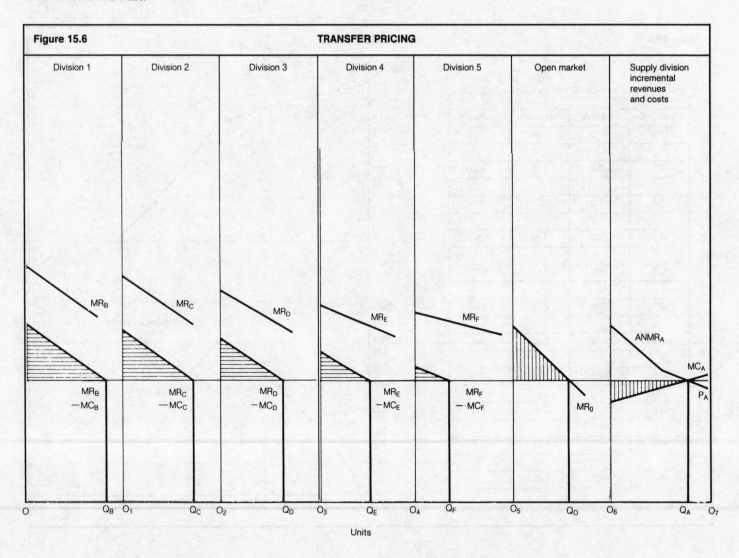

Figure 15.6 TRANSFER PRICING

Division 1 — Division 2 — Division 3 — Division 4 — Division 5 — Open market — Supply division incremental revenues and costs

Figure 15.7	**STRATEGIC PRICING**	

PRICING PRINCIPLES

Market segmentation
Need or benefit identification
Development of appropriate image
Creation of 'monopoly'
Price appreciation

Up-market

Down-market

1 FLEXIBLE PRICING By product mix	2 COST PRICING Fixed + variable + profit	3 CONTINGENCY PRICING According to work performed
4 FIXED PRICE Price controlled	5 CONTRACT PRICING Determined by negotiation	6 VALUE PRICING What the market will bear
7 RATIONING PRICE Limiting supplies	8 OFF-SET PRICING Product + 'free' services	9 PENETRATION PRICING To win market share
10 SKIMMING PRICE Improved quality and image	11 COMPETITIVE PRICE Average market price	12 DIVERSIONARY PRICE Total package of services (including Turnkey)
13 DUMPING PRICE Below 'cost'	14 LOSS-LEADERS Attract other profitable business	15 GRADING PRICES Marginal net increases

Figure 15.8	PRICING PROMOTIONS
1	Straight price cut
2	'Sale' price
3	Increase quantity in pack
4	Add a gift
5	Provide free credit
6	Money voucher
7	Quantity discount
8	Additional free service
9	Package deal
10	Limited period price concession
11	Club membership
12	Cash discount
13	Early settlement discount
14	Joint promotion
15	Seasonal discount
16	Special 'trade only' discount
17	Trial price
18	Banded pack
19	Trading or savings stamps
20	Introductory offer
21	Contractual period discount

Preparing for Contingencies 16

A company is like a living being – it has a brain, a heart, a personality and a reputation, and, like any living organism, must adapt to its environment in order to survive. The appetite of a company is nourished by profit and the greater the nourishment, the greater grows the appetite. In modern business philosophy there is only one rational reason for any business activity and that is the maximization of profits. Some companies are well known for their 'social service' and 'patriotic' policies but these are secondary objectives and are frequently adopted to help attain a favourable public image.

No matter how carefully a business may plan, certain objectives will always prove more difficult to achieve than others. Marketing planning is no panacea for all industrial and commercial ills. Ideally, the marketing plan should include the appropriate action to be taken in order to avoid diminution of profitability. Even if actual performance exceeds all expectations, there should be provision for further exploitation of the favourable conditions that have prevailed. If the total marketing plan has been constructed with care and diligence, the contingency section should be straightforward, being no more than the detailed consideration of alternative courses of action. It should include action that may need to be adopted in the short term to minimize or maximize possible consequences of deviations from plan, and medium to long-term action to exploit a changed environment.

To ensure that the appropriate action is taken at a time calculated to achieve the best results, it is essential that a barometer of company and industrial performance is developed and steps are taken to monitor actual results against forecast company sales and forecast market shares. There are specialist organizations offering performance comparisons within an industry at reasonable cost. A company using such an organization will only need to develop an internal early warning system. This can be done effectively for the long term by plotting orders received by principal product groups against the purchasing industry by standard industrial classification.

In the short term, signals can be provided by relating actual enquiries, quotations, orders received and sales by principal groups, against the forecast objectives. If the average time-lag between enquiry and order is six weeks and a delivery period four to six weeks, then, automatically, the company will have nearly three months' notice of an imminent drop in sales. For example, if the company volume in value of enquiries is only 80 per cent of the forecast, and the conversion ratio remains unchanged, in three months' time sales will only be 80 per cent of target. While it would be unwise to take remedial action on the strength of one deviation from forecast (for fluctuations do occur), once a trend becomes apparent on the graph the cause will be established and appropriate action can be taken.

Apart from showing industrial performance as a whole, some specialist organizations quote the detailed performance of unspecified companies against which one's own company performance can be measured. At this point the company should be able to judge to what extent it will be able to exercise influence on the market situation. If the entire industry is suffering a similar deteriorating position, it is probably wise to curtail expansion plans, as provided within the contingency plan. The timing of such cut-backs, and to what extent they are implemented, should be incorporated into the total marketing plan. The plan should show detailed profit and loss statements for 70 per cent, 80 per cent, 90 per cent, 110 per cent and 120 per cent actual performance against forecast. Each of the profit and loss accounts should include appropriate departmental budgets and head counts. The two most important principles are to preserve a net profit and to indemnify future net profit. Often, in practice, these two considerations prove incompatible and a working compromise may be needed. Sometimes profit comes from the last 15 to 20 per cent of sales, after overheads have been covered and when costs become marginal. Under such circumstances a drop of 20 per cent in sales volume will warrant perhaps a cut of 30 per cent in expenditure in order to maintain net profit at par value.

Occasionally a company can avoid the disasters of a temporarily poor market position by acquisition of another company. Study of the competitive profiles in the marketing plan, followed by a detailed investigation of suitable partners, may reveal a competitor which would supplement or, ideally, complement the company's own operation. The first consideration will always be to make a takeover bid, but management must be realistic and not discount the advantage of soliciting for a bid to be made for one's own company – this course of action may prove more prudent.

A logical part of any contingency plan should be a detailed consideration of both rationalization and diversification policies. There is almost always conflict between a company's sales department, anxious to meet individual customer requirements, and the production department needing long production runs and the elimination of cost-consuming specials. Some firms have reconciled these opposing needs by adopting a market segmentation policy and produce specials for each industry group. They have become so well established within these industries that they have achieved long production runs of specials.

A diversification policy may be adopted, in order to spread the risk of activity across a broader front, so minimizing business risk. Many of the economies of scale may be achieved with a diversification policy.

It frequently happens that additional marketing costs necessary to fill surplus capacity from the established market, with an established product, are uneconomic because of competitive pressures. The spare capacity available may be used more profitably for another product, possibly in a different market. When products reach saturation point company growth is confined to that obtainable at the expense of competitors. Government economic measures are, frequently, the cause of sudden changes in demand. Companies adversely affected by such a change have no alternative but to diversify if they wish to survive. Many products are traditionally seasonal, and manufacturers of these products must endeavour to stimulate sales at other times of the year or to move into other fields. It is not always possible to pass on increasing costs to the customer by raising selling prices, either because of competitive pressures or because the market will not bear it. Some firms have adopted a strategic diversification by offering a related facility in order to sell its regular product.

Where there is a strong possibility that a scientific breakthrough will bring product obsolescence, affected companies should endeavour to concentrate future plans upon a less vulnerable field of operations.A side-step into a related industry or technology is a natural and logical move for most companies, for it is an area where their technology and management expertise may be put to best use.

Figure 16.1 Standard costs – by product in period

The profit on any particular product varies according to the number of units manufactured at any one time. In forecasting its future profitability every company must endeavour to establish its basic economic manufacturing batch. The whole basis of sales forecasting is to provide the production department with advance warning of required volume. Inaccurate forecasts inevitably mean a build-up of stock, and this means production schedules have to be varied from day to day, with uneconomic batches produced. To assess the consequences of these events, each company should prepare a standard cost for each product against which every trading cost makes a contribution. The standard costs are those which are expected to be incurred when the product is being manufactured in its most economic quantity and against which actual costs as incurred during trading can be compared. The cost structure shown in this illustration provides many combinations of costing criteria, each of which can be used as control figures in estimating end-of-year profit based on actual operating costs compared to the standard costs.

Figure 16.2 Pricing schedule

Many companies have built a successful organization based on the bulk of production being sold at a price which recovers all operating costs and relying on the balance of sales to provide a profit. In certain circumstances this policy can be justified, but it must always be based upon a position of strength rather than one of weakness.

All markets have a broad range of pricing sectors with the majority of suppliers concentrating around the competitive area. The strong firms predominate in the higher price sector and the weaker firms are found usually in the low price sector. There is constant pressure within individual companies to push prices towards the top of the pricing range while its market is endeavouring to deflate the pricing structure. Usually the argument for reducing prices is the increase in volume which it is expected will result; conversely, it is always possible that the same volume will be achieved even if prices are raised. Whether a company decides on a high price or a low price, the ability of its sales force and the power of its promotional activities will need to be superior to those of competitors if the market potential is to be fully exploited. A company will need to provide strong supporting services for buyers to be willing to pay a premium price for its products. Similarly, buyers do not change sources of supply giving them good service over a period of time simply to obtain a marginal price advantage.

Figure 16.3   Break-even chart
Once a company has established standard costs for each item in its range, based upon expected volume for each product, it is able to work out the variable costs which must be incurred during the period of the manufacturing cycle. Ideally, in preparing for all contingencies, the company should chart a break-even point at all levels of sales achieved and at every percentage point of manufacturing capacity. Once the break-even point has been established for each level, it becomes possible for the company to apply varied selling prices to different industrial groups in order to achieve maximum penetration according to sales potential within each group. Certain industries often have a more fundamental need for particular products than others, and additional marketing costs can be incurred in penetrating a particular industry or industries, especially where there is a high degree of elasticity in demand, based significantly on price. By varying its pricing structure according to industry and according to the demand within each industry, a company is best able to exploit the conflicting demands of sales volume and low price and high margins at low volume.

Figure 16.4   Lost business and opportunities
Senior management of many companies is reluctant to admit that its products are not of a suitable standard, that its pricing strategy is at fault or that its total marketing effort is misdirected or weak. It is only by evaluating carefully the reasons for lost business and opportunities that the weaknesses of a company's operations become apparent. Every significant enquiry not resulting in an order should be recorded, and the reasons why the business was lost investigated. Every effort should be made to develop a method of overcoming that weakness so that future enquiries can be processed with earlier faults being rectified.

Of much more significance are the opportunities lost because an enquiry was never made to the company in the first place. It may be because the company has not informed its market adequately of the products it has to offer, or of the services that it provides. It may be because the sales force is not concentrating enough effort on winning new

213

business, because it is too busy dealing with established customers and not making enough cold calls, or because the sales force is simply weak in presenting the company to its prospects.

Frequently, causes can be isolated if the company splits business and opportunities into geographical areas, standard industrial classifications or product groups. Weaknesses can then be isolated according to their significance to the company and its markets.

Figure 16.5 Rationalization schedule

It is not unusual for a company that has been in existence for several years to carry in its range products that have long lost significance to the greater proportion of its customers and are being bought only by customers who stick to traditional products and ideas. Obviously, a progressive company does not want to rely for future business and prosperity upon customers not prepared to meet modern conditions. Once a product has lost its usefulness it is far better to remove it from the range completely, rather than to produce uneconomical quantities and carry stocks of slow-moving products which, in all probability, do not even make a realistic profit contribution.

It is only when operating cost, analysed into major sections, is compared to other products that some indication of its value becomes apparent.

In this illustration, sections are used for viewing trends for a product over a period of ten years with year 1 having an index of 100 and a sales trend pattern for the last twelve months with month 1 having an index of 100. From this information it is possible to assess the future sales life of a product consistent with its profit contribution, and to programme the date at which the product is likely to be withdrawn from the range.

Figure 16.6 Contingency action plan

Profit is the first charge to the business enterprise but inevitably, in practical terms, it is the money left over at the end of the year's trading, and it is therefore imperative that the performance from which profit is derived is forecast as early as possible in each operating year. After some four or five months of the trading year it should be possible to establish trends from which end-of-year results can be predicted. Obviously, because no company operates in isolated periods, and its trading is continuous, monthly results for the previous year, month by month, can be used as the foundations against which the results in the current year can be accumulated. This gives an established pattern over many months of activity, so allowing a measure for projection into the future, to the end of the current year. Where the trend shows an unsatisfactory result, remedial action may be taken well in advance (assuming that variations in operating costs can be isolated and their cause established!).

Figure 16.1 Date					**STANDARD COSTS – BY PRODUCT IN PERIOD**								Prepared by	
Cost item	This period Standard costs	Last period Standard costs	This period Actual costs	Last period Actual costs	This period Standard costs per unit	Last period Standard costs per unit	This period Actual costs per unit	Last period Actual costs per unit	This period Standard over actual	Last period Standard over actual	This period Actual over standard	Last period Actual over standard	This period Prior year actual = 100	Last period Prior year actual = 100
Manufactured material														
Bought-In parts														
Purchased material														
Overhead														
Labour														
Total manufacturing														
Salaries and wages														
Overhead														
Total administration														
Salaries and wages														
Overhead														
Total research and development														
Salaries and wages														
Advertising														
Public relations														
Sales promotion														
Marketing research														
Consultancy services														
Product line														
Distribution														
Direct selling expense														
Total marketing costs														
Total costs														

Figure 16.2
Date

PRICING SCHEDULE

Prepared by

Product	Volume A break-even point					Volume B 10% return						Volume C 20% return					
	Mnfg costs		Overheads and marketing		Unit price	Mnfg costs		Overheads and marketing		Unit price	Gross margin	Mnfg costs		Overheads and marketing		Unit price	Gross margin
	Fixed	Variable	Fixed	Variable	Pence	Fixed	Variable	Fixed	Variable	Pence	%	Fixed	Variable	Fixed	Variable	Pence	%

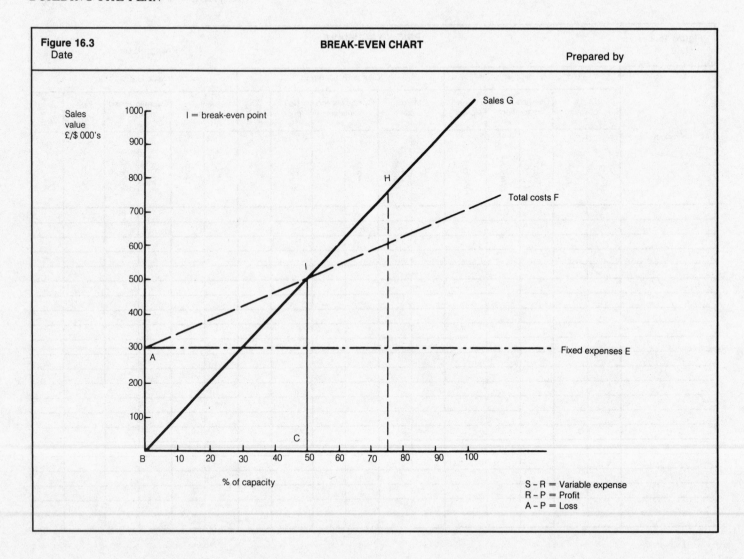

Figure 16.3
Date

BREAK-EVEN CHART

Prepared by

Sales value £/$ 000's

I = break-even point

1000 — Sales G

Total costs F

Fixed expenses E

% of capacity

S – R = Variable expense
R – P = Profit
A – P = Loss

Figure 16.4 Date		LOST BUSINESS AND OPPORTUNITIES						Prepared by		
Prospect name	Geographical area	SIC	Product group	Value at par	Gross margin %	Amount in budget	Contingency action proposed	Value	Target date	Rating %

Figure 16.5 Date							RATIONALIZATION SCHEDULE					Prepared by	
Product	Unit direct costs	Unit indirect costs	% manufacturing capacity	% total sales	% sales force costs	% publicity costs	% total marketing costs	Average delivery period	Sales trend last 10 years (year 1 = 100)	Sales trend last 12 months (month 1 = 100)	Expected product sales life (months)	Expected product withdrawal date

Figure 16.6 Date	CONTINGENCY ACTION PLAN								Prepared by			
	Budget figure to date	Actual figure to date	Variance figure to date	% performance against budget	Budget figure year-end	Forecast figure year-end	Variance figure year-end	% performance year-end	Action year ending forecast			
									80 %	90 %	110 %	120 %
Sales product group A												
Sales product group B												
Sales product group C												
Sales product group D												
Total sales												
Gross margin												
Marketing expenses												
1 Salaries and wages												
2 Vehicles												
3 Publicity												
4 Rent and rates												
5 Commissions												
6 Depreciation												
7 Government charges												
8 Taxes												
9 Interest charges												
10 Other expenses												
Net profit												
Employees												
1 Management and supervision												
2 Salesmen												
3 Administration												
4 Clerical												
5 Other												
Notes on courses of action												

17   Formulating the Campaign Plan

No matter how good the plan, it remains an academic document until it is put into action and becomes a campaign. The production of a marketing plan will help achieve an integrated campaign, with all elements of the marketing mix appropriately co-ordinated. Almost all campaigns are unique, necessarily so if the principles suggested in this text are applied. A consumer goods company of some size will choose advertising as its spearhead, an industrial goods company uses its sales force, a service company uses sales literature, and a retail concern concentrates on merchandising. Each distinct method is supported by all other elements in the mix.

The campaign plan is the product of the marketing plan. It is the implementation of the conclusions drawn as a result of the study, interpretation, understanding, reasoning, and judgement exercised in developing the plan. The campaign plan is all judgement – there are no guaranteed facts which will produce a definite solution. The marketing plan should contain the ammunition for decision-making, so reducing the element of risk, but is indicative not conclusive.

Whether the campaign be advertising, selling, promotional, or merchandising it has basic ingredients. These are the *right*:

1 product
2 target market
3 target position
4 message
5 presentation
6 media
7 timing.

What is right in each case is a question of judgement. However, once a judgement is made on the *right* target market then all other decisions are determined accordingly. This is the ideal situation, usually only possible when a new product is about to be launched and the *right* product has been developed preferably for that *right* market.

Most campaigns are for established products, and therefore the *right* product has to be reborn and endowed with subjective values unless it has some unique functional attribute that makes it *right* already. That functional attribute becomes the determining factor for all other decisions. Unfortunately, few products have or will continue to have any such functional uniqueness. The problem facing most marketing managers is the discovery of a quality to attach to a product that is unique, has sufficient appeal, and can be cost-effectively promoted. That is judgement. Getting it right is the core of success.

While this book clarifies *how*, it does not attempt to tell *what* is to be done. Deciding what to do is possible only when the marketing plan is complete and the necessary resources are made available. However, assuming a competitive product in an established, typically-fragmented market, and an ambitious company (a description applying to 80 per cent of readers) it is possible to suggest a platform on which to build

Firstly, identify a consumer need, in subjective terms, and then create an aura about the product that couples the subjective need with a product feature. Make sure that the subjective need is not being exploited by a competitor. The product is now potentially capable of satisfying a select number of people's basic attitudes, hopes, fears, or needs. Having established the *right* product and the *right* target audience, it is now necessary to select an initial target position in the market, the share you aim to achieve, the *right* position, and so develop the *right* message, *right* presentation, *right* media and *right* timing all determined by the *right* product and *right* target audience.

These are the foundations, and all the elements in the marketing mix now have to be realigned to the projected image. You are selling a dream, a way of life that is true of a significant proportion of the population that is unique to you. Get it right and you have a brand monopoly. Believe that people do not make entirely rational decisions, for decisions are almost invariably made impulsively or compulsively.

Monitoring the results of the campaign will supply information on how to refine the strategy being used.

The charts in this chapter concentrate on advertising, but other communications channels are covered elsewhere in this book.

Figure 17.1   Understanding the user/consumer
Developing a full awareness of the needs and behaviour of potential customers is of fundamental importance since marketing is customer-orientated. No company can know too much about its markets and the people who live within them.

Figure 17.2   Purchasing decisions
Consumers make purchasing decisions according to their own perception of value. They decide on what they need from a brand and choose according to this need. This chart identifies the usual alternatives and which type of buyers are involved. Selecting the most appropriate for investment and concentrating the company strategy on that choice provides a competitive edge.

Figure 17.3   Advertising objectives/themes
Setting specific objectives (a) and producing the appropriate themes (b) to achieve them is essential to successful advertising. Deciding on the required response to advertising messages is the format for establishing such objectives. The theme provides the association of ideas with which customers may identify their own needs, benefits, and feelings.

Figure 17.4   Advertising strategy and tactics
Advertising strategy is concerned with the advertising campaign, while advertising tactics are involved with the advertisement or commercial. The advertising appropriation is a strictly limited quantity and no matter how it is spent it is confined to permutations of:

1   impact
2   frequency
3   coverage
4   duration.

Where there is a need for considerable *impact* then a substantial proportion of the appropriation may be spent on creativity and the production specification of the advertising platform or theme. Under more usual circumstances the creative element and production will amount to about 10 per cent of the total campaign expenditure. Any additional amount will be spent at the expense of one or more of the other strategic elements. The sacrifice may be in *frequency* – repetition of the message nightly, daily or weekly may have to be reduced, or advertisements limited to one per issue rather than appearing on several pages of the same issue. Similarly, *coverage* of the target audience may be limited to the prime part of the market rather than to the whole of the selected market, and, furthermore, penetration may be restricted if the *duration* of the campaign is confined in any way.

The style of the advertisement will be decided according to the nature of the product, the profile of the consumer, and the particular characteristics of available media.

Figure 17.5   Developing advertising copy

Writing copy is the work of a skilled communicator, and building-in the proved stages and using the accepted creative effects needs to be tackled professionally. The rules and techniques are numerous, and their selection critical to the campaign. Too often media expenditure is wasted because of economies sought in copy production.

The stages shown and the creative effects listed constitute the most common criteria used by the copywriter. They are the format for originating ideas appropriate to products, markets, and media.

Figure 17.6   Campaign planning control data

The supplementary objectives shown in this illustration are provided to assist in the formalization of the media plan. They provide a link between the media and advertising subsets of the publicity mix.

Figure 17.7   Developing the media plan

The marketing mix forms a combination which is unique to each particular company, as is the media plan. The marketing mix is the means by which marketing objectives are achieved, and the media schedule is a blend intended to attain the advertising objectives of the firm. Moreover, as advertising objectives are steps taken towards the realization of marketing objectives the final media selection is determined by the company's specific needs. Therefore, media selection is an integral part of the company's marketing plan.

To arrive at a reasoned and qualified media schedule it is necessary to progress through all the steps inherent in the marketing plan. The media planner or buyer should become involved, ideally at the development of the marketing mix, but certainly no later than the consideration of the marketing communications channels. From this point onwards the planner's expertise will be critical in reaching the company's markets in the most cost-effective manner. This illustration shows the progression of media from research to the publicity programme and then the subsequent feeding back to research.

Figure 17.8   Advertising expenditure planning
Pressure on advertising budgets has forced consideration of more economic means of spending available funds. The techniques which have proved the most cost-effective are shown in this illustration. The most suitable choice is dependent on the advertising objective. In turn its selection will be influenced by the proportions of the target audience which are *unaware*, *aware*, *comprehending*, *convinced*, or in *action* stages of awareness. Clearly, the more people convinced or in action, the more likely the advertising is to be a reminder, and the less likely is the need to provide saturation promotions. If brand switching or market development is the strategy involved, then economy campaigns will probably be used.

Figure 17.9   Monitoring the advertising
Advertising effectiveness is most often measured through the specialist research companies identified in Chapter 2 for the UK and the USA and similar organizations for other parts of the world. For industries and countries where such research is not undertaken, a company may be able to use multi-client organizations mentioned in Chapter 7. Alternatively, a company may make its own assessment by studying its promotional copy, seeking impartial opinion, and establishing whether the essence of advertising appeal has been incorporated. Advertising, to be effective, should reflect the features shown on this chart.

Figure 17.1	UNDERSTANDING THE USER/CONSUMER
1	What is the target group of buyers?
2	What satisfaction/values does this particular group hope to obtain?
3	Which of these satisfactions are they least able to obtain from other sources?
4	From which sources do they get it now?
5	What is the availability of other sources of satisfactions?
6	How well does the product serve the perceptions of values to be fulfilled?
7	Where or how does the buyer obtain the product?
8	When does he buy it?
9	What is the basis of choice between this and other sources of the same kinds of satisfactions?
10	What is the extent of loyalty towards a company or a product?
11	Who is involved in the purchasing decision?
12	What part in the purchasing decision does each play?
13	What appeals are most likely to influence them?
14	What is the most cost-effective way to communicate with each party involved?
15	How can we obtain information about each of them?
16	What specific benefits are needed?
17	What are the current pricing and financial incentives?
18	
19	
20	

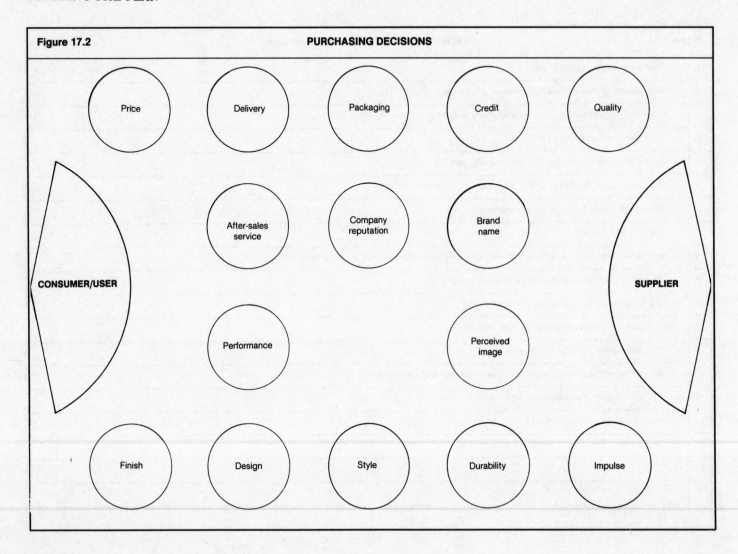

Figure 17.2 **PURCHASING DECISIONS**

Price

Delivery

Packaging

Credit

Quality

CONSUMER/USER

After-sales service

Company reputation

Brand name

Performance

Perceived image

SUPPLIER

Finish

Design

Style

Durability

Impulse

Figure 17.3

(a) ADVERTISING OBJECTIVES

To establish an immediate sale	To combat competition
To bring prospect closer to a sale	To reassure customers
To build a long-term franchise	To enter new markets
To increase consumption among users	To create awareness
To initiate first move towards a sale	To support retail trade
To give sales force a supporting service	To promote incentive marketing
To gain market support	To counter price competition
To deepen penetration	To overcome memory lapse
To open distribution	To defend present position
To develop image	To establish market lead
To impart information	To reinforce reputation monopoly

(b) ADVERTISING THEMES

Prestige	Fun	Health	Excitement	Mystery
Style	Sophistication	Quality	Exotic	Trust
Future	Interest	Fashion	Bargain	Herd instinct

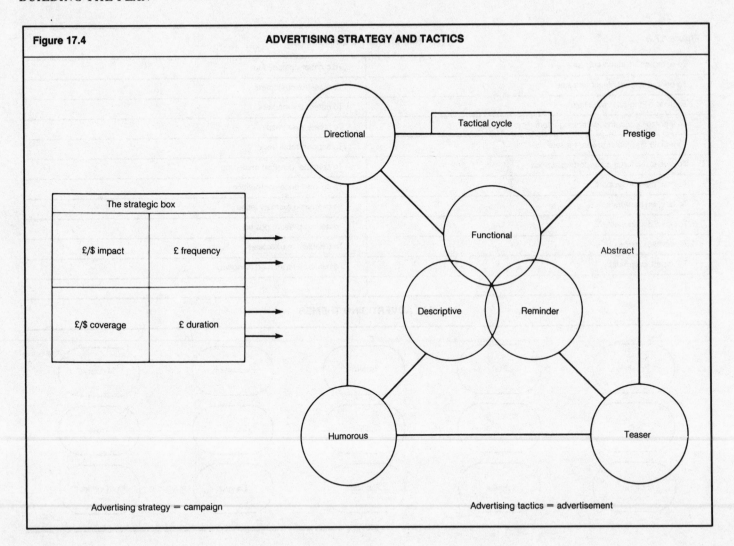

Figure 17.4 ADVERTISING STRATEGY AND TACTICS

Tactical cycle

Directional

Prestige

Functional

Abstract

Descriptive

Reminder

Humorous

Teaser

The strategic box

£/$ impact	£ frequency
£/$ coverage	£ duration

Advertising strategy = campaign

Advertising tactics = advertisement

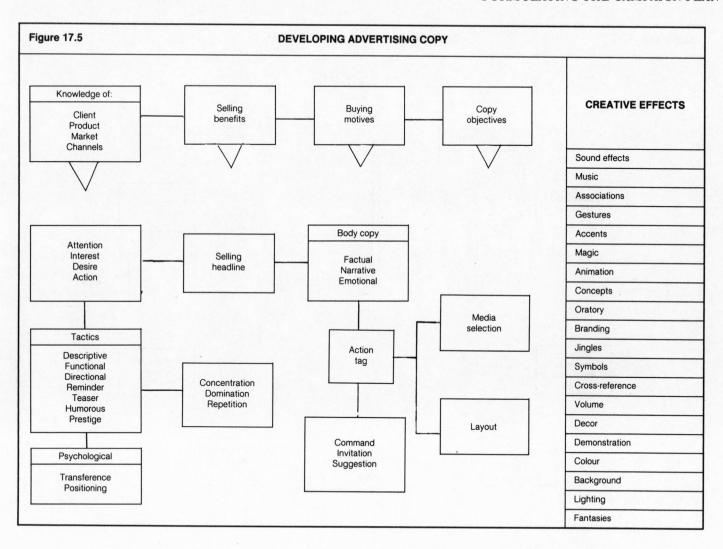

Figure 17.5 — DEVELOPING ADVERTISING COPY

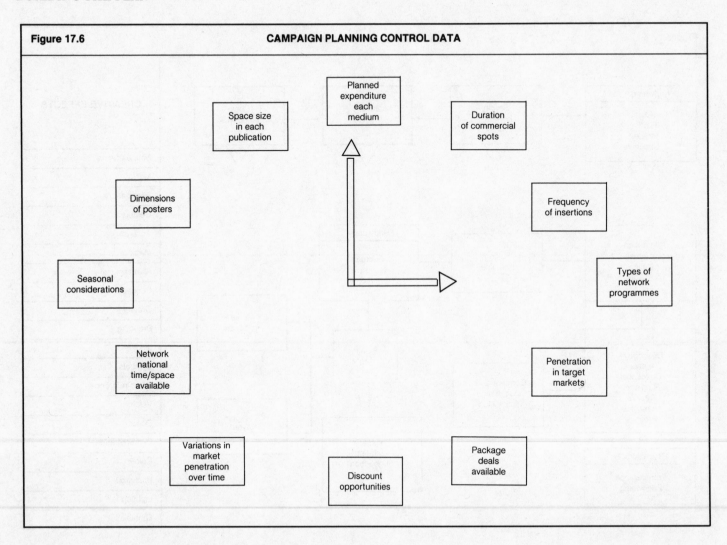

Figure 17.6   **CAMPAIGN PLANNING CONTROL DATA**

Figure 17.7   **DEVELOPING THE MEDIA PLAN**

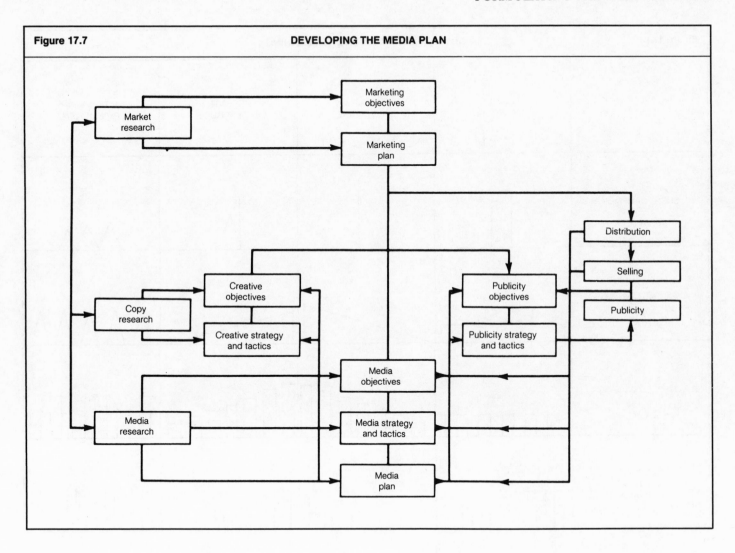

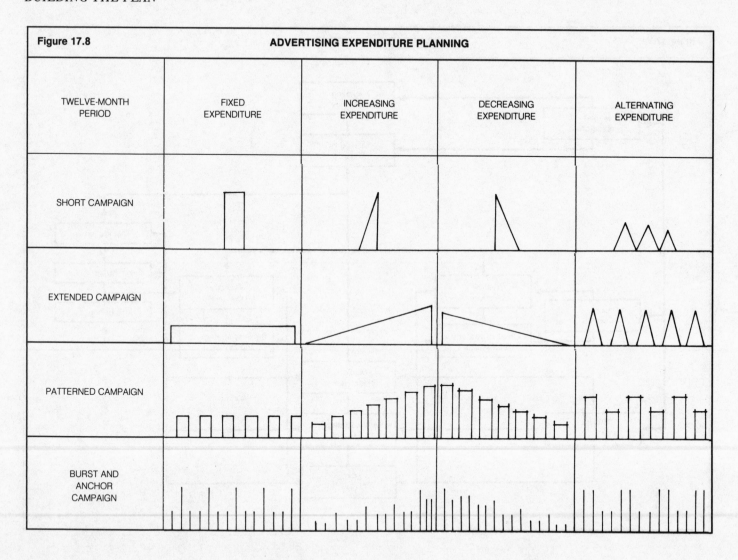

Figure 17.8

ADVERTISING EXPENDITURE PLANNING

TWELVE-MONTH PERIOD	FIXED EXPENDITURE	INCREASING EXPENDITURE	DECREASING EXPENDITURE	ALTERNATING EXPENDITURE
SHORT CAMPAIGN				
EXTENDED CAMPAIGN				
PATTERNED CAMPAIGN				
BURST AND ANCHOR CAMPAIGN				

Figure 17.9   **MONITORING THE ADVERTISING**

Does your promise offer:

Hope – Identification – Cognition –
Superiority – Reassurance – Pleasure –
Reward – Value – Compatibility

Does a purchase suggest:

Ego gratification
Maternal traits
Romantic rewards
Emotional security
Sexual reassurance
Social acceptability
Required recognition
Self-esteem
Winning ways

Does your advertisement:

A Create awareness
    Ensure conviction
    Reach an audience
    Inspire action

B Attract attention
    Arouse interest
    Stimulate desire
    Compel action

Does your message have:

Impact
Involvement
Recall
Image
Credibility

18 Making the most of Packaging

At one time packaging was limited in scope to paper used to cushion the contents of parcels or to fill empty spaces in a package. In more recent years it has included wrappings and the parcelling of goods. But more significantly it has become recognized as one of the most significant marketing communications channels.

Today, packaging provides the security for the contents of a parcel during distribution and a vital means of communication between the manufacturer and the customer, or even the actual consumer. The package passes through every distribution channel and can therefore be used to convey any message to a particular channel. In this day of unit packaging it is likely that a different *skin* can be used according to the distribution point. Wholesalers break bulk and the container they receive may carry an appropriate message. Supplied in cartons to the retailer a further communication may be made. On show in the shop the display box will carry information to persuade the customer, and, finally, the unit pack will have copy intended to influence the consumer or user. In many ways packaging is the ultimate in communications channels.

Some companies are beginning to recognize that packaging does not end with the pack. Within the last few years certain packages have become part of the product itself. Aerosols are inseparable from their contents, while providing an invaluable benefit to the product itself. Similarly, frozen foods provide a complete merger between package and contents. These two products would not have the same value without the package. Similarly, gifts offered with an attractive pack add more to the value of the item than the additional cost would suggest. So clearly the package may improve the product and the value of the product itself.

The packaging industry is, therefore, only one step removed from the experts in industrial design. The body of the motor car, the shape of the domestic cooker or the style of household appliances are all elements of packaging, for they provide security of contents and a communications channel – by design as well as by word.

Using an industrial designer

It is fairly clear that industry in general underrates the extent to which an industrial designer should become involved with packaging problems. The profession is still comparatively new, and there are conflicting views among its members, involving much heated discussion on the scope of activities.

Some years ago the Design Council produced a definition which it hoped would clarify the position. Briefly, the council said that the function of the industrial designer is to give form to objects and services by producing a hypothesis for a possible product, to co-operate with other specialists to develop a feasible version and to determine a final form for the product. It was believed that the actual scope of the industrial designer embraced practically every type of human artifact especially those that were mass produced and mechanically actuated.

It seems from this definition that many well-known conventional shapes can be expected to disappear. Many of the present designs for everyday goods are based on out-of-date conventions. The gas or electric cooker found in every home is a typical example. Originally the household cooker was based on a fire-range with coal, coke, or wood being the main source of heat. Of necessity the oven and hot-plates had to be combined with one heat source. Now that gas and electricity are readily available, it is no longer necessary for oven and boiling plates to be part of a single unit. But because of convention the single unit is still bought in preference to alternatives.

Packaging as a promotional vehicle

Packaging today incorporates considerable selling power and, with merchandising, had to assume the vital role of selling at the point of sale. It is a means by which the consumer is able to distinguish one product from another, either because of a real additional facility that that package provides or because of the psychological satisfaction it brings.

Colour is one of the means by which psychological messages may be conveyed. Everyone has a natural or a developed association of ideas between colour, people, events, happenings, opinions, attitudes, and beliefs. In some cases the association of ideas relevant to particular colours is common. For example, everyone will associate white with cleanliness and purity because of advertising of detergents, wedding dresses, hospitals and medical staff. Other common associations are:

Black – strong, overpowering, dramatic
Blue – cool, melancholy, latent excitement, moody
Brown – utility, soothing
Gold – royal, rich, cheap, simplicity, vulgar
Green – natural, quiet, jealous, superstition
Orange – warmth, mobility, vibrant, gay
Purple – lush, extravagant, royal
Red – hot, danger
White – pure, clean, fresh, crisp
Yellow – warm, sunshine, wholesome, tranquil, insipid
Silver – cold, hard, cynical, sophisticated, precision, reflective

Different shades of these colours may strengthen or soften the ideas conveyed. For added emphasis a combination of colours may be used.

Equally, the shape or form of a package conjures up associated ideas. In many cases a particular design has become linked with a specific event or happening, or perhaps a concept or object. Circular objects, rectangles, squares, or triangles bring their own preconceived ideas of form. Certain advertising programmes leave an imprint on the mind. Phallic symbols, period furniture and architecture, impressions of affluence and romantic associations all suggest an environment for establishing a message, whether it be a slogan, image, or benefit. Packaging may prove to be the most effective medium for symbolic form.

Figure 18.1 Packaging for strategic marketing
Design is obviously a necessary part of marketing philosophy. To satisfy the individual needs of worldwide markets, products have to be developed so as to give the maximum possible value for money. This means that the industrial designer has to be brought in at the product planning stage with access to all the marketing research information.

Designers will need to know who is to use the product, what they will use it for and why, where it will be used and how it is to be used. Once this information is available they can, in true marketing fashion, apply their specialist knowledge when producing new ideas.

The advantage of using an outside specialist frequently outweighs the economic advantages of an in-house specialist because the latter will soon become enmeshed with a company's established ideas and ways of thinking, so limiting a radical approach.

Designers may well produce a product design that gives the company a leading advantage in the market-place – the unique selling proposition (USP). They may develop a design which enables the product to be manufactured more economically than would normally be expected. This could be because the shape is more easily machined or because the choice of more suitable materials enables the company to reduce its raw materials purchasing cost. Often designers will produce a concept that improves the performance of the product itself. The modern car and aircraft are good examples of superior performance due to design of the 'package'. In some cases the designer will assist with the development of product innovation.

Figure 18.2   Packaging as a marketing tool
Significantly, designers have made their contribution to halting the imminent decline of long established products. This has been done by the creation of new or convenience packaging. Tea-bags have become widely accepted and the money spent by the consumer has brought increased revenue without necessarily affecting volume. The sealed-in jam pack has helped jam sales, while the use of luxury packs with soft margarine has enabled the product to compete effectively against butter.

Figure 18.3   Packaging and legal requirements
Packaging is subject to more statutory regulations than any other element in the marketing mix. Short of considerable study and a legal background the marketing specialist should use the best possible counsel to meet the legal requirements of both home and international trade. This illustration itemizes some of the rules and regulations applicable to packaging.

Figure 18.4   Packaging as a marketing communications channel
Products of fashion and taste carry a high premium, and therefore packaging design may

enhance their sales prospects. It provides additional value and suggests, perhaps subconsciously, that the recipient is worthy of attention and consideration. It is a most subtle form of paying a compliment.

Repeat-selling consumer goods, however, carry a more blatant message. The message is intended to incite repeat purchases. Packaging promotes the product in the store, on the way home, in the home, to visitors, and, when empty, acts as a reminder that the contents have gone, been enjoyed, and need replacing. No other form of advertising can match this for timing, place and motive. This illustration lists the main attributes of packaging as a communications channel.

Figures 18.5 and 18.6   Packaging check-lists
It has already been emphasized that packaging design is for the professional. The items listed in the two illustrations should reinforce this point. Packaging design has the additional advantage of providing the marketing department with prior knowledge of the areas with which the specialist will be concerned. Preparing necessary information in advance helps to ensure control of the cost of professional help.

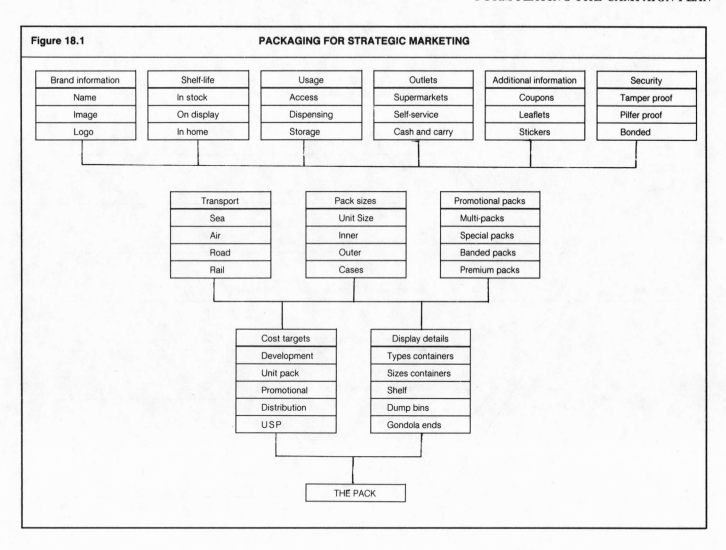

Figure 18.1 **PACKAGING FOR STRATEGIC MARKETING**

Brand information
Name
Image
Logo

Shelf-life
In stock
On display
In home

Usage
Access
Dispensing
Storage

Outlets
Supermarkets
Self-service
Cash and carry

Additional information
Coupons
Leaflets
Stickers

Security
Tamper proof
Pilfer proof
Bonded

Transport
Sea
Air
Road
Rail

Pack sizes
Unit Size
Inner
Outer
Cases

Promotional packs
Multi-packs
Special packs
Banded packs
Premium packs

Cost targets
Development
Unit pack
Promotional
Distribution
USP

Display details
Types containers
Sizes containers
Shelf
Dump bins
Gondola ends

THE PACK

Figure 18.2   **PACKAGING AS A MARKETING TOOL**

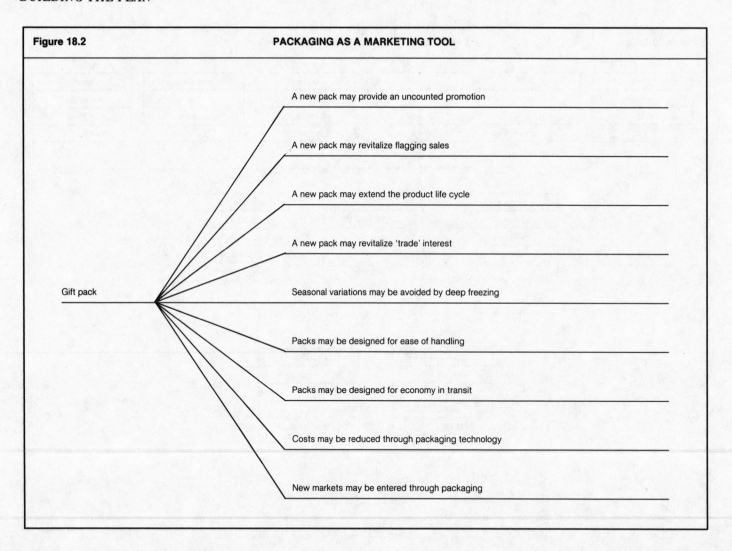

Gift pack

A new pack may provide an uncounted promotion

A new pack may revitalize flagging sales

A new pack may extend the product life cycle

A new pack may revitalize 'trade' interest

Seasonal variations may be avoided by deep freezing

Packs may be designed for ease of handling

Packs may be designed for economy in transit

Costs may be reduced through packaging technology

New markets may be entered through packaging

Figure 18.3	PACKAGING AND LEGAL REQUIREMENTS		
Weights and Measures Act 1963	**Food and Drugs Act 1955**	**Dangerous Drugs Act 1951 *et al***	**Trade Descriptions Act 1968 *et al***
Adequate packaging materials Weight marketing, metric and imperial Minimum lettering sizes Contrasting colours necessary Definition of pre-packed	Name of packer/labeller/trader General name to appear Ingredients (descending order, weight) Declaration of preservative Print regulations applied Limitations on colour usage Specific hygiene factors	Limited distribution and sale Limits on storage and containers Declarations on labels Recognizable by touch Identification possible Safety of contents	False description unlawful Prohibition misleading design Offence to mislead in promotion

TRANSPORT AND HANDLING
Petroleum Acts and Regulations and Voluntary Labelling System 1953 (Hazardous Containers)

Specified manner of conveyance
Particular conditions for containers
Regulations on conveyance, storage, sale

Product name to appear
Signal word denoting degree of danger
Specified type of hazard
Necessary precautions
Appropriate remedial action

SEA	AIR (IATA)	ROAD	RAIL
Declaration of identity Class of hazard Packed, marked and labelled	Hazards Maximum weight Construction Survival tests	No 'packaging' regulations	Hazards specified Specified acceptable packages

Figure 18.4   **PACKAGING AS A MARKETING COMMUNICATIONS CHANNEL**

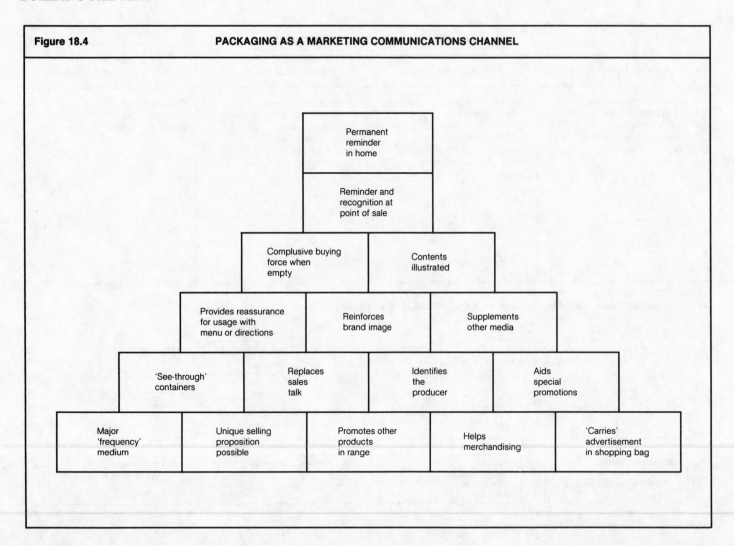

Figure 18.5	PACKAGING CHECK-LIST–1
ARTICLE/COMMODITY FOR PACKAGING	
Nature	Desirable storage conditions
Size	Cost
Construction	Possible substitutes
Packing density	Re-use value
Weight	Opening devices
Number of units	Resealing/closures
Shape	Moisture loss
Fragility	Aroma retention
Surface finish	Colour retention
Corrodibility	Catering use
Value	Industrial/commercial usage
Usage	
PARAMETERS	
Limits of temperature	
Relative humidity limits	
Barometric pressure limits	
Use for display	
Dispensing/discharge	
Maximum/minimum weight	
Intermediate containers	
Infrequent usage	
Single trip or returnable	

Figure 18.6	PACKAGING CHECK-LIST–2
POSSIBLE PROBLEMS	
Interaction with package	Odour migration
Contamination by residue	Water vapour transmission
Contamination by adjacent goods	Acidity
Ullage or vacuity	Expansibility
Pilferage	Combustibility
Physical limitations	Poison
Statutory	Shock
Tropical or Arctic destinations	Compression
Transit on space, weight, pallet	Impact
Handling	Vibration
Storage	Handling
Insect or rodent attack	Perishability
Mould growth	Gas transmission
Dew formation	Ecological
Rainwater	
Sea water	
Dust conditions	
Sunlight	
Artificial light	
Artificial heat	
Bacteria attack	
Odour contamination	

Evaluating Media

To the advertiser, media planning is a process of allocating resources to achieve marketing objectives. It is, however, rare for a media researcher to exercise much influence on the development of the original plans. This is an anomaly. Often the media-planner has a better idea of the validity of communications processes than any other member of an agency team, and may well be able to advise that a given advertising objective is unattainable within the limits of available expenditure. Too often the media-planner is left in the position of making the best possible use of arbitrarily allocated funds. Clearly, it is necessary for marketing planners to establish that objectives are obtainable in the circumstances rather than to impose plans on media-buyers that are achievable but perhaps in some other way than that prescribed.

Media planning needs to be operated as a business activity under exactly the same rigorous control as production or even accounting. This is clearly an aim, for media planning cannot produce exact results. As no one has managed to isolate the actual contribution an advertising campaign has on sales performance, it eliminates the possibility of establishing any correlation between advertising and sales. Moreover, the effects of the marketing mix on the market and the collective influence of individual scales of preference denies any measurement of the effectiveness of one marketing activity in isolation, particularly as the whole will almost certainly exceed the sum of the collective parts in the operation. Furthermore, the time-lag between an advertisement's impact and a purchasing decision may make the establishment of any link unrealistic. It is possible, however, to develop an indicative link statistically between advertising and sales through regression analysis (see the Appendix).

Advertising objectives
In order to measure the significance of a campaign it is necessary to establish some objective, related to sales performance, that is measurable. If, for example, the company decides that the most appropriate objective is to 'get the target audience to take the first step towards a sale' it will then be possible to calculate the effectiveness of the campaign

by counting, say, the number of people sending in coupons for more information, or the number of brochures handed out following visits to a showroom or, perhaps, customer visits made to a random selection of sales outlets during a given period of time.

The media plan is the means by which the advertising objective is achieved. It incorporates the selection of media which reach a chosen target audience and provides the characteristics necessary to carry the message in its most effective manner. The evaluation process is the means by which the media are measured as a vehicle. Clearly, it is necessary to draw distinctions between the effectiveness of a campaign because of good media selection and the impact of a campaign because of inspired creativity. Media weightings will usually be the means by which the different media will become almost comparable.

Figure 19.1   Stages in the media plan
As an integral part of the marketing planning process, media selection becomes involved with the comparison of marketing communications channels. Although few companies acknowledge the contribution that could be made by planners at this stage, it is apparent that they are the ideal people to advise on the choice between the different channels. Until recently the marketing communications channels were openly considered as a form of media, principally because they can be used to achieve results similar to direct advertising – the principal user of media. It is, however, necessary to distinguish between the various channels because the steps necessary to achieve similar results are different. They differ principally in the use of advertising strategy and tactics.

Figure 19.2   The media planners' signpost
Although there are almost no scientific rules in media planning, there are, nevertheless, a number of 'rules of thumb'. These rules have been developed following successful application over a number of years. They will not work in every case but there is a high expectation of success. It is an unfortunate fact that such observations tend to be typical of the marketing profession. Often it is the man that breaks the rules who succeeds while those who stick to the rules remain undistinguished. The 'rules of thumb' are shown in this illustration and they show the need for clear and positive thinking about the aims and goals of a campaign.

Figure 19.3   Media evaluation
Deciding between the use of one medium as opposed to another need not be decided by the power of personal persuasion but by direct comparison of comparable characteristics. Each advertising medium has a number of qualities that makes it the most effective channel for certain objectives. In combination with some other medium it may become the most cost-effective method for a wide range of goals.

If an advertiser of, say, soft furnishings considers colour essential to the promotion of a new range of designs, then he is immediately limited to television, cinema, consumer magazines and posters. Cinema is a restricted age group audience, and consumer magazines have their own reproduction standards. Posters provide the widest target audience in colour, but as the medium tends to be a 'reminder' medium and lacks sales impetus as such, it should follow or run concurrently with a primary campaign. It is comparing these characteristics that provides the most powerful ingredient of the media-planner's work.

Figure 19.4   Quantitative analysis
In making comparisons the older media planner uses both experience and judgement. The younger planner may be more inclined to apply quantitative methods for decision-making. These will usually be numerical values applied to qualitative assessments established through the flair and skill of the more experienced. Weightings are applied to the assessments so as to reflect a more realistic valuation. An example of media weights is shown where a weighting is incorporated with insertions. Impression cover is the result. An example of consumption weights is also shown, where certain age groups, and the relative costs of reaching them, are linked to consumption factors. By applying these weights the relative importance of different media is revealed.

Figure 19.5   Housewife television viewing behaviour
Audiences for television channels are subject to constant change with migration across channels and with differing life-styles throughout the population. In order to secure cost-effective communication to specific target audiences and to reduce wastage the media planner using past records and personal expertise will predict viewing patterns throughout a proposed campaign period. The media buyer will then be able to negotiate spots or time segments appropriate to the rigours of the campaign.

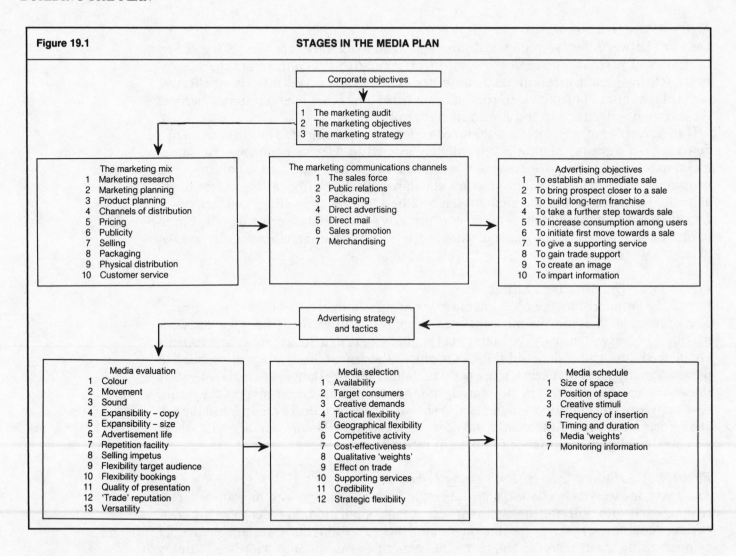

Figure 19.1   **STAGES IN THE MEDIA PLAN**

Corporate objectives

1 The marketing audit
2 The marketing objectives
3 The marketing strategy

The marketing mix
1   Marketing research
2   Marketing planning
3   Product planning
4   Channels of distribution
5   Pricing
6   Publicity
7   Selling
8   Packaging
9   Physical distribution
10 Customer service

The marketing communications channels
1 The sales force
2 Public relations
3 Packaging
4 Direct advertising
5 Direct mail
6 Sales promotion
7 Merchandising

Advertising objectives
1   To establish an immediate sale
2   To bring prospect closer to a sale
3   To build long-term franchise
4   To take a further step towards sale
5   To increase consumption among users
6   To initiate first move towards a sale
7   To give a supporting service
8   To gain trade support
9   To create an image
10 To impart information

Advertising strategy
and tactics

Media evaluation
1   Colour
2   Movement
3   Sound
4   Expansibility – copy
5   Expansibility – size
6   Advertisement life
7   Repetition facility
8   Selling impetus
9   Flexibility target audience
10 Flexibility bookings
11 Quality of presentation
12 'Trade' reputation
13 Versatility

Media selection
1   Availability
2   Target consumers
3   Creative demands
4   Tactical flexibility
5   Geographical flexibility
6   Competitive activity
7   Cost-effectiveness
8   Qualitative 'weights'
9   Effect on trade
10 Supporting services
11 Credibility
12 Strategic flexibility

Media schedule
1 Size of space
2 Position of space
3 Creative stimuli
4 Frequency of insertion
5 Timing and duration
6 Media 'weights'
7 Monitoring information

Figure 19.2   **THE MEDIA PLANNERS' SIGNPOST**

THE PRODUCT OR SERVICE		SELLING STRATEGY		MEDIA
1 Repeat selling consumer	→	Mass — Extensive	→	TV Press
2 Durable consumer	→	Mass — Intensive	→	Consumer magazines
3 Repeat selling industrial	→	Selective — Service	→	Trade magazines
4 Durable industrial	→	Selective — Technical	→	Direct mail
5 Expensive luxury	→	Exclusive — Prestige	→	High-class glossy
6 Special interest	→	Specific — Utility	→	Related magazines

THE PURPOSE OF THE CAMPAIGN

New product in established market
- Strategy — Impact and frequency
- Tactics — Functional/descriptive
- Media — Primary — Television or national press
- Media — Secondary — Provincial dailies/consumer magazines

New market new product
- Strategy — Impact and coverage
- Tactics — Descriptive
- Media — Primary — Television and national press
- Media — Secondary — Outdoor — Posters and transport

Facelift established product
- Strategy — Impact and frequency then duration
- Tactics — Descriptive then functional
- Media — Primary — Television then national press
- Media — Secondary — Radio and outdoor

To maintain established product
- Strategy — Coverage and duration
- Tactics — Reminder
- Media — Primary — Radio/posters
- Media — Secondary — Consumer magazines

To increase sales from competitors
- Strategy — Impact/frequency and coverage
- Tactics — Functional
- Media — Primary — Television and national press
- Media — Secondary — Evenings/radio/provincial press

To build long-term franchise
- Strategy — Coverage and duration
- Tactics — Prestige
- Media — Primary — National press/consumer magazines
- Media — Secondary — Outdoor/cinema

251

Figure 19.3 | **MEDIA EVALUATION**

MEDIA CHARACTERISTICS \ MEDIA CHANNELS	National press	National Sundays	Colour supplements	Provincial dailies	Provincial Sundays	Provincial weeklies	Consumer magazines	Independent Television	Channel 4	Cable television	Breakfast television	Teletext	Satellite television	Community television	Outdoor-posters	Outdoor-transport	Cinema	Bingo halls	Radio	Yellow pages	Directories	Free sheets	Trade and technical	Professional	Direct mail	Sponsorship	Packaging	Sales promotion	Public relations	Other
Colour																														
Movement																														
Sound																														
Expansibility–copy																														
Expansibility–size																														
Advertisement life																														
Repetition facility																														
Selling impetus																														
Flexibility target audience																														
Flexibility bookings																														
Quality of presentation																														
'Trade' reputation																														
Versatility																														
For: transference																														
For: positioning																														

Figure 19.4 **QUANTITATIVE ANALYSIS**

MEDIA WEIGHTS

Formula	Media Weight W	0.2	0.3	0.4	0.5	0.6	0.7	0.8	0.9	Impression cover
$1-(1-W)^N$ N = insertions W = media weight	N	%	%	%	%	%	%	%	%	1 Is high when weight is over 0.5 *or* 2 When number of insertions high
	1	20	30	40	50	60	70	80	90	
	2	36	51	64	75	84	91	96	100	
	4	59	76	87	94	98	100	100	100	
	8	83	94	98	100	100	100	100	100	

CONSUMPTION WEIGHTS

Index of consumption	
Age groups	Index
4–14	150
15–24	250
25–34	120
35–44	60
45+	17

000's of individuals per £100					
	4–14	15–24	25–34	35–44	45+
Television	60	28	32	34	96
Press	15	54	44	35	111
Cinema	20	45	15	8	12

Medium	4–14		15–24		25–34		35–44		45+	
Television	60	15	28	12	32	6	34	3	96	2
Press	15	4	54	23	44	9	35	4	111	3
Cinema	20	5	45	19	15	3	8	1	12	–

FORMULA POSTERS

Coverage
$$C = \frac{AS \times 100}{AS + 3.5}$$

Repetition
$$R = AS + 3.5$$

Sites
$$S = \frac{3.5 \times C}{A(100 - C)}$$

C = Coverage %
S = Sites
R = Repetition
Log $A = -0.7284$
Population
('000) + 1.4317

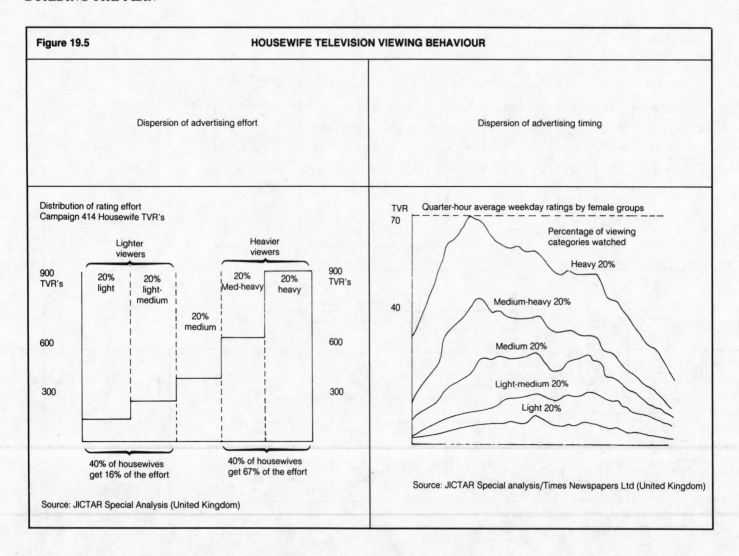

Figure 19.5 **HOUSEWIFE TELEVISION VIEWING BEHAVIOUR**

Dispersion of advertising effort

Dispersion of advertising timing

Distribution of rating effort
Campaign 414 Housewife TVR's

Lighter viewers

Heavier viewers

20% light

20% light-medium

20% medium

20% Med-heavy

20% heavy

900 TVR's

600

300

900 TVR's

600

300

40% of housewives get 16% of the effort

40% of housewives get 67% of the effort

Source: JICTAR Special Analysis (United Kingdom)

TVR 70

40

Quarter-hour average weekday ratings by female groups

Percentage of viewing categories watched

Heavy 20%

Medium-heavy 20%

Medium 20%

Light-medium 20%

Light 20%

Source: JICTAR Special analysis/Times Newspapers Ltd (United Kingdom)

Figure 19.6   Basis for comparison
Quantitative intermedia comparisons are frequently based on housewife ratings, cover, 4+ cover, frequency, and gross OTS according to the determined media objective. This illustration compares television and women's magazines, on the basis of a £100 000 level of investment. The housewife ratings for magazines are gross coverage levels and are directly comparable with TVRs. The comparison is made in terms of weekly build-up (cumulative coverage) for short-burst advertising. It is based on a burst strategy and suggests that magazines can be used to achieve a frequency, cover, and 4+ cover substantially greater than that of television during a four-week campaign. This is not to suggest that magazines are a better advertising medium than television, only that there is a basis for comparison and that in this particular case magazines offer a better quantitative return than television.

Figure 19.7   Media objectives
Media advertising is usually the most expensive element in a publicity campaign. To achieve the best possible return on this investment it is necessary to determine just what the expenditure is expected to achieve. The advertising objective is the normal determinant, and to help achieve that objective the media planner suggests how to reach particular target audiences and the alternative means by which this may be achieved. In order to set a target and to provide the means by which success of the media may be measured, it is necessary to establish a formal media objective. The objective may be penetration of a selected group, or a measure of advertising strategy identified in the different ways listed in this illustration.

Figure 19.6   **BASIS FOR COMPARISON**

'BURST' STRATEGY

THROUGH TV AND

MAGAZINES

COVERAGE

BUILD-UP

COMPARISONS

Cumulative penetration
all housewives

Source: JICTAR and JICNARS NRS

Housewife ratings, cover,
4+ cover, frequency,

OTS

Through TV	ALL H/W	ABC1C2 under 45 H/W	Through magazines	ALL H/W	ABC1C2 under 45 H/W
H/W TVR	319	276		480	511*
H/W COVER	75%	72%		84%	88%
4+ COVER	31%	28%		53%	57%
FREQUENCY	4	4		6	6
GROSS OTS	56m	16m		89m	31m

* Gross coverage level,
directly comparable with TVRs

Weekly build-up for
short burst advertising

Through TV					Through magazines				
Weeks	H/W TVR	COV*	4+ COV	AVE FREQ	Weeks	H/W TVR	COV*	4+ COV	AVE FREQ
1	100	54%	—	1.9	1	248	79%	28%	3.13
2	200	67%	20%	3.0	2	348	82%	42%	4.24
3	319	78%	32%	3.9	3	418	83%	48%	5.04
4					4	480	84%	53%	5.75

* based on total housewives

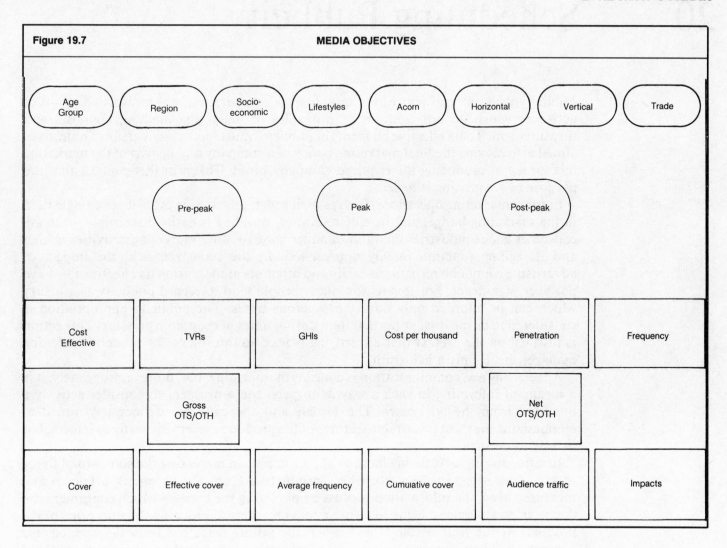

Figure 19.7 — MEDIA OBJECTIVES

Age Group · Region · Socio-economic · Lifestyles · Acorn · Horizontal · Vertical · Trade

Pre-peak · Peak · Post-peak

Cost Effective · TVRs · GHIs · Cost per thousand · Penetration · Frequency

Gross OTS/OTH · Net OTS/OTH

Cover · Effective cover · Average frequency · Cumulative cover · Audience traffic · Impacts

20   Scheduling Publicity

Publicity is an integral part of the total marketing operation, not an isolated group of activities which do not conform to principles of marketing method, appraisal and measurement. To be effective all forms of publicity must have clearly-defined objectives aimed at achieving the total marketing policy of a company and be part of the marketing mix aimed at producing the required company profit. Taken in this context, the true purpose of advertising is to sell.

In some marketing operations, such as mail order, advertising is the largest single item in the marketing budget and its true relevance to selling is easily discernible. In many consumer goods industries the ratio of advertising to other marketing activities is high and its selling function readily appreciated. In the industrial field the impact of advertising cannot be recognized easily and attempts at measuring its effectiveness have not been significant. For this reason many people tend to regard publicity as a luxury which can be afforded only during prosperous times. The publicity appropriation is considered to be the least important item during times of economic pressure. This action is justified on the pretext that advertising is used to inform; to the modern marketing manager this is only a half truth.

Advertising as a communication is a means of informing, but, more appropriately, it is a means of informing in such a way as to persuade a prospect to consider actively a purchase from the advertiser. The visuals and the copy are deliberately aimed at emphasizing the most favourable features of the product concerned, partly to inform, but mainly to persuade.

In a free society advertising has a vital part to play in increasing the standard of living of the population. In a society where products are created to satisfy a known and measured need, the information process emphasizing the benefits which consumers can derive from a purchase helps to create a mass market, so reducing the unit price of the product. At the time of the launch when the selling price has been determined, the company will have forecast the volume of sales expected, based on a measured demand at a given price level. Without advertising, the company marketing such a product would have to rely upon word of mouth and many years may pass before the required volume and economic price can be achieved. The time span may be such that the company may be forced to charge a premium price in order to recover its investment, so making the purchase price too high for the majority of people who could have used and enjoyed the product. By stimulating demand with publicity, every company is contributing towards a higher level of employment by providing jobs for workers and by ensuring a satisfactory return for those seeking an income from their investments.

The advertising world of today offers such a broad range of promotional services that its activities are now more appropriately called publicity services. Advertising agents now offer marketing research activities as well as specialist departments devoted to public relations, direct mail, promotional film production, design and production of sales promotion literature and press-cutting services. The role of the advertising agent in the future will continue to change as will the total concept of advertising, particularly in its approach to company problems.

Historically, advertising has been used as a means of stimulating increased sales volume. With an increase in the standard of education, combined with increasing company size, an advertising approach will be developed towards the protection of market shares, avoiding the erosion in profit which comes from overemphasis on pricing tactics in marketing practice. In addition, advertising strategy will be developed in such a way that it will become easier to concentrate the approach on predetermined consumer or industrial groupings. By concentrating strategy on individual groups it is possible to generate more specific, and, therefore, more compelling benefits where characteristics or needs tend to be similar.

In future years, publicity expenditure will become increasingly subject to scientific methods of measurement for effectiveness. While it is still not possible to measure the exact contribution advertising makes to sales volume, it is possible to measure the effectiveness of the objectives of advertising, and publicity in any form, as an investment of company resources. Advertising expenditure must be justified in the same way as any other form of investment. The pattern of advertising campaigns in the future will be divided into specific and logical steps. It will be necessary to define specific advertising objectives. The company must choose the message to be communicated to its markets in order to achieve the predetermined objectives. Copy, layout and even impact of advertisements must be pre-tested before the appropriation is committed to their use. More emphasis is likely in the projection of media in terms of cost-effectiveness through coverage and opportunity to see by the selected audience most appropriate to the advertiser. The effectiveness of the total campaign can then be measured by comparing actual results with the original objectives.

Several specialist companies provide much valuable information for advertisers. The National Readership Survey (see Figure 20.1) is essential for press media selection. Audits of Great Britain Ltd (see Figure 20.2) provide detailed analyses of television viewing and comprehensive reports on advertising expenditure by individual companies in selected media grouped by industry. Some of the principal advertising media provide their own reading and noting studies. Sometimes, in conjunction with advertisers, they provide information on response rates and, occasionally, conversion rates of enquiries into orders.

Pre-testing advertisements has been undertaken on a limited scale by exposing alternative campaigns to audiences, selected at random or by quota and judging their reaction to these trials – presupposing that the sample will be representative of the characteristics of the total market. While these tests are never likely to produce the stroke of genius that characterizes the company that achieves rapid growth in a short period of time, they do tend to ensure that total failure is eliminated. For companies spending vast sums on advertising the cost of research may be so minimal that even a marginal increase in sales volume covers research expenditure.

To many companies the selection of an advertising agency presents one of the most difficult and critical tasks in ensuring their future prosperity. The justification for using an agency is simply the need for professional skill which would be uneconomic for the advertiser to obtain by recruiting the necessary staff, even if such staff were readily available. In hiring the services of an agency the company expects the agency to provide creative thinking, competent media knowledge, realistic commercial comprehension, and an understanding of progressive and enlightened business attitudes. Although the company may not require the full range of services the modern agency can provide, it will expect the agency to have experience of similar products, a broad experience of the market, other industries and products, initiative, speed and considerable enthusiasm for its product. The illustrations shown in this chapter are designed to ensure that companies apply the principles of marketing planning to their publicity appropriation.

Figure 20.1   NBRS average issue readership
The National Readership Survey, providing much valuable information for the selection of press media in the UK.

Figure 20.2   Analysis of television viewing
Audits of Great Britain Ltd provide detailed analyses of television viewing.

Figure 20.3   Media analysis
Cost-effective advertising communication is achieved through penetration and relative cost of media. Compiling information on comparative penetration and cost and then relating these to target audience coverage by each medium provides a quantitative inter-media comparison. Compiling the information by publications, channels, and stations makes possible comparison between one vehicle of communication and others.

Figure 20.4   Appropriation analysis
The basis of this form is to relate the publicity function to achieving the objectives closely associated with the forecast sales volume. Budgeted expenditure covers the full time span of the marketing period, and actual financial expenditure on publicity does not have to be correlated to forecast sales volume. Expenditure is to be devoted to the achievement of year-by-year objectives in terms of increasing market awareness of the company, its products, benefits, and the additional services provided which, within themselves, must be closely related to the industries which will be served. The geographical areas in which industries are located and within which the company plans to achieve a greater degree of penetration than in the past must also be considered. In establishing its goals the company must decide whether its approach to advertising is to win new business at the expense of competitors, or whether it intends to expand the total market by penetration, by developing a unique selling proposition, so as to ensure brand loyalty from its customers. This form provides an analysis of expenditure on established products and on new products. It goes on to divide the appropriation between the available media. Ideally, for control purposes, each medium used and the money planned to be spent on each medium should be divided into established products and new lines. A product can be classified as new to the company for whatever period of time the company concerned chooses, but it is advisable to classify products as new until such

time as development costs have been fully recovered and the product is making its planned contribution to profitability. This would normally not be longer than three years.

Few companies would use the full range of media listed but the form is recommended for use as a checklist of available media before the appropriation is finally settled. Justification for and against each medium should be prepared in line with the advertising objectives.

Figure 20.5 Advertising/business systems mailing/weeks/Appropriation schedule
The appropriation schedule is a much simpler form and, apart from the two historical years, is a complete analysis of advertising cash flow for each month of the first year of the marketing plan. A personal choice can be made as to whether each sub-heading is divided by product, by geographical area or by specific publicity medium. Ideally, each schedule should be subdivided into customer applications – that is, the use to which customers actually employ a product to any significant degree in terms of value. Each of the applications can then be categorized into an established or new product.

Careful preparation of the schedule well in advance of the year concerned will ensure a satisfactory cash flow is provided for the benefit of the company's accounting procedures. By deciding well in advance at which time of the year the company plans to spend money on various forms of publicity, each must be related to some particular objective. Objectives may be related to other events, such as major exhibitions, special features being planned by the press, direct mail campaigns, premium promotions, or the launching of a new product.

It is always advisable to allocate a small contingency allowance in the appropriation to avoid inflexibility during any periods when events occur which the company considers should be exploited, rather than upset the planned schedule in any way. The danger of using this contingency allowance as a buffer for extravagance in progressing other planned promotions must be avoided. Use of the contingency fund should be subjected to the same justification, appraisal and measurement as other items in the budget.

The percentage growth section for each year is an indication of any increased expenditure through particular media but can also be used as a guide to increases in the rate card for some magazines or newspapers. This will, itself, justify an immediate investigation into the cost-effectiveness of that medium compared to others which may not have increased their rates to the same extent.

Figure 20.6   Advertising deployment

Deploying the advertising appropriation over time is finding the mid-point between product sales trends and media reading, viewing, or listening. Because the pattern of consumption may differ between product sales and media behaviour, it is necessary to equate the divergent trend lines. Clearly the purchasing cycle creates time lags between an effective communication and a consequent purchase, so the time period has to be adjusted in the calculations. This system may be used in conjunction with advertising expenditure planning.

Figure 20.7   Progress production record/ Press advertising monitor

It is not unusual for advertisers and advertising agencies to lose track of the detailed administration necessary to programme advertising campaigns properly. Often, at the last possible moment, a publication will remind its client that blocks are required urgently and it is at this point that everyone has to abandon other pressing tasks temporarily, in order to gather together, hastily, people responsible for copy, visualizing, artwork, photography and blockmaking. It is not surprising that campaigns developed in such a way tend to be ineffective. The only way in which this haphazard practice can be avoided is for each campaign to be planned well in advance with the individuals responsible clearly briefed and target dates set for work to be completed. Only by setting critical dates with properly recorded lead times for the preparation of material can full production and a progressing system be developed.

Each date can be carefully noted in the master record and a follow-up system introduced. The system recommended is the preparation of files numbered 1 to 31 with each number signifying the appropriate day of the month; each morning, before commencement of the day's activities, the documents for that particular day are extracted from the file and actioned as necessary. The master chart should be incorporated in the total marketing plan booklet, and, should any documents be required urgently, a check on the master record will indicate the date in the follow-up system to which the necessary documents relate.

If the function of advertising is to sell, effectiveness of advertising is to be related where possible to the achievement of its function. The monitor shown in part (b) of the illustration allows for analysis of enquiries received by publication with an indication of the status of the enquirer. Its particular significance is to indicate to a company the decision-maker in any particular enquiring company. Set against these enquiries are ratios for measuring the cost and effectiveness of queries produced. Some publications produce high enquiry responses but may be poor in conversion into orders, thus cost per order would be correspondingly high. This is the only true measure of cost-effectiveness for advertising purposes and is the best method of assessing the extent to which advertising improves sales performance.

Figure 20.8   Space records
Once a company starts to justify in detail its expenditure with any specific publication or medium, it often finds that its knowledge of the publication concerned is inadequate. Although the advertisement managers of publications are always willing to supply information and media planners of advertising agencies have much data available, the final responsibility for the selection of media must always rest with the executive in the company responsible for authorizing money spent on advertising. It is not enough for executives to plead that they rely upon the guidance of the agency, for some agencies will be biased towards their own vested interests as, in general, more money spent by their clients will mean a higher return for the agency concerned.

Agencies are also in business to make a profit and occasionally to the surprise of companies they recommend a higher level of expenditure than might be justified in the circumstances. In addition, media planners are visited by sales promotional executives from different publications, each of whom can produce plausible evidence that their publication will be more effective than others. To avoid such possibilities company executives should develop their own records based upon their own requirements and insert the information available from reliable sources according to their own definitions, or, at least, according to definitions which are strictly comparable, so eliminating as much bias as possible. The record card suggested in this illustration will help to ensure that unavoidable costs which may well be hidden in the information supplied are understood and agreed in advance. Detailed information may be obtained from *British Rate and Data* in London or from *Standard Rate and Data Services (SRDS)* in New York.

Figure 20.1

NBRS AVERAGE ISSUE READERSHIP

PRESS

Publication	Average Issue Readership All Adults %	Net Sales '000s	Page B/W £	Page Clr £	C/000 Circ. B/W £	C/000 Circ. Clr £
NATIONAL DAILIES						
Tabloids						
Daily Express	11	1879	16,170	44,000	8.61	23.42
Daily Mail	11	1808	16,632	33,250	9.20	18.39
Daily Mirror	20	3018	21,300	–	7.06	–
Daily Record	5(53)+	760	5,630	8,250	7.41	10.86
The Star	10	1438	8,820	23,000	6.13	15.99
The Sun	26	4079	23,562	–	5.78	–
Today	3	400*	3,600	7,600	9.00	19.00
Daily Mirror/Record	25	3804	26,120	–	6.87	–
Broadsheets						
Daily Telegraph	7	1179	22,400	–	19.00	–
Financial Times	2	183	17,472	21,870	95.48	119.51
The Guardian	4	506	14,000	18,150	27.67	35.87
The Times	3	475	11,500	–	24.21	–
NATIONAL SUNDAYS						
Tabloids						
Mail on Sunday	11	1624	15,300	–	9.42	–
News of the World	29	4954	24,549	–	4.96	–
Sunday Mail	6(55)+	838	5,500	9,710	6.56	11.59
Sunday Mirror	21	2998	22,770	–	7.60	–
Sunday Post	9(64)+	1482	5,814	–	3.92	–
Sunday Today	3	400*	3,900	8,300	9.75	20.75
The People	19	2983	19,570	–	6.56	–
Broadsheets						
The Observer	6	757	18,500	–	24.44	–
Sunday Express	15	2413	36,000	–	14.92	–
Sunday Telegraph	5	682	16,500	–	24.19	–
The Sunday Times	9	1200	28,000	–	23.33	–
LONDON EVENINGS						
The Standard	2 (14$)	505	6,650	9,900	13.17	19.60
COLOUR MAGAZINES						
Observer Colour Magazine	6	757	5,600	8,250	7.40	10.90
Sunday Times Magazine	9	1200	8,000	12,500	6.67	10.42
Sunday Express Magazine	14	2413	16,000	20,350	6.63	8.43
Sunday	27	4954	24,000	27,500	4.89	5.55
Telegraph Sunday Magazine	5	682	4,600	5,500	6.74	8.06
You	12	1624	7,675	10,900	4.73	6.71

PENETRATION OF VARIOUS MEDIA

	Qualifying Period	Adults %	Men %	+ Housewives %	Adults '16–24
PRESS*					
Publication group:					
Any National Morning	Yesterday	68	72	64	70
Any National Sunday	Past 7 days	75	77	72	76
Any General Weekly	Past 7 days	41	45	38	49
Any Women's Weekly	Past 7 days	26	9	35	31
Any General Monthly	Past 4 weeks	36	47	28	42
Any Women's Monthly	Past 4 weeks	32	18	39	38
TELEVISION*					
ITV-1	Past 7 days	93	93	96	89
Channel 4	Past 7 days	82	81	84	76
TV-am	Past 7 days	24	21	28	25
RADIO					
Any ILR	Past 7 days	35	39	31	46
Radio Luxembourg	Past 7 days	3	3	2	7
CINEMA	Past 6 months	24	25	19	55

* Based on average issue readership. Includes informants who read or looked at one or more publications in the group during the qualifying period. TV is based on March 1986 data
+ Male and Female Housewives

PROFILE OF AVERAGE AUDIENCE – ALL ADULTS

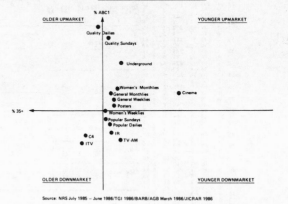

Source: NRS July 1985 – June 1986/TGI 1986/BARB/AGB March 1986/JICRAR 1986

Figure 20.2　　　　　　　　ANALYSIS OF TELEVISION VIEWING

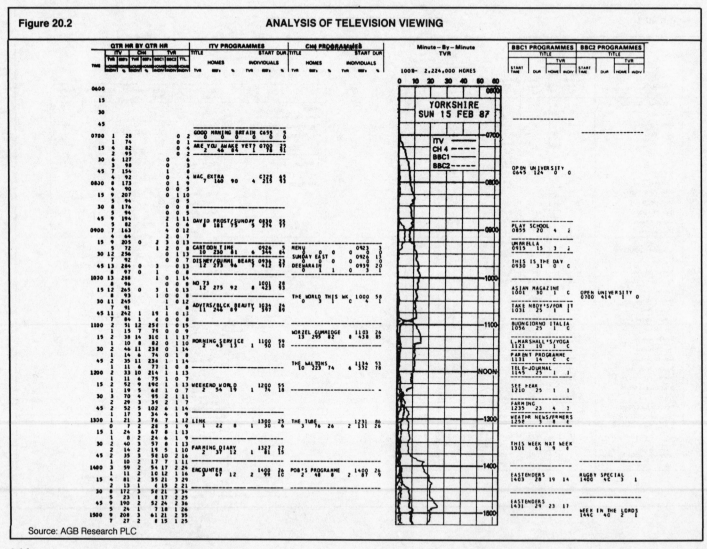

Figure 20.2 (concluded)   ANALYSIS OF TELEVISION VIEWING

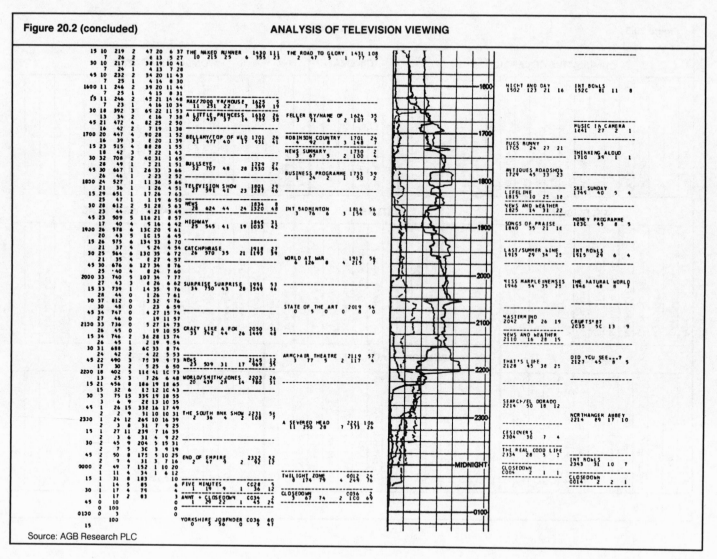

Source: AGB Research PLC

Figure 20.3

MEDIA ANALYSIS

CUMULATIVE COVERAGE

All women 1	3	6	ABC_1C_2 1	Women 3	6	15–34 1	Women 3	6	Single 1	Women 3	15–24 6	All housewives 1	3	6	Housewives 1	with children 3	0–15 6	

CINEMA

ITV area	Number of screens	Cost 1 week 30'			

WOMEN'S MAGAZINES

Frequency	Cover price	Total circulation	Readership adults	Women	H/W	Basic rates colour	Basic rates b/w	Copy dates colour	Copy dates b/w	Page type area mm	Readership age group	Readership soc grade							

TELEVISION

Area	Contractor	ITV homes	ITV homes with colour	Number 000's	Share of N/W%	Share of N/W 000's	Penetration %	AB	C_1	C_2	DE	16–34	35–44	45–54	55+	Cost

POSTERS

Area	BP PSCs standard	Units	Rate A month	Rate AA month	Rate AAA month	48 sheet units	Rate A month	Rate AA month	Rate AAA month

NATIONAL NEWSPAPERS

Publication	Cover price	Circulation 000's	Readership A 000's	Readership A %	Age profile 15–24	25–34	35–44	45–54	55–64	65+	Class profile AB	C_1	C_2	DE	Cost SCC	Cost page b & w		

RADIO

Area	Station	Sales	Area pop 15+ 000's	Reach weekly 000's	Reach weekly %	Prime segment max	Prime segment min	Average ½ hr reach	CPT Max	CPT Min		

GENERAL MAGAZINES

Publication	Circulation 000's	Readership A 000's	Readership A %	Sex profile M	Sex profile W	Sex profile H/W	Age profile 15–34	Age profile 35–54	Age profile 55+	Class profile ABC_1	Class profile C_2	Class profile DE	Page cost b & w	Page cost colour	

DEMOGRAPHICS

Adults 15+	Sex M/W/HW	000's	%	Age groups	000's	%	Social grades	000's	%	Standard regions	000's	%	ITV areas	Adults 16+	000's	%

SOURCES

Figure 20.4				APPROPRIATION ANALYSIS											

Prepared by:

Prior year actual		Current year. budget		Media	Plan year 1		Plan year 2		Plan year 3		Plan year 4		Plan year 5	
Value	%	Value	%		Value	%	Value	%	Value	%	Value	%	Value	%
				Established products New products Total										
				National dailies National Sundays Colour supplements Provincial press Consumer magazines Trade and technical press										
				Independent Television Channel 4 Cable Television Breakfast Television Satellite Television Community Television Teletext										
				Outdoor advertising Commercial radio Cinemas Directories Direct mail Sponsorship Sales literature Co-operative promotions										
				Total										
				Public relations Seminars Exhibitions Press Total										
				Agency charges										
				Budget total										

Figure 20.5   **(a) ADVERTISING/BUSINESS SYSTEMS MAILING/WEEKS**

	w/page	w/page (f/m)	⅔ page	½ page	½ page (f/m)	Week 1	Week 2	Week 3	Week 4	Response	Conversion	Remarks
J												
F												
M												
A												
M												
J												
JY												
A												
S												
O												
N												
D												
Cost												

(b) APPROPRIATION SCHEDULE

Prior year actual	Current year budget	Media	1	2	3	4	5	6	7	8	9	10	11	12
		Television												
		Press												
		Posters												
		Sales promotion												
		Public relations												
		Others												
		Totals												

Figure 20.6   ADVERTISING DEPLOYMENT

%	J	F	M	A	M	J	JY	A	S	O	N	D	%
20													20
18													18
16													16
14													14
12													12
10													10
8													8
6													6
4													4
2													2

	J	F	M	A	M	J	JY	A	S	O	N	D	
Product consumption	15	10	9	8	5	5	4	3	6	8	12	15	100%
Media consumption	16	11	9	7	5	4	3	2	5	8	13	17	100%
Product + Media consumption	31	21	18	15	10	9	7	5	11	16	25	32	200%
Mid-point	16	10	9	7	5	4	3	2	5	8	12	19	100%
Deployment of £100 000	16	10	9	7	5	4	3	2	5	8	12	19	£000's

Figure 20.7   **(a) PROGRESS PRODUCTION RECORD**

Publication	Product	Advertisement reference	Insertion date	Copy date	Press date	Proofs required	Voucher checked	Account agreed

(b) PRESS ADVERTISING MONITOR

Publication	Actual enquiries						Actual expenditure	Enquiries period circulation	Cost per 000's	Orders booked per thousand	Cost per order
	Board director	General manager	Department manager	Senior executive	Other	Total					

Figure 20.8
Date

SPACE RECORDS

Prepared by:

RECORD CARD

Publication _____

Address _____

_____

_____

Telephone _____

Contact _____

Copy _____weeks   Colour _____weeks

Classified _____weeks   Publication _____

Cancellation _____weeks

Date of latest rate card _____

Standard rates

	Page	Colour	Cover	Special
	½ page			
	¼ page			
	S C I			

Mechanical data

Type page size	Bleed plates
½ page	Column length
¼ page	Column width
Trim size	Number of columns
Portrait/landscape	Screen

ABC _____

Circulation _____

Readership _____

SIC	Readership		Circulation	
1				
2				
3				
4				
5				
6				
7				
8				
9				
10				
11				
12				
13				
14				
15				
16				
17				
18				
19				
20				
21				
22				
23				
24				
25				
26				

A		Region 1
B		Region 2
C_1		Region 3
C_2		Region 4
D		Region 5
E		Region 6

Figure 20.9   Percentage of population seeing an advertisement a number of times/Space register

As mentioned earlier, some of the principal advertising media provide their own reading and noting studies.

No matter how much information is obtainable about different publications, that information serves no useful purpose until it is analysed or used as a comparison against its counterparts. The common denominator of the advertising world is cost-effectiveness measured as either cost per single column cm or cost per thousand readership/viewers. While these are valuable guides, they give no indication about coverage by socio-economic groups, geographical area or vocation. Part (b) in this illustration allows for much more detailed information and makes direct comparisons between a number of publications, channels or stations which may be more easily related to the objectives of the company concerned. The illustration is intended to indicate the sort of information advertisers can use to justify their selection in each publication or channel.

Figure 20.9　　　　**(a)　PERCENTAGE OF POPULATION SEEING AN ADVERTISEMENT A NUMBER OF TIMES**

Number of occasions	ITV 1	ITV 2	ITV 3	ITV 4	ITV 5	ITV 6	ITV 7	ITV 8	ITV 9	ITV 10	ITV 11	ITV 12	ITV 13	ITV 14	ITV 15	Channel 4	Average frequency
1																	
2																	
3																	
4																	
5																	
6																	
7																	
8																	
9																	
10																	
Average																	

(b)　SPACE REGISTER

Publication	Circulation	Readership	Cost per single column cm	Cost per page	Cost per 000 circulation	Gross OTS	Average frequency	TVR homes	TVR housewives	GHI	Penetration	Profile	Cumulative index	Other	
1															
2															
3															
4															

21　Using Sales Promotion

While the main objective of all selling and advertising effort is to persuade people of the advantages of ownership and of the benefits its use will bring, sales promotional techniques have been used to incite people to buy and to buy now. So sales promotion has been used to supplement the process of advertising and to complement the selling procedure by reminding people, often at the critical decision-making stage, of the benefits of an immediate purchase. Advertising tends to be longer term and is a strategic activity, while sales promotion is short term and tactical.

Incentive marketing is the modern equivalent of sales promotion. It provides for increasing the value of a particular brand promotion at one point in time; it can tip the balance between indecision and a purchase. In its earlier days it gave the impression of bribery, and of inferior goods competing against well-established brands by cheap gifts or meaningless discounts.

Nowadays, incentive marketing is another marketing communications channel. While incentive marketing and advertising have many distinctions, they do have communications in common, with an objective devoted towards establishing a favourable impression of the product or brand concerned, whether real or to be perceived. In this sense the term 'incentive marketing' is already obsolescent.

As a marketing communications channel, it follows that a brand may be given an individuality, so separating it from its competitors. As marketing is concerned with establishing a particular identity for a brand, incentive marketing enables a manufacturer to develop one brand's distinction from others, providing a pre-determined image, and helping to cultivate a reputation monopoly. Ideally the advertiser will be showing that it is concerned about its customers, is anxious to provide value for money and is not just concerned about selling to them.

In many cases an incentive may be the provision of some related item, a premium, of sufficient attraction in its own right. Ideally the incentive will consist of an established branded product with a known selling price, although securing such a deal often cuts into the normal market for the premium, and suppliers are well aware of this situation.

Normally, an established company will allow such a deal if it is about to launch a new model or is discontinuing the line. Many successful incentive schemes have worked through the provision of a unique educational incentive: being able to identify an inexpensive package attractive to young and old alike, possibly from an encyclopaedia, and providing information necessary to make incentive marketing work.

Some of the more successful schemes have provided a wide range of uniquely related items, often for collection over time, and tied to continuing proof of purchases. Where possible, the goods will be consistent with the company image, so providing a continuing reminder of the brand while it is in use in the home.

Incentive marketing is therefore an aggressive or active promotional technique. It is used to stimulate demand pull or to initiate sales push. Promotions aimed at the consumer are expected to provide demand, while those aimed at the distributive trades are to gain dealer co-operation in display and selling effort. Combining a consumer and a dealer promotion often produces solid sales growth.

Competitions are considered to be a main contributory force to image building, and usually provide the opportunity to list brand or product benefits for consumers to study. They typify the pressure that may be applied to retailers both in brand selection and in product display.

Pricing promotions may be one of the oldest forms of incentive to purchase, but appropriately handled they may prove highly-effective. Often money-off offers may be matched by competition, and may still be at a price disadvantage compared to the retailer's own brand. To gain the maximum advantage, therefore, an advertiser will calculate the gross sum of savings for all consumers likely or possible during the promotion, and publicize that figure. It gives the impression of vast savings, with which consumers will identify, particularly if the savings are possible for a range of the advertiser's branded goods.

Alternatively, the advertiser may make an offer of a reduction on a subsequent purchase. As the number of people who make use of the offer is small relative to those who purchase because of the offer, it is possible to make a far greater reduction offer than is possible with a reduced price. A cut of 3p from the purchase price is snapped up by all buyers, whereas 9p off a later purchase may be taken by less than one-third of them, so that the cost will be less and the increase in sales volume from the promotion may be greater.

Incentive marketing is not solely an aggressive promotional tool but an invaluable defensive technique. It is capable of maintaining effective distribution, of retail display, and of countering attempts by retailers to confine stocks to their own label and that of the market leader. It may also be used to hold market share while alternative longer-term plans are being made.

Incentive marketing is not confined to the fast-moving goods industry. It is a technique available to industrial marketing organizations. The baker's dozen (13), quantity discounts, turnkey operations, seasonal gifts, special inducements, and credit dispensations are frequently used. There is much scope for further imaginative approaches.

Figure 21.1   Sales promotion objectives
The objectives listed in this illustration will normally be quantified so as to be consistent with objective formalization.

Figure 21.2   Types of sales promotion
This checklist of promotions provides a reminder of the range available to advertisers. It is comprehensive but features only those with proved value on a significant scale.

Figure 21.3   Sales promotion matrix
Monitoring the success of particular campaigns against specific objectives provides the foundations for sophisticated controls. Using formal documentation with all incentive promotions helps to ensure full integration with the other elements in the marketing plan.

Figure 21.4   Check-list for developing incentive marketing promotion
Although the promotional programme will be unique to each company, there are areas of activity which are common to many companies. The check-list shown in this diagram identifies the more usual information need required by a specialist consultancy. To arrive at good answers or solutions to company problems it is necessary to ask good questions. The brief will need to incorporate both questions and answers.

Figure 21.1   **SALES PROMOTION OBJECTIVES**

Consumer promotions	Trade and industrial promotions
Matching competition	Extending distribution network
Increasing amount of purchase	Meeting competitive activity
Combating 'own' labels	Stimulating distributor co-operation
Inducing immediate purchases	Overcoming seasonal fluctuations
Providing retailer sales push	Introducing new product
Stimulating demand pull	Opening new accounts
Retaining established customers	Increasing average value of order
Reaching specific markets	Prompting salesmen to sell full range
Extending effective distribution	Enlisting support from publicity
Overcoming seasonal patterns	Encouraging advance stock holding
Developing brand awareness	Gaining merchandising support
Controlling selling effort	Pushing supporting products
Acquiring market intelligence	Educating the trade
Inducing consumption of range	Reclaiming lost or dormant business
Evaluating media effectiveness	Securing media news coverage

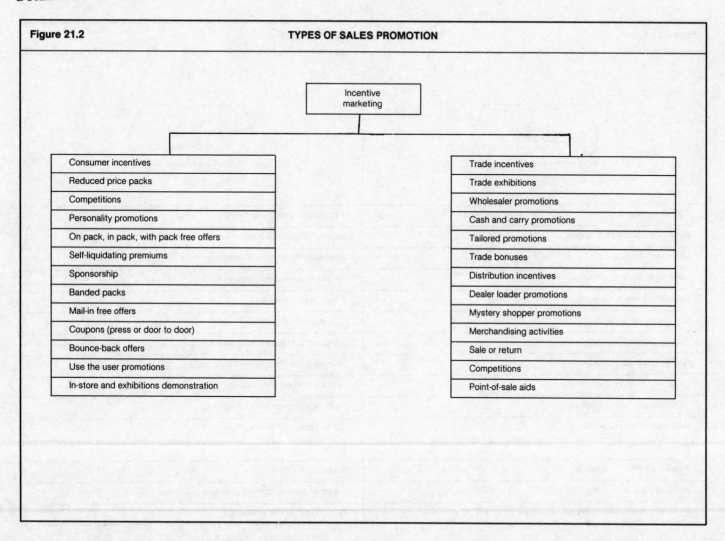

Figure 21.2   **TYPES OF SALES PROMOTION**

Incentive marketing

Consumer incentives
Reduced price packs
Competitions
Personality promotions
On pack, in pack, with pack free offers
Self-liquidating premiums
Sponsorship
Banded packs
Mail-in free offers
Coupons (press or door to door)
Bounce-back offers
Use the user promotions
In-store and exhibitions demonstration

Trade incentives
Trade exhibitions
Wholesaler promotions
Cash and carry promotions
Tailored promotions
Trade bonuses
Distribution incentives
Dealer loader promotions
Mystery shopper promotions
Merchandising activities
Sale or return
Competitions
Point-of-sale aids

Figure 21.3		SALES PROMOTION MATRIX											
Objective	Promotion	Competitions	Money-off purchase	Money-off vouchers	Personality promotions	Premium offers	Sampling	Self-liquidating	In-store	Banded pack	Advertising	Selling	Merchandising
To try the product													
To repeat purchase													
To build customer loyalty													
To increase consumption among users													
To stimulate immediate buying activity													
To incite consumer response													
To open new markets													

Figure 21.4	CHECK-LIST FOR DEVELOPING INCENTIVE MARKETING PROMOTION

Sales
promotion
brief

Brand name(s) of products, its pack and outer details

Brand pricing policy and how it matches competition

Promotional details of other known brands

Size of sales and merchandising, force and journey cycle

Promotional budget available

Profiles of existing consumers and target audience

Seasonal and/or regional variations in sales or distribution patterns

Media strategy and planned creative platform

Product limitations and particular brand benefits

Proposed duration of promotional campaign

Quantitative and qualitative objectives

Promotional background and consumption details

Figure 21.5   Conflicting objectives, manufacturer and retailer
Although the retailer is the normal sales outlet for branded goods manufacturers, it is not always appreciated that the particular objectives for each of the two parties are often in conflict. The diagram illustrates these conflicts. Incentive marketing promotions often provide the bridge between the two and help to bring about a co-ordinated effort of mutual benefit. Certainly retail co-operation in sales push brought about by manufacturers demand pull may cement a profitable relationship.

Figure 21.6   Selecting a premium gift
Many companies may be considering an incentive marketing promotion for the first time, and therefore a check-list of appropriate types of premium is included in this illustration. It is basic but reliable.

Figure 21.5   **CONFLICTING OBJECTIVES, MANUFACTURER AND RETAILER**

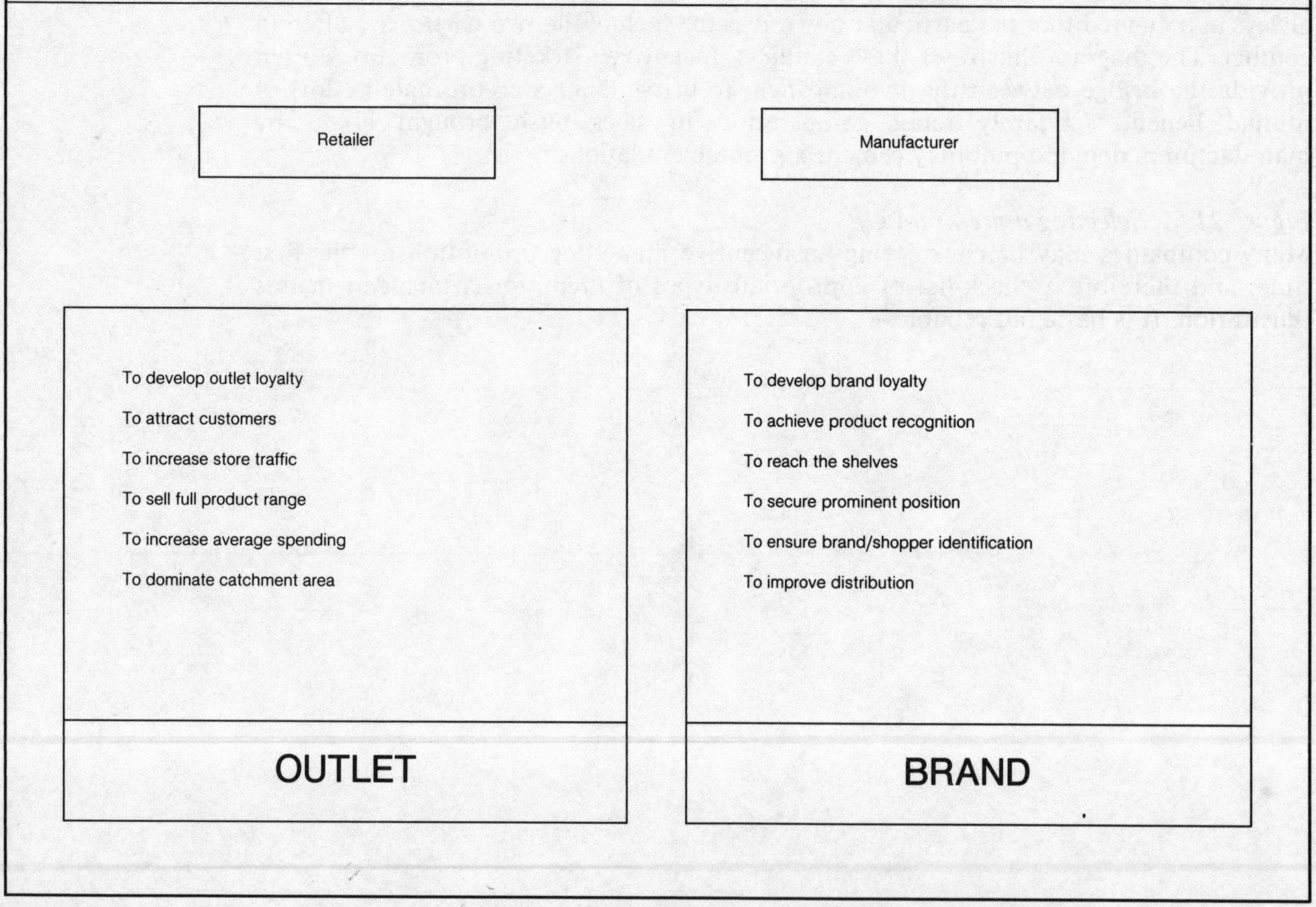

Retailer	Manufacturer

OUTLET	BRAND
To develop outlet loyalty	To develop brand loyalty
To attract customers	To achieve product recognition
To increase store traffic	To reach the shelves
To sell full product range	To secure prominent position
To increase average spending	To ensure brand/shopper identification
To dominate catchment area	To improve distribution

Figure 21.6	SELECTING A PREMIUM GIFT

THE PREMIUM CHECK-LIST

DOES IT HAVE EYE APPEAL?	A product attractive to the eye is essential at the point of sale
HAS IT BEEN NATIONALLY ADVERTISED?	A product with established consumer acceptance will be an aid to the promotion
IS IT OF EXCEPTIONAL VALUE?	A product should represent comparable value to other known brands
IS ITS USE WIDELY KNOWN?	A product well known and with simple method of application provides added value to the promotion
IS IT A HOUSEHOLD PRODUCT?	A product with housewife appeal is an established attraction in promotions
WILL IT ATTRACT TARGET AUDIENCE?	A product must be aimed at and attractive to the selected target audience
CAN IT BE HANDLED BY THE TRADE?	A product must be capable of easy and economical handling by the retail trade
WILL IT SUIT AS A BRAND REMINDER?	A product should be one suitable for constant use in the home, particularly the kitchen
IS IT SUITABLE FOR PUBLICITY?	A product must be such that it is easily advertised
ARE ADEQUATE SUPPLIES AVAILABLE?	A product must be readily available to match demand

22   Deploying Public Relations

Public relations activity is the means by which management secures eyes and ears in essential places and has a voice to express its view when sought or when considered appropriate. Public relations provides for open management. Supplying information on problems, lost business, limitations, and social welfare as well as achievements, new opportunities, aspirations and profits is the means by which companies establish credible images. Significantly, a company may be able to condition what is said about it. By making regular announcements about its development and proposed future actions the company may be able to avoid doubts or suspicions.

One of the most important roles of public relations is to provide a two-way communications link. Where a particular image is needed to reach a marketing objective, often at the cost of advertising expenditure, the public relations team will supply a monitor. The team collects media information on both the company and its industry, and feeds management with a full assessment of the results of the marketing effort. Should a change of direction become necessary, management will be able to respond to the need by distributing information through the various communications channels. So public relations executives gather information reflecting the company's image and disseminate supporting or countering information accordingly. In many cases a close relationship is established with the media, so that unfavourable news will be checked by journalists with the company executives. Where open management has been clearly established, mutual trust will result.

Often during difficult times certain marketing activities are hard to mount or to sustain; necessary price rises, increased advertising expenditure, rationing of scarce supplies, extensive promotions, extended delivery dates, credit control or debt collecting, and restrictions on new product development or the extension of customer services have to be explained fully to customers. Public relations executives secure the cooperation of the media in explaining the background to such marketing action and policies. Public relations is therefore an essential part of marketing practice.

In an age when consumerism is a constant source of pressure on politicians and legislators it is necessary for the voice of industry to provide a balance among views expressed. As both marketing and consumerism have common philosophies, it is often the route to providing satisfaction for society which causes dispute. Public relations efforts may therefore sway public opinion or information suggesting a change of direction by management. Either way, the company will be able to secure appropriate goodwill in the market-place. Public relations, however, has a positive role to play in the marketing programme.

In some notable cases a brand name is also the company's name. Media references to these companies have much the same significance as brand promotions and so provide an element of advertising in newscasting or reporting. Such companies are able to distribute news of a strictly factual nature without it being considered just a product puff.

In addition many companies are now sponsoring sporting events or cultural programmes, bringing an awareness of the name of the company to the community which helps to establish a favourable impression of that company's social awareness and participation. Similarly, some companies have found it necessary to publicize their technological progress or their contribution to economic or social development. They may advertise these achievements in order to ensure control of the wording and to guarantee repetition of the communication. This is advertising but it is aimed at public relations objectives. These advertisements may often come as a direct result of an earlier successful media information release.

Competitive homogeneous brands which vary little in price or usage are usually distinguished in the minds of consumers by the reputations of supplying firms. Public relations is a support to advertising action in promoting predetermined reputations and in the establishment of an advantageous image for a brand name. In many such cases, public relations actions are an integral part of the total marketing plan. In service organizations or industrial marketing firms where single assignments or contracts are secured it is often the firm with an established and approved reputation which receives the commission.

While dispute may arise as to which particular marketing or management activities are strictly public relations, it is appropriate to say that all business activities are subject to public scrutiny and equally therefore should be treated as subject to public relations coverage. PR, therefore, may act as a monitor on the course of management action.

Figure 22.1   Public relations objectives
Setting objectives is an essential feature of any marketing plan, and even a so-called abstract function such as public relations will conform to this principle. When formalized in this way, public relations ceases to be an intangible and uncontrollable activity. When operated on basic marketing principles of customer orientation and realistic employee or industrial relations it becomes as controllable as company brands or products, and so offers similar opportunities for acceptance through its own channels. The objectives shown in this illustration will normally be quantified in terms of the particular areas chosen for a particular campaign.

Figure 22.2   Public relations budget control
All marketing expenditure is an investment, and public relations activity is no exception. Preparing budgets in advance, appropriate to achievement of objectives contained within the marketing plan, provides for control of public relations performance. The information listed is provided as a check-list covering the normal budget items for this department. An attempt is also made to include hidden costs, so that a true picture of the function is shown.

Figure 22.3   Sources and impressions in an organization
Finding every opportunity for news coverage is the important role of public relations executives. Having to rely on information filtering through from other departments is unreliable and good opportunities may be missed. Publishing a list and gaining executive co-operation during planning time permits advance preparation and efficient control of resources. The list offered in this illustration has been compiled according to expressed interest of editors in media. They are keen to secure well-written, reliable news information for their readers' interest. Usually they want to publish or broadcast good stories as much as the originators want them to be published. Too often media information is of too poor a quality, both in content and presentation, for publication.

Figure 22.4   Publics for a PR campaign – motor cars
Identifying specific groups of influential people and maintaining contact is half the battle. In this illustration a list of publics is suggested for the motor-car industry to give

an indication of the breadth possible. Each firm preparing its marketing plan will identify its own appropriate contacts and set out to establish a mutual relationship. It should be recognized that feeding information to such persons or organizations imposes a responsibility on the firm to provide reliable and honest information. Furthermore, once established, the relation will be nourished only if the firm responds to the needs of the contact, respects its aims and policies, and co-operates on mutually beneficial projects. Seeking the advice of its contacts when formulating policy helps to ensure co-operation on implementation.

Figure 22.5   The communications network
The process of communications is often complex. Identifying the important issues and allowing for attitudes and motives of individuals in society enables a company to speak the language and to satisfy the latent needs of appropriate sections of the community.

Figure 22.6   The media in public relations/ The underlying role of mass media
Possibly the most neglected area in public relations activity is the media that carry the communications. Applying the marketing concept to public relations suggests that readers and viewers should be regarded as media consumers and the media owners as distributors of information. One must therefore discover what these consumers want and need and how they can be satisfied.

The vertical circulation publication is aimed at all levels within one or related industries while the horizontal is aimed at one level throughout all industry and commerce.

Part (b) illustrates the underlying role of mass media and originates from an IPC publication. It suggests the uses and gratifications of mass media. Understanding these distinctions enables the writer of media information to formulate ideas and to develop an appropriate central theme.

Figure 22.7   The rules for preparing media information
Media information is written for publication, and therefore needs to be fitted into the editorial format of the chosen medium and be of interest to its target audience. Editorial formats for publications are easy to identify, since practical specimens appear in each

issue. Making media information appealing to target audiences and, therefore, the media owner requires study of the chosen publications and the preparation of material accordingly.

The rules suggested in this illustration are those applicable to many types of media vehicles. Where any particular publication uses a different approach, then noting it and making necessary adjustments to particular releases increases publication opportunities. Issuing one standard release to all media according to these rules will increase press mileage, and issuing variations where appropriate will increase the rate of coverage by the media.

Figure 22.8   Communications selection
Certain types of news story are best handled in particular ways. The suggestions in this chart indicate the most favourable selections.

Figure 22.9   Opportunities in sponsorship
Sponsoring a major event or personality provides access to those people who do not give much time to the commercial media. Indirect promotion is possible when normal sales resistance is low and people are relaxed. The best investment is that made in instances where universal acclaim has not yet been attained. Sponsoring a future star through a contract can bring a substantial promotion for a modest sum. Investing in several which are 'on the fringe', even if only one makes the grade, is still a sound proposition.

Figure 22.1   **PUBLIC RELATIONS OBJECTIVES**

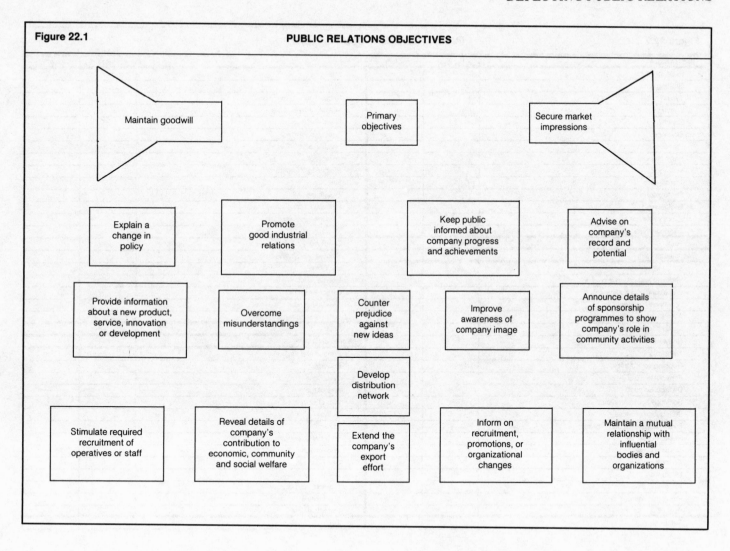

Figure 22.2			PUBLIC RELATIONS BUDGET CONTROL		
Media release	Budget	Actual	Exhibitions	Budget £/$	Actual £/$
Executive time			Space		
Drafting fees			Stand		
Typing			Decorating and materials		
Printing			Maintenance and cleaning		
Paper			Freighting outwards		
Envelopes			Freighting inwards		
Postage			Loading and unloading		
Hand delivery			Installation		
Mailing list			Freighting literature		
Translations			Electricity		
Photographs			Telephone		
Enclosures			Personnel travel subsistence		
Clipping service			Personnel accommodation		
Telephone charges			Photography		
Total			Direct mailing		
Documentary film			Related advertising time		
Script-writing fees			Staff time		
Shooting and sound recording			Executive time		
Processing and editing			Exhibition clothing		
Location expenses			Hired personnel		
Actors', commentators' fees			Lost sales during exhibition		
Music composition			Total		
Copyright fees			Press conference		
Translations			Printing and stationery		
Dubbing sound-track			Postage		
Print costs			Telephone		
Distribution costs			Hire of room		
Bookings administration			Hire of equipment		
Distribution services			Buffets		
Film maintenance and repairs			Drinks		
Preview costs			Media releases and press packs		
Media release			Photography		
Advertising			Samples		
Direct mail			Identification badges		
Accommodation costs			Captions and displays		
Projection charges			Electricity		
Executive time			Executive time		
Total			Total		

Figure 22.3	SOURCES AND IMPRESSIONS IN AN ORGANIZATION

SOURCES OF AN INDUSTRIAL OR COMMERCIAL NEWS STORY

1	An important development of an existing product or service	16	Technical developments
2	Company awards	17	Participation in exhibitions – home and overseas
3	Use of the product by some personality or prestige installation	18	Management and staff changes
4	Anniversaries	19	A new use for an existing product
5	Sponsored events in conjunction with other organizations	20	Promotions and achievements by employees
6	Important price changes	21	Extensions to existing factories and offices
7	New advertising campaigns, packs and promotions	22	Speeches and appearances by management
8	Trade mission participation	23	How local events will affect the company
9	Additions to an existing range of products or services	24	New factories or offices
10	Dealer and stockist promotions	25	Large and unusual orders – home or export
11	An ingenious method of meeting some unusual demands	26	Long service awards and retirements
12	New production plant	27	Business visits overseas by management
13	How national and world events will affect the company	28	New product or service
14	Production records	29	Appointment of agents home or overseas
15	Company charity educational sponsorships and awards	30	Sponsored events and competitions

SOURCES OF IMPRESSIONS IN PUBLIC RELATIONS

Advertising	Press reports
Television coverage	Radio coverage
Corporate image	House style
Van livery	Buildings
Offices	Products
Photographs	Publications
Exhibitions	Conferences
Promotions	Sponsored events

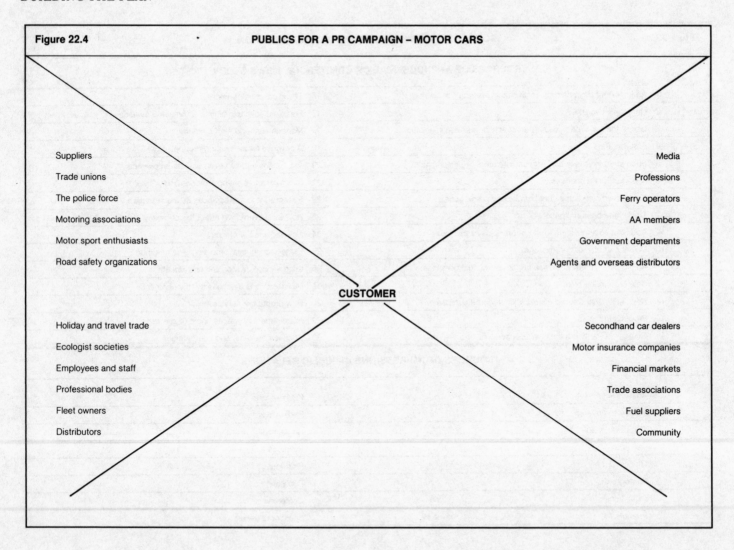

Figure 22.4   ·   **PUBLICS FOR A PR CAMPAIGN – MOTOR CARS**

Suppliers

Trade unions

The police force

Motoring associations

Motor sport enthusiasts

Road safety organizations

Media

Professions

Ferry operators

AA members

Government departments

Agents and overseas distributors

CUSTOMER

Holiday and travel trade

Ecologist societies

Employees and staff

Professional bodies

Fleet owners

Distributors

Secondhand car dealers

Motor insurance companies

Financial markets

Trade associations

Fuel suppliers

Community

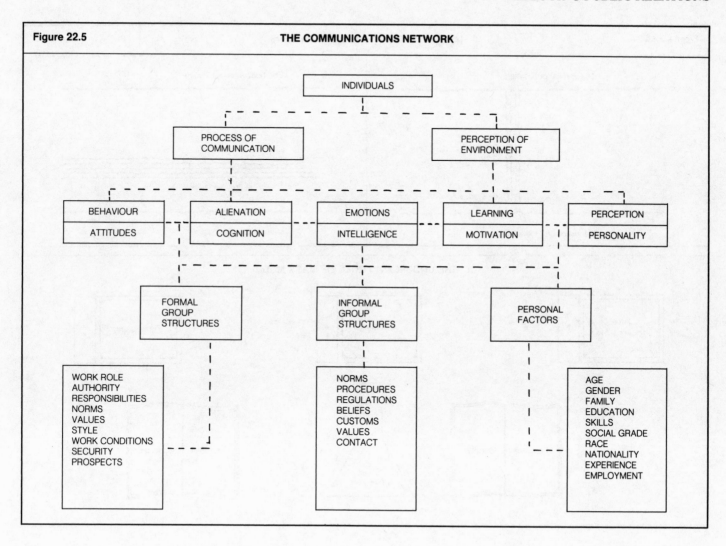

Figure 22.5 — THE COMMUNICATIONS NETWORK

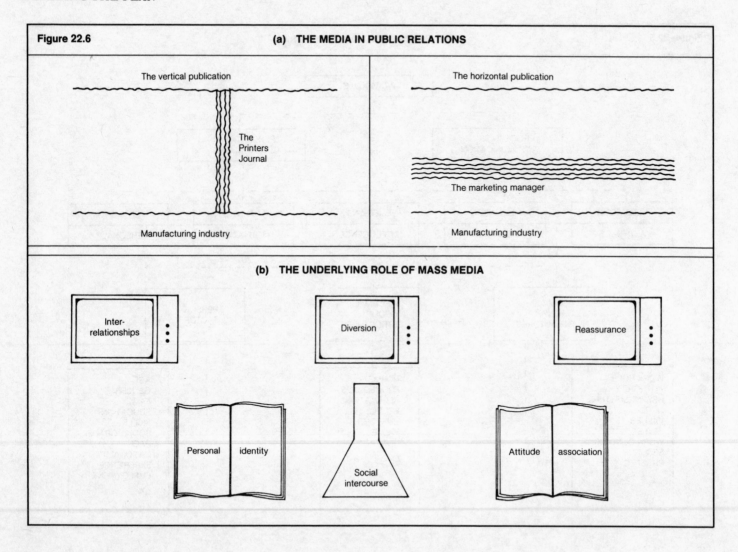

Figure 22.6

(a) THE MEDIA IN PUBLIC RELATIONS

The vertical publication

The horizontal publication

The
Printers
Journal

The marketing manager

Manufacturing industry

Manufacturing industry

(b) THE UNDERLYING ROLE OF MASS MEDIA

Inter-
relationships

Diversion

Reassurance

Personal   identity

Social
intercourse

Attitude   association

Figure 22.7   **THE RULES FOR PREPARING MEDIA INFORMATION**

Media information	
Marketing Planning Ltd	
Paper size	International A4 210mm × 297mm (8¼" × 11¾")
Identification	Name, address, telephone number, further information
Title	Simple, identity central theme
Underlining	Do not use at all
Margins	1½" (38mm) either side of text
Indentation	No indentation at start, three spaces after
Spacing	Double space typing essential
Sub-headings	Avoid if possible
Carry-over of text	Use only one side of paper; do not run over mid paragraph. Use 'more' and 'ends'
Continuation sheets	Repeat title; number 1 of 1; 2 of 3 etc.
Names of persons	Use first or forenames as well as surnames
Company and brand names	Avoid capitals or quotation marks
Date	Use as current media style
Reference number	Use reference number
Embargo procedure	Avoid where possible
Captions – affixing	Attach to bottom of picture
Captions – title	Use as news – release
Captions – lead-in	Relate to text in news – release
Captions – picture shows	Paragraph beginning picture shows . . . .
Source and date	Name, address, telephone, date
Negative number	Provide reference number
Copyright	Provide any stipulations

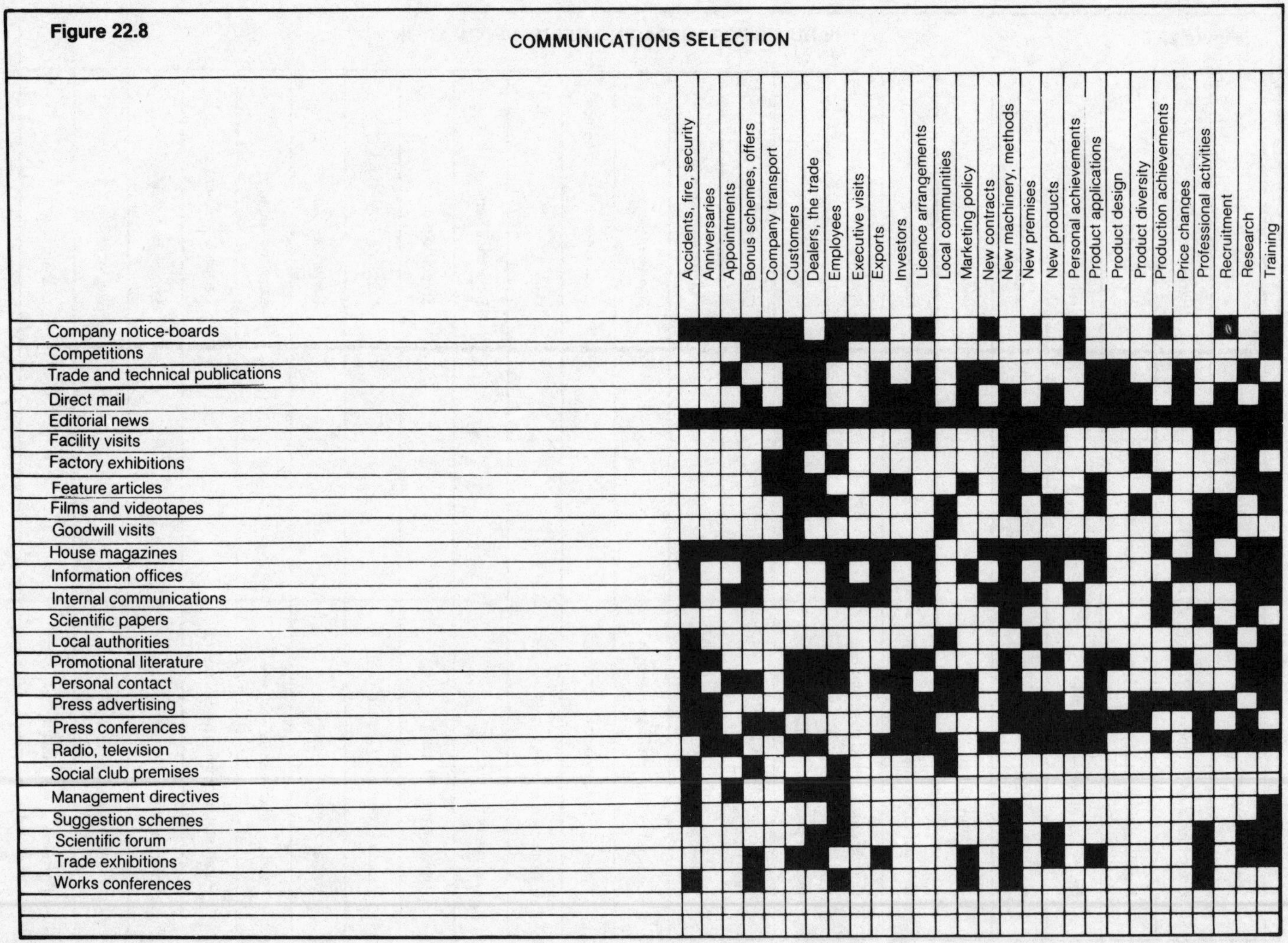

Figure 22.8

COMMUNICATIONS SELECTION

Column headers:
- Accidents, fire, security
- Anniversaries
- Appointments
- Bonus schemes, offers
- Company transport
- Customers
- Dealers, the trade
- Employees
- Executive visits
- Exports
- Investors
- Licence arrangements
- Local communities
- Marketing policy
- New contracts
- New machinery, methods
- New premises
- New products
- Personal achievements
- Product applications
- Product design
- Product diversity
- Production achievements
- Price changes
- Professional activities
- Recruitment
- Research
- Training

Row labels:
- Company notice-boards
- Competitions
- Trade and technical publications
- Direct mail
- Editorial news
- Facility visits
- Factory exhibitions
- Feature articles
- Films and videotapes
- Goodwill visits
- House magazines
- Information offices
- Internal communications
- Scientific papers
- Local authorities
- Promotional literature
- Personal contact
- Press advertising
- Press conferences
- Radio, television
- Social club premises
- Management directives
- Suggestion schemes
- Scientific forum
- Trade exhibitions
- Works conferences

SPONSORED SPORT (UK)					% PROFILE	CONNECTION
Figure 22.9		**OPPORTUNITIES IN SPONSORSHIP**				
Angling	Archery	Association football	Athletics	Badminton		Obvious link with chosen sport
Ballooning	Baseball	Basketball	Billiards and snooker	Bowls		Audience identification
Boxing	Canoeing	Chess	Cricket	Curling		Geographic link
Cycling	Darts	Equestrianism	Fencing	Gliding		Potential television coverage
Golf	Greyhound racing	Gymnastics	Hang-gliding	Hockey		Potential press coverage
Horse-racing	Lacrosse	Land yachting	Lawn Tennis	Motor sport		Potential radio coverage
Netball	Orienteering	Parachuting	Powerboat racing	Rowing		Indirect association with related activities
Rugby League	Rugby Union	Sailing	Shooting	Skiing		Employee link
Speedway	Squash	Surfing	Swimming	Table Tennis		Transference towards corporate image
Tennis/ Rackets	Ten-pin bowling	Volleyball	Water skiing	Weightlifting		Reaching minority segments

23　Realizing Plans

The need for improved efficiency and the constant search for improved productivity have long been accepted for manufacturing processes in industry. A similar need has been recognized for some time in the marketing function, but has never been resolved satisfactorily because of the difficulties in developing and applying accounting principles to a business activity which is considered part art and part science. Although many marketing activities operate under disciplines not widely appreciated, let alone understood, by management, the practice of marketing is still an investment in company resources and, if control is to be maintained, will be subject to the same accounting appraisal as any other form of investment. In using the principles and charts set out in this book, it is possible for various costs to be collated and analysed so that the expenditure on marketing activities and their effects upon profitability can be ascertained. Activities are shown by customer and by products, some of which may prove unprofitable on investigation.

If stock levels are controlled with great accuracy the cost of handling orders of various sizes can be ascertained. It may be more profitable to refuse orders below a certain uneconomic level. Such selective selling often increases profitability. The location of warehouses, the planning of sales territories and the routes of salesmen can be planned, based on accurate cost statistics rather than by intuition. Improved direction and supervision of salesmen by the setting of performance and activity targets can increase selling and operating efficiency.

Management of many businesses is unable to recognize that its products or service are mediocre and sometimes inferior. Where such blindness exists the company is unlikely to introduce methods or procedures which would help to rectify or overcome the problem.

Technological change is causing a greater demand for information to be employed in decision-making. As companies grow, investment decisions become vast and more complex and the executive must endeavour to forecast growth potential and factors likely to influence the company's penetration of that potential, in an effort to reduce the risk facing every business enterprise. In marketing there has long been a need to concentrate information into quantitative and yet practical forms, to provide the basis for a company's marketing information system and to help ensure more effective marketing control and the development of increased profit opportunity. The effect of marketing planning and the integration of the marketing *function* into proper accounting procedures is intended to produce a higher return than would be possible in totalling the performance of the constituent parts.

Companies should be able to state the influences on their main activities and how they are being controlled to the benefit of the total organization. They should be able to assess the extent to which the information provided is relevant to current management needs. Executives need to eliminate unused material being prepared and to discover additional information. Such research into the marketing effort will help to ensure that the most economic level of expenditure is being maintained. For marketing, planning and control will help to reduce misdirected effort in all promotional activities by selective selling policies and the concentration of publicity, energy and expense, thus reducing the actual cost of producing and selling goods. Appropriate marketing policies should ensure that all products are developed according to market needs and resources are not wasted on products unsatisfactory in the market-place.

The recent change of emphasis to impersonal selling techniques, such as advertising, is one of the more important developments in marketing consumer goods. However, personal selling still has an important role in industrial marketing. Improvement in the function and performance of industrial sales forces justifies more attention than is now necessary in the consumer goods selling effort. Unless they are given adequate direction, salesmen cannot be expected to sell the ideal product mix nor can they, without guidance, differentiate between products when considering profitability. The level of profit responsibility must be not only decided but widely communicated, to ensure satisfactory implementation of the most critical of business activities.

The marketing plan and all documents ancillary to the plan must be used by executives as a day-to-day evaluation control and development manual. Every effort should be made to avoid treating the planning process as a once-a-year political exercise which is suffered by busy executives performing other tasks. Planning, organization, direction and control are the basic jobs of management; in a successful marketing-orientated company they will fill the working day of the management. Each manager must understand the interactive nature of the individual tasks which have to be completed during each period of the marketing plan. The timing of each step, at all levels and in each function, is critical if the total plan is to be satisfactorily co-ordinated and the anticipated results achieved. A flexible attitude to planning principles must be adopted so that management recognizes the need for contingencies and the control of these within corporate strategy. Unforeseen events often create a different scale of priorities; flexibility in the interpretation of policy as provided for in the plan must be recognized if the company's interests are to be best served. Monitoring actual performance against forecasts has a definite value in personal development and in operating efficiency, as does the preparation of forecasts itself.

In every marketing-orientated company, final responsibility for marketing policies remains with the chief executive. The marketing manager of any company provides advice in the field of marketing and may well carry a line responsibility, but if the marketing concept is to be adopted the entire company, and in particular the management team, must be devoted to its customers' satisfaction.

In the immediate future, most businesses will increasingly become involved with computerization. Even if not directly involved as users, companies will become affected by the use to which suppliers, competitors and even customers have become enmeshed with electronic data processing. It is essential that marketing staff should see how the computer is applied to marketing problems. They need some appreciation of the effects of computers on present-day and future marketing decisions. At present, management has tended to utilize computers for administration and control because they are close to the accounting function. Little use of data processing techniques has been made in decision-making because they often involve operational research techniques.

The introduction of the personal computer is bringing about a revolution in data storage and use. Marketing executives are beginning to use desk-top machines to process operational data. Some are having success in planning for future performance, often with simulated models, and they are assessing opportunities, analysing cash flows, measuring profit potential, and exercising controls. Using built-in programs they can undertake complex mathematical calculations without having to learn appropriate mathematical skills. They choose the right technique, input the required data and obtain the conclusions needed for decisions.

A number of manufacturers provide ranges of software while specialist suppliers are offering increasingly sophisticated packages. During the next few years many of the planning guides contained in this edition will be incorporated into software programs, making the planning process easier to implement (see Figure 23.1).

Figure 23.1   Personal computer data printout
In this chart are a selection of printouts from a Pegasus Software Ltd package, involving eight modules: sales ledger, purchase ledger, nominal ledger, invoice/sales order processing, stock control, payroll, job costing and bill of materials, together with two complementary programs, the report generator and information manager.

A need for a basic change in accounting procedure is becoming apparent. Inflation accounting has its supporters but this is only a step in a new direction. Marketing expenditure is a business investment, it brings short, medium, and long-term returns but is usually treated as a short-term expense. Charging the expenditure as an expense brings short-term advantages in taxation but distorts the balance sheet. Even a liquidated company leaves behind an unrealizable asset – its market connection.

Whilst governments may not be willing to allow marketing expenditure to be treated like tangible assets for taxation purposes, they do not stop companies producing internal accounts on the investment nature of its expenditure, using discounted cash-flow techniques, showing therefore a more realistic appraisal of its value to the company. Another advantage to the company executive is that it reduces the amount of current expenditure in the books, indicates a more realistic profit, and increases the real worth of the company. For functional executives it encourages necessary expenditure for future growth, rather than limiting current expenditure to a level consistent with current revenue. The present accounting procedure encourages attention to what is acceptable rather than what is appropriate for now *and the future*. In marketing planning the company is dealing with now *and* the future. In the marketing plan the *market connection is given an asset value.*

Figure 23.1   **PERSONAL COMPUTER DATA PRINTOUT**

Date 07/04/87   Marketing Output Budget Matrix   Page 1

Mission	Marketing	Production	Research	Personnel	Mission Budget
01 Electrical Parts Mission	80000	10000	25000	35000	150000
02 Industrial Engines Mis.	75000	160000	60000	70000	365000
03 O.E.C. Systems Mission	80	120000	20000	60000	200080
04 Aerospace Supply Mission	25000	37000	12000	35000	109000
05 Univ. Installations Mis.	10000	24000	8000	20000	62000
06 Corporate Support Mission	10000	5000	2500	9000	26500
07 C.S.C. Development Mis.	45000	125000	30000	40000	240000
08 B.P.C. Systems Mission	12000	23000	7500	27000	69500
09 Project Sales Mission	35000	110000	30000	170000	345000
10 AT Resource Div. Mission	21000	80000	7000	45000	153000
Functional Budgets:	313080	694000	202000	511000	

Market share analysis computing companies

% share × 10

Legend: Software, Hardware, Services

Company 1, Company 2, Company 3, Company 4

Electro-Systems International p.l.c.

07.04.87   ABC Analysis of Stock   Page 1

Stock Code	Units Used	Units %	Turnover	Turnover %
205	600.00	.59	40800.00	20.40
203	3000.00	2.97	35400.00	17.70
208	500.00	.50	28800.00	14.40
201	1400.00	1.39	28000.00	14.00
202	25000.00	24.75	22500.00	11.25
209	10000.00	9.90	17500.00	8.75
206	4000.00	3.96	12000.00	6.00
210	40000.00	39.60	7600.00	3.80
204	6500.00	6.44	5200.00	2.60
207	10000.00	9.90	2200.00	1.10

Electro-Systems International p.l.c.

07.04.87   Usage/Turnover Report–Stocks   Page 1

Stock Code	Annual Usage (units)	Unit Costs	Annual Turnover
201	1400.00	20.000	28000.00
202	25000.00	.900	22500.00
203	3000.00	11.800	35400.00
204	6500.00	.800	5200.00
205	600.00	68.000	40800.00
206	4000.00	3.000	12000.00
207	10000.00	.220	2200.00
208	500.00	57.600	28800.00
209	10000.00	1.750	17500.00
210	40000.00	.190	7600.00
	101000.00		200000.00

Source: Pegasus Business Software.

Figure 23.2   Major action programme

In a properly co-ordinated management policy programme each planned activity must have direct and indirect consequences on all other planned activities. Eventually all management actions are interrelated and it is imperative that every task assigned to individual managers should have a clearly specified time of action and established completion date. Even senior managers need the discipline of an agreed deadline date for the finalization of reports and project activities. By including major management actions in the marketing plan, other managers become aware of the activities of their colleagues and will be able to see the effects of each other's activities on all other functions as a clear policy of objectives is established and co-ordinated. Ideally, a standby should be nominated for each task, reducing to a minimum any delay caused by the nominated executive becoming ill or being otherwise indisposed. It will not be necessary for the standby to become involved to the same extent as the nominated executive, but the person would simply be kept informed and be provided with up-to-the-minute reports on progress.

Figure 23.3   Performance barometer

An essential early warning signal for eventual sales performance can be provided by establishing the relationships between enquiries, quotations, orders and sales at the time of developing objectives. Normally, for most companies, there is a time-lag between the receipt of an enquiry and the conversion to sales. If time periods can be established by products for each of these steps from enquiry to sale, it is possible to provide early warning of sales volume according to the time-lag. If enquiries during one period achieve only 80 per cent of forecast, then, without remedial action or change in conversion, sales to 80 per cent of forecast will be achieved. Indications in advance of sales shortfall give management the opportunity to investigate quickly a cause and take any necessary action to rectify the situation and, where possible, to concentrate effort in order to either shorten the normal time-lag or to improve the conversion ratios.

Ideally, remedial action should be incorporated into the plan from the outset and implemented as soon as justified according to terms specified in the plan.

| Figure 23.2 Date | | | MAJOR ACTION PROGRAMME | | | | | | | | | | | Prepared by | | | | | |

MAJOR ACTION PROGRAMME

Manager	Stand by	Action and completion date																
															Following year			
		Jan	Feb	Mar	Apr	May	Jun	Jul	Aug	Sep	Oct	Nov	Dec	¼	½	¾	1
Marketing manager							Revise marketing strategy programme										
Publicity manager			Prepare new sales literature														
Marketing research manager						Research market by SIC											
Sales manager										Report new sales office location							
Customer service manager			Develop new progressing system														
Product line manager						Produce new product programme											
Field sales manager												Write new sales manual					
Branch manager			Recommend new journey cycles														
Personnel manager								Select staff with management potential									

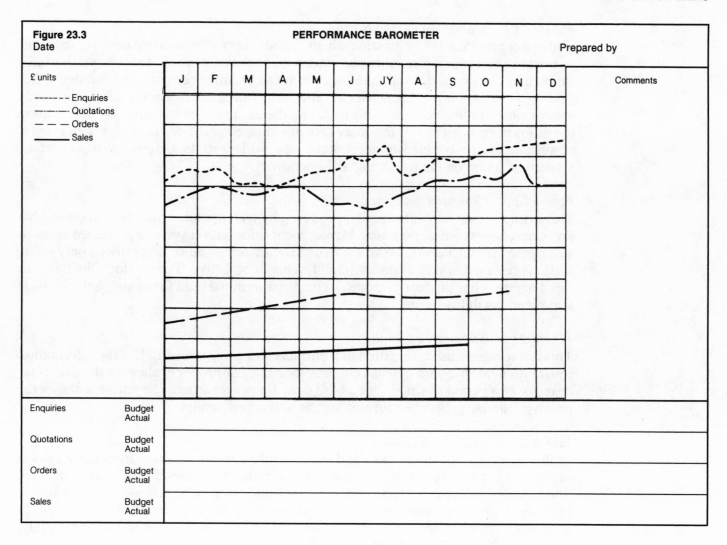

Figure 23.3
Date

PERFORMANCE BAROMETER

Prepared by

£ units

------- Enquiries
-·-·-·- Quotations
- - - Orders
——— Sales

	J	F	M	A	M	J	JY	A	S	O	N	D	Comments

Enquiries	Budget	
	Actual	
Quotations	Budget	
	Actual	
Orders	Budget	
	Actual	
Sales	Budget	
	Actual	

Figure 23.4   Management results ratios
This is a comprehensive illustration which includes far more standard controls than will be used by most companies. Although extensive, however, it is only a representative indication of the many guides and monitors which can be introduced into the company. The guiding principle for any management ratio is the fullest consideration of the standards against which ratios are to be compared, and the use to which management can employ the ratios in carrying out its everyday task of management. The chart suggested is most significant to the company's accountant who will need to determine the effect of marketing action on the total company operation.

Figure 23.5   Computer printout
There is no reason why information produced by a computer should be indecipherable for management control purposes. Management information systems processed through a computer are intended to be an aid to decision-making and should provide only information presented in such a way as to fulfil its major objective. The printout illustrated in this diagram is one produced through a computer terminal used for its simplicity in operation, and flexibility in use.

Figure 23.6   Summary of results
This is a comprehensive valuation of a business as a going-concern. It is the information sought for a takeover bid or by a company 'doctor'. For proper evaluation the data is indexed over a period of time, with a base date 3/5 years earlier. The variance shows the relative differences between current budget and actual results.

Figure 23.7   Profit performance
In this chart secured future sales and secured future profit resulting from these sales is identified, but as a result of past and current marketing expenditure. It indicates the future return from the market connection. Initially, it may be difficult to assess but an analysis of time-lag following earlier promotions up to the point where sales begin to drop will indicate recent short-term promotional investment – all other continuing sales are the result of past investment over time.

Figure 23.4 Date	Operating profit/ operating assets	Operating profit/ sales %	Sales/operating assets (times per year)	Production costs of sales	Distribution and marketing costs	General and administration costs	Materials costs	Works labour costs	Other production costs	Operating assets	Current assets	Fixed assets	Stocks	Work in progress	Debtors	Land, buildings	Plant, machinery equipment, vehicles
MANAGEMENT RESULTS RATIOS — Prepared by																	
Ratios																	
Return on assets																	
Profit margin on sales																	
Turnover of assets																	
Departmental costs % of sales																	
Production costs % of sales value of production																	
General asset usage £s per £1000 of sales																	
Current asset usage £s per £1000 of sales																	
Fixed asset usage £s per £1000 of sales																	

Figure 23.5   **COMPUTER PRINTOUT**

```
DEBTORS SCHEDULE CLIENT 6009 CENTREBROOK INDUSTRIES                          STATEMENT DATE 31/ 3/80 PAGE 12
                                                                            RUN DATE      13/ 4/80

CUSTOMER NO  CUSTOMER NAME    TURNOVER  CREDIT  T                                                      FLAGS
                             THIS      ALLOWED C  TOTAL   ************* AGED DEBT *************    A V T
                             YEAR         M      OWING   THIS PERIOD  1 PERIOD  2 PERIODS 3 PERIODS+ C A I
                                       VALUE E                                                        T L M
             97985  ROSE HOLLAND    296    200 2   197.78   123.34    74.44      -        -
             98531  J G SMYTHE      190    250 2      -        -        -        -        -           5
             98566  SPEARMAN       3974   4000 3  3072.86   1474.06   500.00   701.07   397.73       *
             98582  THAMES VALE     122    250 2   121.45    57.54    63.91      -        -
             98590  TORSON SAILS   5340   2000 3  1701.00   733.32   449.28   518.40     -
             98612  TRADERS         549    250 2   548.99   548.99      -        -        -          *
             98620  USEFUL CO        80     50 1    63.44    27.86    35.58      -        -          * *
             98655  VICEROY ASSOC   814    650 3   323.27   219.11      -      104.16     -
             98663  VICTORY CLEAN  1364    700 2   698.82   600.04    98.78      -        -
             98671  WALLACES        172    450 2    64.05    64.05      -        -        -
             98736  WHITEWAYS      3966   1100 3  1030.21   227.40      -      606.41   196.40       *
             98752  WILLIAMS BROS   320    859 2   320.16      -        -        -      320.16     *  *
             98768  WORDSWORTHS    2856   1000 2   674.12   279.86   394.26      -        -
             98795  YOUNG & CO      891    703 2   221.28   104.16   117.12      -        -
             98809  ZENITH FARMS    474    250 3   155.29    53.20    41.39    47.12     6.42-

             TOTAL DR           86.854          26.929.23  7.434.52 5.186.73 5.976.27 8.331.71
PERCENTAGE OF TOTAL DEBT                                     27.6%    19.3%    22.2%    30.9%
             TOTAL CR                           1.010.88-   350.44-  145.63-  272.28-  242.53-

             FINAL TOTAL                       25.918.35
                                                         06009/050/00012


CLIENT 2682 TAB NO 1 CENTREBROOK INDUSTRIES LIMITED                          DATE 11/01/80 PAGE 1
                                        PURCHASE DAY BOOK
                      INTERNAL                      VAT      THIS MONTH            YEAR TO DATE
TRANSACTION TYPE      DOC.REF.  SUPPLIER  DD MM YY CODE   DR/CR    VAT/DISC     DR/CR      VAT/DISC
INVOICES        E  6583  MONUMENT      27 03 80 15    98.78     12.88
                   6584  ROPERS        01 04 80 15  1.376.77   179.58
                   6585  BEARING SERV. 01 04 80 00   808.05
                   6586  BADDELEY      12 04 80 15   284.93     37.68
                   6587  BADDELEY      09 04 80 15   209.68     27.35
                   6588  BIRD STEVENS  14 04 80 15    55.00      7.17
                   6590  MONUMENT      11 04 80 15   526.60     68.69
                   6591  FDK FIELDS    16 04 80 98    13.59

       TOTAL E                                     3.377.40    333.35   18.913.44   1.931.40

JOURNAL CREDITS H  107   CALOR GAS     16 04 80      50.50
                   108   HEBON         16 04 80      10.00

       TOTAL H                                       60.50               423.57

JOURNAL DEBITS  J  107   CALOR GAS     16 04 80      50.50-
                   108   I C I         16 04 80      10.00-

       TOTAL J                                       60.50-              423.57-

CREDIT NOTES    P  78641 CALOR GAS     17 04 80 15   47.01-      6.13-
                   78642 AIR PRODUCTS  31 03 80 15  321.41-     41.92-
                   78643 ARCSPEED      01 04 80 15   34.20-      4.46-
                   78644 AIR PRODUCTS  01 04 80 15   59.75-      7.79-

       TOTAL P                                      462.37-     60.30-   1.757.00-    349.74-

CASH PAID       T  270895 ALL-STAR     02 04 80      87.10-      2.19-
                   270896 E C G D      02 04 80     809.25-
                   270897 AUTO CATERING             55.62-      1.39-
                   270898 B MATHIESON  02 04 80     494.20
                   270899 HEBON        03 04 80      29.48-
                   270900 MONUMENT     03 04 80     981.36-     49.06
                   270901 ROPERS       03 04 80     612.17-      7.65-
                   270902 BIRD STEVENS 07 04 80      55.00-

       TOTAL T                                    3.127.78-     55.29-  13.436.55-    237.74-

GRAND TOTAL                                         209.75-    217.76    3.719.89    1.343.92
```

Figure 23.6 **SUMMARY OF RESULTS**

OBJECTIVES	INDEX Budget	INDEX Actual	VARIANCE Budget	VARIANCE Actual
Corporate: P/E ratio				
Return on investment				
Capital appreciation				
Financial: Costs ratio				
Credit control				
Cash flow				
Manpower: Management results				
Labour productivity				
Training input				
Marketing: Market share				
Marketing costs				
Profit contribution				
Sales: Sales revenue				
Sales volume				
New products				
Selling: Order values				
Cost per call				
New accounts				
Advertising: Market awareness				
Market penetration				
Market franchise				
Pricing: Price elasticity				
Competitive ranking				
Promotional discounts				
Distribution: Outlet penetration				
Geographical profile				
Unit costs				
Public relations: Media impressions				
Supplier reflection				
Community image				

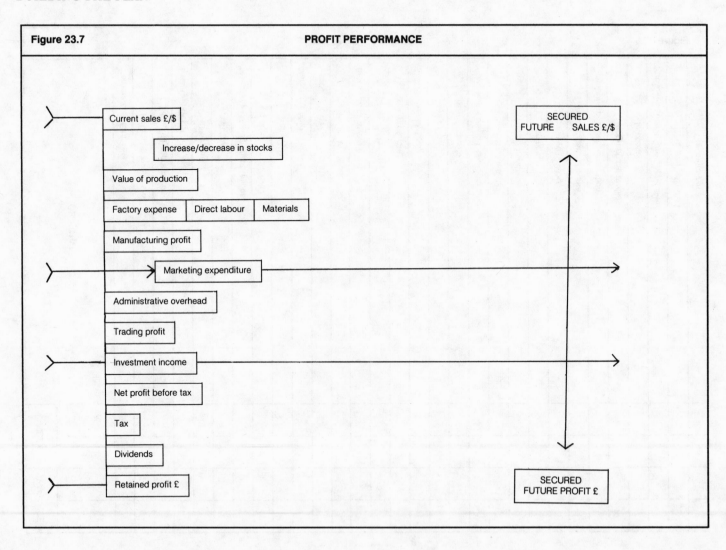

Figure 23.7 **PROFIT PERFORMANCE**

Current sales £/$

Increase/decrease in stocks

Value of production

Factory expense | Direct labour | Materials

Manufacturing profit

Marketing expenditure

Administrative overhead

Trading profit

Investment income

Net profit before tax

Tax

Dividends

Retained profit £

SECURED FUTURE   SALES £/$

SECURED FUTURE PROFIT £

Figure 23.8   Balance sheet

In this chart the market connections, namely patents, brand franchises, market reputation and trade marks are all valued. They are not required for taxation purposes or for registration under the Companies Acts but are nevertheless invaluable as a measure of company performance. They are the only assets that, suitably maintained, can appreciate in value and so are the only true indicator of the company's future.

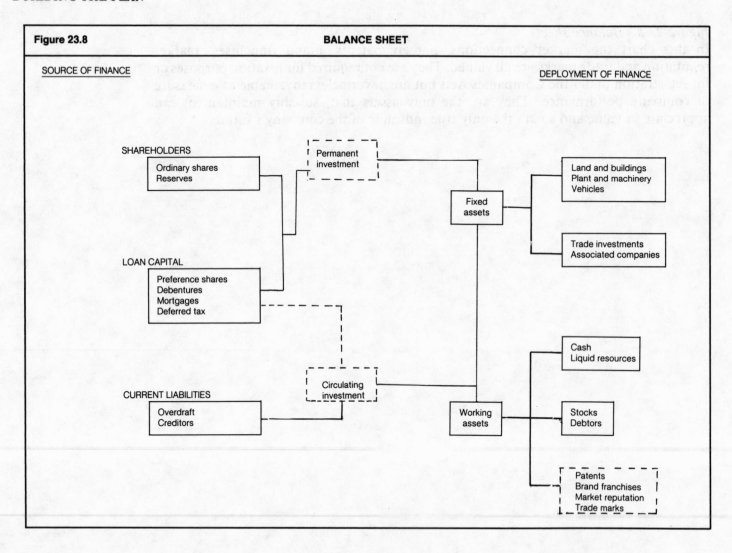

Figure 23.8 **BALANCE SHEET**

SOURCE OF FINANCE

DEPLOYMENT OF FINANCE

SHAREHOLDERS
- Ordinary shares
- Reserves

Permanent investment

LOAN CAPITAL
- Preference shares
- Debentures
- Mortgages
- Deferred tax

CURRENT LIABILITIES
- Overdraft
- Creditors

Circulating investment

Fixed assets
- Land and buildings
- Plant and machinery
- Vehicles
- Trade investments
- Associated companies

Working assets
- Cash
- Liquid resources
- Stocks
- Debtors
- Patents
- Brand franchises
- Market reputation
- Trade marks

Appendix: Using Statistical Methods

Statistical methods have become an important feature of marketing decision-making and future marketing executives will need to be well versed in the available techniques. These techniques represent not only a decision-making facility but an international language understood by numerate executives worldwide.

The use of statistical methods does not preclude qualitative assessment nor judgement in decision-making. In most cases the results of an analysis will confirm an opinion or indicate a path. Often they will highlight an opportunity or clarify complex situations. In the examples shown here, statistical methods were not essential but their use eliminated much mental effort and hours of time. They are therefore an essential aid to modern marketing management efficiency. Formulae for most statistical methods will be found in *Statistical Methods for Business Decisions* by Clarke and Schkade (South-Western Publishing Company, Cincinnati).

COEFFICIENT OF CORRELATION

THE BRIEF

The marketing manager of a direct marketing company is about to organize a major expansion and asks the advertising manager for advice on the relationship between company advertising expenditure and sales revenue as an indicator to future prospects.

The advertising manager decides to use the coefficient of correlation to establish the closeness of relationship between the two variables and then a regression analysis for future trends.

THE ARITHMETIC MEAN – 1

a) Add the five years' sales revenue together and divide by five (years of data).

b) Add the five years of advertising expenditure together and divide by five (years of data).

c) You now have the arithmetic mean ($\overline{Y}$) for sales and the arithmetic mean ($\overline{X}$) for advertising.

THE STANDARD DEVIATION – 2

Y	$Y - \overline{Y}$	$(Y - \overline{Y})^2$	X	$X - \overline{X}$	$(X - \overline{X})^2$
85	- 45	2025	3	- 2	4
140	+ 10	100	5	0	0
150	+ 20	400	6	+ 1	1
160	+ 30	900	7	+ 2	4
115	- 15	225	4	- 1	1
	$\sum(Y - \overline{Y})^2 = 3650$			$\sum(X - \overline{X})^2 = 10$	

$$\sqrt{\frac{3650}{5}} = \sqrt{730} \qquad \sqrt{\frac{10}{5}} = \sqrt{2}$$

$$\sigma Y = 27.02 \qquad \sigma X = 1.41$$

THE DATA

Over the past five years data has been:

Year	Sales 000's	Advtg. 000's
1	85	3
2	140	5
3	150	6
4	160	7
5	115	4

THE ARITHMETIC MEAN – 2

Y	X	YX
85	3	255
140	5	700
150	6	900
160	7	1120
115	4	460
$\sum Y = 650$	$\sum X = 25$	$\sum YX = 3435$

$$\overline{Y} = \frac{650}{5} = 130 \qquad \overline{X} = \frac{25}{5} = 5$$

THE CALCULATIONS

a) Multiply X times Y for each year.
b) Add together the product XY (XY)
c) Apply coefficient formula, so that

$$r = \frac{3435 - 5 \times 5 \times 130}{5 \times 1.41 \times 27.02}$$

$$= \frac{185}{190.49}$$

$$= .97$$

THE FORMULA

The formula for a coefficient of correlation is:

$$r = \frac{\sum XY - n\,\overline{XY}}{n\sigma X \sigma Y}$$

Where X = Advertising expenditure
Y = Sales revenue
$\overline{X}$ = Arithmetic mean of X
$\overline{Y}$ = Arithmetic mean of Y
σX = Standard deviation of X
σY = Standard deviation of Y
n = Number of data years.

THE STANDARD DEVIATION – 1

Standard deviation = $\sqrt{\dfrac{\sum(X - \overline{X})^2}{n}}$

a) Deduct from each year of sales revenue the average sales ($\overline{Y}$).
b) Square the subtraction $(Y - \overline{Y})^2$
c) Add together the product of each years $(Y - \overline{Y})^2$.
d) Divide by number of years data.
e) Find the square root of the sum $(\sum(Y - \overline{Y})^2)$.
f) Repeat the process for advertising X.

THE CONCLUSION

r = + .97   (Perfect positive correlation is + 1.00) therefore this correlation shows a high positive correlation, i.e. sales revenue and advertising expenditure are closely linked. Now see the chart on regression analysis to ascertain the sales revenue possible from different levels of advertising expenditure (subject to available demand).

GEOMETRIC MEAN ANALYSIS

THE BRIEF

The advertising manager wishes to advertise in three trade journals, each of which reaches substantial parts of the company target audience, and to gain maximum gross impacts in terms of cost efficiency, market penetration, and unit costs. A decision has to be made on how much money to spend in each publication, and so the manager decides to use geometric mean analysis.

Formula $\sqrt[n]{X_1 \quad X_2 \quad X_3 \quad X_n}$

THE PRINCIPLES

a) **Media with equal cost effectiveness are entitled to an equal share of the budget.**

b) Media with equal penetration of the market are entitled to an equal share of the budget.

c) Media with an equal unit cost are entitled to an equal share of the budget.

THE DATA

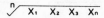

$\sqrt[n]{X_1 . X_2 . X_n}$	Pub A		Pub B		Pub C	
	£	%	£	%	£	%
Insertion cost	480	22.3	750	34.9	920	42.8
Penetration 000's	233	16.5	460	32.6	716	50.9
000's per £	.49	26.1	.61	32.4	.78	41.5

THE INSTRUCTIONS

1. a) Add together insertion costs for each possible publication.
   b) Take percentage for each.
   c) Add together penetration for each possible publication.
   d) Take percentage for each.
   e) Add together 000's per £ for each possible publication.
   f) Take percentage for each.

2. Each possible publication now has a set of three percentages.
   a) Multiply together the percentages in each set.
   b) Find cube root for the product of each set (find log. divide by three and then antilog).
   c) Each set now has a geometric mean.

3. From the three geometric means
   a) Add all three together
   b) Take percentage for each.
   c) The resulting percentage is equal to the share of the budget for each publication.

4. Book series of advertisements to the value of each share.

PUBLICATION A

$\sqrt[3]{22.3 \times 16.5 \times 26.1}$

$\sqrt[3]{9,603}$

Log. 9,603 is $\dfrac{3.9824}{3}$ = 1.3275

Antilog. = 21.26 (rounded = 21.38)

PUBLICATION B

$\sqrt[3]{34.9 \times 32.6 \times 32.4}$

$\sqrt[3]{36,863}$

Log. 36,863 is $\dfrac{4.5665}{3}$ = 1.5222

Antilog. = 33.29 (rounded = 33.48)

PUBLICATION C

$\sqrt[3]{42.8 \times 50.9 \times 41.5}$

$\sqrt[3]{90,408}$

Log. 90,408 is $\dfrac{4.9562}{3}$ = 1.6521

Antilog. = 44.89 (rounded = 45.14)

THE CONCLUSION (Budget £ 100 000)

Publication A   21.38% is £21 380
Publication B   33.48% is £33 480
Publication C   45.14% is £45 140
_____
£100 000

From original work by A. Philips and S.N. Ghosh

LINEAR PROGRAMMING FOR PHYSICAL DISTRIBUTION

THE BRIEF

The distribution manager of a national consumer goods firm has to decide how to deploy two sizes of lorry to distribute 750 orders of the company's standard washing machine to a distribution warehouse in the south. Available are:

1) Six lorries capable of carrying 125 machines each.
2) Ten lorries capable of carrying 50 machines each.
3) Eleven drivers each capable of driving either vehicle type.

Financial constraints are

1) Available budget is £4000
2) Cost of journey for larger lorry £550.
3) Cost of journey for smaller lorry £200.

Find the most profitable solution.

THE CALCULATION

Let the larger lorry = X

Let the smaller lorry = Y

The conditions imposed by availability and financial constraints are therefore:

1) At most six large lorries: $X \leqslant 6$
2) At most ten small lorries: $Y \leqslant 10$
3) At most eleven drivers and therefore no more than eleven lorries: $X + Y \leqslant 11$
4) 750 machines to be carried:
   $X(125) + Y(50) \geqslant 750$
   or $5x + 2y \geqslant 30$ (when divided by 25)

The combination of vehicles satisfying these inequalities simultaneously are shown in the shaded area of diagram B.

The number of pairs satisfying these requirements are therefore: (3,8); (4,5); (4,7); (5,3); (5,4); (5,5); (5,6); (6,0); (6,1); (6,2); (6,3); (6,4); (6,5), with the larger lorry shown first in each case.

The most profitable solution:

Each of these possible solutions is not equally economic, for in some cases lorries will be travelling with spare capacity: (6,1); (6,2); (6,3); (6,4); (6,5), while in others the solutions will be more costly, (5,4); (5,5); (5,6); (4,6); (4,7).

So therefore the most profitable solution is from (3,8); (4,5); (5,3) and (6,0). We can find the best solution by comparing the costs involved in each case. The cost is £ (550x + 200y) and as the budget available is £4 000 then (550x + 200y) = 4000 OR 11x + 4y = 80 (after dividing both sides by 50).

When this cost line is drawn on to the graph the region to the left of this line represents all profitable solutions, i.e. when costs are less than the budget. In fact the further to the left the solution point lies then the lower the cost to the company. Of the four possible solutions (3,8); (4,5); (5,3); (6,0); the point (4,5) is the furthest away and therefore represents the lowest cost.

SOLUTION 4 large and 5 small lorries with two drivers resting.

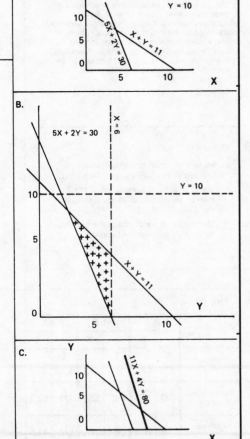

REGRESSION ANALYSIS FOR SALES AND ADVERTISING

THE BRIEF

Finding a coefficient of correlation at + .97 the advertising manager now wishes to advise the marketing manager of the level of sales indicated by varying amounts of advertising expenditure. In order to do this regression analysis is used.

$\Sigma Y = an + b x$
$\Sigma XY = a x + b x^2$

where a and b are constants and $Y = a + bx$ is a straight line.

Line of best fit

Substitution

As b = 18.5 substitute the number 18.5 for b in the equation:

So $650 = 5a + 18.5 \times 25$

Therefore

$650 = 5a + 462.5$
So $5a = 650 - 462.5$
$5a = 187.5$

Therefore a = 37.5

THE CALCULATIONS

X	Y	XY	X^2
3	85	255	9
5	140	700	25
6	150	900	36
7	160	1120	49
4	115	460	16
$\Sigma X = 25$	$\Sigma Y = 650$	$\Sigma XY = 3435$	$\Sigma X^2 = 135$

Using formula and calculations.

1) $650 = a \times 5 + b \times 25$
2) $3435 = a \times 25 + b \times 135$

Multiply 1) x 5 and 2) x 1, so as to equate a x 5 and a x 25.

Therefore

1) $3250 = 25a + 125b$
2) $3435 = 25a + 135b$
Deduct 1) from 2)
So $185 = 10b$. Therefore $18.5 = b$.

To calculate sales where advertising is ....?

Apply a = 37.5 and b = 18.5 to the equation for a straight line

$Y = a + bx$

So $Y = 37.5 + 18.5 \times$ (advertising expenditure)

When the level of advertising expenditure is applied to this equation then the applicable level of sales revenue may be calculated.

Straight line $Y = a + bx$

The regression of Y on X

$\Sigma Y = an + b \ \Sigma x$
$\Sigma XY = a\Sigma x \quad b \ \Sigma x_2$

Where n = the number of pairs of figures; Y = sales; and X = advertising
a and b are constants.
Find a and b so that calculations may be made whatever the variable of X advertising expenditure may be.

Sales results based on different levels of advertising expenditure.

Where advertising = £8 000
$Y = 37.5 + (8 \times 18.5) = £185\ 500$ sales

Where advertising = £15 000
$Y = 37.5 + (15 \times 18.5) = £315\ 000$ sales

Where advertising = £20 000
$Y = 37.5 + (20 \times 18.5) = £407\ 500$ sales.

Index